To Gary H
with my warmest good
wishes

God bless you!

July 23 1989

But for the Grace of God

« Monsignor Carroll-Abbing, in these last 25 years of our history has been unfailingly close to the people of our country. His penetrating spirit was able to understand the needs of our populations, the problems of our children. There was something magical, something unbelievably delicate in it. Monsignor Carroll knew how to become one with the populations that he assisted, with the ragged children that he gathered from the street, one with the wounded soldiers, one with those who fought for the cause of Liberty. He faced every risk; during the occupation, under the bombardments, on the battlefields. When the war ended he continued his own battle. When the others demobilized he remobilized his energies and was an apostle of good in the period of reconstruction. That uniform of idealism, that social combativeness have not been laid aside. He is standing in the breach, with the same indomitable enthusiasm of the very first days ».

Speech of the representative of the Italian Government at the official celebrations in the Capitol of Rome for the 25th Anniversary of Mons. Carroll.

« While human solidarity lay in ruins, Monsignor Carroll-Abbing, with indomitable and constructive fervor, reawakened in the face of the peoples crushed by the war and in the hearts of lost children, without consideration for differences of race and creed, the certainty of the Christian message of renewed concord among men.

« The City of Rome decorating Monsignor J. Patrick Carroll-Abbing with the Gold Medal on the occasion of his 25th priestly anniversary wishes to give testimony to him of its thankfulness and gratitude ».

Gratitude of the City of Rome.

First published in the United States of America
1965 by Delacorte Press

Litostampa Nomentana - Roma
Printed in Italy

Pope Paul VI, a close friend of the Boys' Towns
of Italy, with their founder Monsignor Carroll-Abbing.

But for the Grace of God

JOHN PATRICK CARROLL-ABBING

THE STORY OF AN IRISH PRIEST WHO
BECAME A RESISTANCE LEADER AND
LATER A FATHER TO THOUSANDS OF
CHILDREN IN THE BOYS' TOWNS OF
ITALY

Published by O.N.C.R.
Lungotevere Marzio, 12
Rome, Italy

Contents

PART ONE
Rome Occupied and Liberated, 1943-44

PART TWO
Germany's Withdrawal and Surrender, 1944-45

PART THREE

Child Victims in the Aftermath of War, 1945-63

Illustrations

PART ONE

Rome Occupied and Liberated, 1943–44

CHAPTER ONE

Black-Out

THE CLOCK in the bell-tower warned us that it was a quarter to five. The sun had not yet appeared over the Alban hills, but the Roman sky was already aglow with the soft magic of the morning. The dome of St. Peter's, touched by the gentle radiance, rose light as a bubble over the dark grey huddle of the houses; not even the massive bulk of the Vatican basilica could anchor it to earth. The procession of saints atop Bernini's colonnade was etched dramatically against the translucency of a grey-blue sky. In a narrow courtyard flanking the church the early morning light was too weak to dispel the shadows, giving the men who waited there a conspiratorial air. It was June 6, 1943.

I countersigned the papers of consignment that the Vatican official handed me. Hugh Montgomery, Chargé d'Affaires during the temporary absence of Sir D'Arcy Godolphin Osborne, the British Minister to the Holy See, wished me a safe journey. Four stocky young men in cheap, civilian garb entered one of the limousines. They were the English and Canadian prisoners-of-war whom I was to accompany to Lisbon on their return to freedom.

It was several months since they had escaped from their prison camps and made their way to Rome. They had lounged unobtrusively in the narrow streets leading up to St. Peter's, waiting for the right moment to come. A momentary distraction of the guards; some ingenious piece of strategy; once they reached the neutral soil of the Vatican they had been safe.

Safety! That had seemed to be the answer to their every need. Not to be in enemy hands. To have a reasonable hope that they might live to see their families again. Strange that, once they had succeeded in entering the diminutive City-State, the novelty of their new security should have faded so rapidly. A sense of confinement, a feeling of frustration at being out of the fight and yet still so far from home, made them fretful. It had been a relief when an international agreement was reached, allowing their repatriation in return for an equal number of disabled Italian prisoners-of-war.

As the limousines—window curtains tightly drawn—passed silently under the Arch of the Bells, the Swiss Guards sprang to attention. Their medieval halberds rang sharp on the cobble stones. St. Peter's Square was deserted; not a human eye to see the beauty of the giant fountains. Across the border-line, the automobiles of the Italian Police and the Ministry of War were waiting to escort us to the airport.

On the field, the Marchetti-Savoia was ready to depart. It was only a question of minutes. The men were hurried out of the car directly into the plane. I halted for a moment at the foot of the steps to sign the last official receipts. Soon the plane was speeding along the runway. We felt it banking steeply to avoid the slopes of Monte Mario, but the blue-painted glass in the windows prevented us from taking a last look at the city sprawling below us.

In Madrid, that evening, we agreed to stay in our hotel; the Spanish secret police were anxious to avoid the risk of a foreign agent creating an incident in the streets. Even in the spacious salons the heat was uncomfortable. The boys were tense. Now that the long-awaited moment was rapidly approaching, a strange uneasiness seemed to have invaded them. Sunk deep in the luxurious armchairs, their sombre gaze followed the elegant afternoon parade. The well-dressed men and women halting to chat lightly under the crystal chandeliers belonged to a world that the soldiers had not even dreamt could exist. Fugitives from every war-torn country, their foreign bank-accounts allowed them to sit out the war in bored comfort abroad.

"It wasn't for them I did any ruddy fighting."

"So what?" The big Canadian removed the glass from the hand of his companion and pushed the bottle away. The Englishman did not protest. He rubbed his brow wearily and sank back into silence.

Next day we were in Lisbon. It was a relief to find a telegram from Ankara to tell me that the Italian prisoners-of-war had arrived, I could consign the soldiers to the British Embassy, go on to England to see my Bishop,[1] and continue on my way for my first war-time vacation at home.

My last impression of Lisbon was of a little man of indefinable nationality approaching me cautiously at the airport to inquire whether I would be passing that way again: "If you bring some English prints with you—any English prints—I will give you a good price."

The weeks in Dublin passed only too quickly. I had intended to do so many worthwhile things and, instead, I found myself sauntering idly along the Quays, rummaging in dusty bookshops and slipping into the cool twilight of old, familiar churches. Small boys tugged at their caps and housewives in the Coomb knelt on their doorsteps as the priest passed by: "God bless you, Father!" Everything was old and everything seemed new.

There were war-time restrictions in Ireland; there was an unending flow of Jewish refugees from the Nazi-dominated countries to remind us of the horrors on the Continent; but there was peace. Peace could be breathed in like the fresh, clean air blowing from the sea. There was peace in the eyes of kindly men and women, in the smiles of children playing on the sidewalks. I moved as in a dream, seeing only the sunlight filtering delicately through the green tracery of the trees, hearing only the laughter of children racing their wooden boats on the pond, the quiet, humorous conversing of people at peace with themselves.

Many evenings my mother and I sat contentedly on the sea front at Dun Laoghaire, watching the packet-boat from England coming slowly into sight. They were people arriving from another planet, those Irish lads and colleens returning home for a brief respite from Manchester and Liverpool and London. There was heaviness in their walk and a sense of weariness. The startled look in their eyes and the sudden quirk of laughter on their lips betrayed their delight at the unexpected beauty of a country at peace.

I stood on O'Connell Street and looked across at the Post Office that had formed the earliest, dim recollection of my childhood,

---

[1] I was ordained for the Diocese of Salford where I had spent several years of my childhood. Immediately after my ordination, however, I was appointed to a post in the Vatican.

the Post Office that had seen the tricolour hoisted that Easter
Monday morning and heard the poet-patriot, Padraic Pearse, de-
claring Ireland a Republic.

Strange that, after so many tormented centuries, it should be
Ireland that had become a haven of peace in Europe!

My time was running short. I drove down to Arklow, to
Cousin Tommy's farm, for a few days. But the evenings by the
kitchen fire were touched with the melancholy shades of a happier
past. Cousins Joe and Anna were no longer with us. Only now
did I realize how much their quiet presence and gentle humour
had meant to me as a child.

"Do you remember the headless coachman, Tommy? And the
apples we roasted in the ashes?"

Tommy smiled with his eyes. He puffed placidly at his pipe and
his wrinkled face was serene. But his lilting voice no longer
blended into the crackling of the fire; the story-teller's tongue,
that had so often caressed the words of the leprechaun, was silent.
We were old, not with the age of years, but with the weight of a
world that was changing, slipping away from us, never to return.

There were a few precious days in County Tipperary, with the
Royal Rock of Cashel in the distance and the quilt-like pattern of
the Golden Vale—green, yellow and golden brown—spread out
before us. There was joking in the evening with boyhood friends.
They were young and their eyes were bright. I realized with a
shock that I, too, was young and that life stretched before me as it
did for them. But they knew only peace; mutilations had not
seared them, nor hate, nor the power-lust of men.

On July 10 the newsboys were crying it down by the boat as I
walked along the sea-front: the Allies had invaded Sicily.

Dramatic events followed in rapid succession. July 19, the
Allied bombardment of Rome—Pope Pius XII kneeling among
the wounded in the street! July 25, the arrest of Mussolini and the
fall of Fascism! How strange to hear of these things and not to be
there, to be well fed, free from fear and so far removed from the
devastation of war!

It was evident that the German defence line in Sicily was yield-
ing. Once the Allies had taken Mount Etna and crossed the Strait
of Messina, the whole Italian peninsula would become an active
theatre of war. If I was to return to Rome, I must leave at once.

« What goes on in the minds of these
children of the road? ».

« What was to happen to those tiny
victims of man's cruelty to man? ».

The Apostolic Nunciature and the Department of External Affairs prepared my papers and obtained permission for me to board a British seaplane stopping at Shannon. The plane would touch down at Lisbon on its way to Africa. From there I would go to Madrid and so on to Rome.

My mother came to Shannon to bid me good-bye. Our last farewell had taken place four years previously and I knew that, as she continued to wave to me while the boat took me out to the plane, she was wondering, as I was, whether four more years would pass before we would meet again.

It had been in the early summer of 1939 that Cardinal Pizzardo had granted me a leave of absence and I had gone to meet my mother in Switzerland.

Under normal circumstances I would have spent my vacation at home, but that year the war clouds were heavy over Europe. If a conflict should come, Switzerland would probably be a neutral zone along the fracture line. Within a couple of hours I could be back in Italy and mother could be on her way to Paris and home.

The weeks in Lugano and Lucerne had been uneventful. The tranquil mornings on the lakes and the quiet under the trees in the cool of the evening had banished from our minds any thought of war.

Then, on the morning of August 23, the shrill cries of the news-boys running wildly along the waterfront rudely shattered our illusion of peace; Russia and Germany had signed a non-aggression pact. We hastily prepared our luggage and hurried to the railway station. We were already too late.

We looked with dismay at the hysterical crowds besieging the terminal. It was frightening to recognize in the terrified men and women fighting savagely to board a northbound train the respectable tourists who, the previous evening, had sauntered so peacefully along the boulevards.

After several hours, mother succeeded in leaving for Paris. She looked very tiny, gazing down at me from her compartment.

"I don't think that Italy will go to war," I said to console her.

She smiled bravely as the train drew out of the station. I waved until it had disappeared round the bend. There was a lump in my throat as I retraced my steps down the platform. Home had been lonely for her since my father died. My three brothers were already dead.

That same evening, in the solitude of the railway compartment, I looked dismally out of the window into the blackness of the countryside. Only the giant pine-trees could be seen flashing by in spectral procession against the darkened sky. The miles disappeared under the metallic click of the speeding rails. Except for an old man, whom I had glimpsed during a lonely perambulation along the corridor, I was the only traveller on the usually crowded trans-Continental Express.

The clerk in the travel-bureau had eyed me curiously that morning when I had asked for a ticket to Rome. "No difficulty about that," he had said ironically.

At the border the customs officials and frontier guards boarded the train. There was the inspection of my passport, the rapid consultation of a mysterious closely-printed volume, the thud of the metal stamp, a courteous salute, and the group moved on down the corridor.

A few minutes later, pandemonium had broken loose on the platform. The old man was struggling desperately in the grasp of the soldiers. His guttural voice was protesting piteously. He looked up at me with terrified, unseeing eyes as they dragged him away. His fragile body was still straining convulsively, opposing its last useless resistance to the implacable New Order that was descending upon Europe.

A turmoil of thoughts tumbled through my brain as the train pulled out, smoothly, powerfully, inexorably. The world was moving on and the negligible little incident of human tragedy, of brutality and terror, would pass into oblivion. An old man had been crushed and the world did not care. My heart was pounding. I was humiliated by my fear and by the futility of my anger.

I sat in my corner, seeing, not the darkness outside, but the bright sunlight of a summer's afternoon, now gone. It had been warm in the sun, that day in 1934, when I stood on the landing-stage in Linz waiting for a steamer to take me down the Danube to Bratislav. I had glanced curiously at the grey-haired man standing nearby, whose thin frame was racked by a hacking cough. I inquired how far he was going and he told me that he did not really know. He was a Jew and the Nazis had deprived him of his citizenship. Now he was a stateless man, wandering from one country to another, not allowed to work for a wage, forced to move on when his stay-permit expired. His wife and his children had gone back to her parents so as not to starve. "She is a German citizen."

"What will you do?"

"Oh, it won't be long now." He had smiled at me with quiet resignation.

If only we had taken warning from such inhuman episodes! They were the logical outcome of Hitler's ruthless concept of the world, 'where one creature feeds on the other and where the death of the weaker implies the life of the stronger".

The madman could have been stopped at any of the vital stages of his advance to power. But now, in August, 1939, a world war lay inevitably ahead of us. The future was dark as the blackness outside the window of my compartment. The train sped rapidly on its way.

In the morning my mood changed. The smiling Italian country-side was there to reassure me: the church towers, the cypress trees of Tuscany, the vineyards, the ancient cities, the tiny villages carved grey into the rock of the hillsides. Robust peasants were labouring in the fields. Old men and children waved to us in friendly fashion as the train rattled past the level-crossings.

The compartment had filled to overflowing with comfortable citizens: Milanese businessmen, a grey-haired army officer and his wife, a young mother and her little girl. The hysteria of yesterday had vanished like a ridiculous dream. The threat of war seemed to be a million miles away.

Even after September, 1939, this strange feeling of detachment persisted. The very rapidity with which Poland, the Low Countries and France were invaded plunged the Italian people into a deeper fatalism. Their only hope for peace lay in Mussolini. It is true that he talked of war, but it might all end there, in the belligerency of his public utterances. They clung pathetically to each fragile thread of hope. "Mussolini has given orders for work to continue on the 1942 World Fair. He is not going to war." My old professor of archaeology stopped me in the street to give me the glad news.

Then, unexpectedly, on June 10, 1940, war came. The people

had flocked obediently to the Piazza Venezia, hoping that the current rumour was true and that Mussolini would officially confirm Italian non-intervention. Although my home was a mile from the meeting-place, the thunderous applause that greeted his appearance was wafted to me across the intervening labyrinth of narrow streets. I turned on the radio, just in time to hear the fatal words: "Today I delivered to the French Ambassador . . . to the English Ambassador . . . our declaration of war."

An hour later a subdued crowd was still slowly wending its way home. That night the black-out began.

Soon after dark two French planes flew low over the city. The Fascist anti-aircraft corps on the Janiculum hill pointed their guns downwards and sprayed the houses with shellfire.

"If the English don't get us, our own defence will," grumbled one disgruntled citizen as he took refuge in our doorway.

That night of all nights an owl filled our courtyard with its mournful cry. It was an evil omen, as everyone in the *palazzo* knew.

The last sounds I heard were of a tardy homegoer cursing volubly in the alley-way under my window. He had poked his eye into the shaft of an abandoned pushcart.

I was awakened again by a vigorous pounding on the street door. Two officious air-raid wardens were pointing indignantly at a second-floor window.

"There is a light on upstairs. Don't you know we are at war?"

"The lights are all out. That is the reflection of the moon on the glass."

"I don't care what it is. Turn it off."

I kept silent. We were at war. The moon should have known it. In that atmosphere of tragi-comedy we really had gone to war.

Time had flown. For three years Italy had been at war. I had been home to visit my mother. Now I was returning to Rome to see the end of the tragedy.

On the plane the British servicemen in their grey-stripe civilian suits had greeted me cheerfully.

"Where are you going, Padre?"

"To Italy," I had replied.

There had been dead silence. They were going to Italy, too, by way of Africa and Sicily. The last lap for them would not be by passenger plane.

In Lisbon I noticed that the civilian pilots—British, German, Italian—were still taking their meals in the same mess-hall, courteously passing the sugar to their enemies but in complete silence, each one thinking his own thoughts.

It was on August 11, my birthday, that I concluded the last lap of my return journey from Shannon. To my surprise the plane from Madrid landed on the military field at Guidonia, some miles from Rome. The civilian airfield on the Via Salaria had been wrecked that very afternoon by an Allied bombardment.

It was uncanny not to be met with Fascist salutes. My last impression in June had been of outstretched arms saluting me as I turned to enter the plane. Now all the familiar emblems had disappeared and the funereal uniform was nowhere to be seen. The officials who greeted me were courteous but non-committal. It was true that Mussolini was in prison, but who knew what the future might still hold in store?

There were no facilities for passenger clearance at the military airfield. The five travellers, including General Umberto Nobile of North Pole fame and myself, were taken by car to Rome and placed under guard in the doorway of an office building in Via delle Terme.

The Grand Hotel opposite was darkened and subdued. It was no longer the mecca of wealthy travellers. It was difficult even to recall that this street had once sparkled with lights, had been lively with the chatter of tourists.

I watched the grey figures scurrying by on the pavement, anxious to reach their homes before the curfew, and I reflected in the gathering dusk how squalidly dismal Rome was under the black-out.

In the early days of the war it had sometimes seemed that, with the absence of artificial lighting, an older and a more magical city had been reborn. Piazza Santa Maria in Trastevere, bathed in the silvery moonlight, was spectral in its beauty. Piazza Navona became a vast arena, a noble theatre, a seventeenth-century engraving of dramatic highlights and conspiratorial shadows. Castel Sant'Angelo was massively, uncompromisingly outlined against the sky. The pine-trees of Villa Borghese sighed nostalgically and the fountains splashed their centuries-old music in the mellow darkness. It was beautiful, eerily beautiful, unnaturally so. The unrelieved blackness of a twentieth-century city was heavy with foreboding, strangely menacing.

What a contrast to the life of cities outside the circle of war! The thought of Dublin gave me a sudden tightening of the heart. Even in Lisbon, where the war was present in the underground manoeuvring of spies and counter-spies, there was peace: sidewalk cafés, animated boulevards, men and women without the heavy sorrow of bereavement engraved on their faces.

I had paid a visit a few months previously to the Swiss village of Kreuzlingen, practically a suburb of the German city of Constance. The store windows were filled with Christmas dainties; the children were going unconcernedly to school.

Down the street, but across the fragile border-line, German men and women bearing the same names, speaking the same language, linked by the same ties of blood, were at war. There was hunger, fear and suspicion and the constant menace of bombardments. Women were mourning and children were bereaved.

Painful memories tumbled confusedly through my mind as darkness settled upon Rome.

Across the square the half-demolished railway station—its rebuilding indefinitely postponed—loomed uglier than ever. I had gone there every afternoon in those warm days of May, 1940. when Italy teetered on the brink and the foreign seminaries, one after another, were closing their doors for the first time in centuries. I had said good-bye to all of them: English, Scots, French, Belgians. Then, with a heart heavier than lead, I had walked back alone down the Via Nazionale.

One afternoon there had been two trains facing each other on the platform. On one side Italian recruits: country boys in baggy uniforms, ridiculously young and already homesick, staring with friendly interest at the *preti*,[1] younger than they were, who were leaning out of the windows of the Rome-Calais Express. The English seminarians were waving to them and wishing them *"Buon Viaggio"* in their clipped, schoolboy Italian. A few more days and they would be enemies, destined to kill and to be killed, to prove the truth of that strange, arbitrary proposition.

[1] Clerics.

Jerry, round-faced, placid, quietly tenacious, who had played soccer under the pines of Villa Pamphili and had dreamed of a Lancashire parish, would die—a chaplain among his men—landing on a beach in Normandy. Fair-haired Timothy, peering into his cardboard box to see the turtle he was taking back to England, would give up the study of philosophy and join the Navy. He, too, would die, eighteen years old, in the defence of his country.

The wave of depression that had swept over me deepened. Would the war never end and, if it did, what kind of world would it leave behind it? A place of new hatreds and piled-up resentments? The darkness advanced. What a homecoming to Rome! More than an hour went by before the Italian frontier police arrived to inspect our documents and allow us to go on our way.

The Hospital of the Knights of Malta was only ten minutes distant.[1] Inside, all was dark, except for the dim, blue lights in the wards and the diminutive reading lamps on the tables of the night sisters.

I tiptoed between the lines of white beds. A young soldier was moaning painfully in his sleep. I opened the door of my familiar little room: an iron cot, a wash basin, a table and a chair. In four hours, at five o'clock sharp, the night sister would knock at my door as she had done for the past three years and a new day would begin. A strange feeling of contentment surged up within me; I was home again.

---

[1] It had been at the invitation of the Grand Master of the Order, of which I am a member, that I had become the voluntary chaplain of the Roman hospital. Although the Sovereign Military Order of Malta no longer rules over any territory, it is still recognized internationally as a sovereign power. Even the invading German armies respected its extra-territorial privileges and immunities.

CHAPTER TWO

Eyes that have Wept

IT MAY seem strange that I should look back to the four years I spent in the military hospital of the Knights of Malta with a feeling almost of nostalgia. It is not because the passage of time has left only the memory of the more serene moments. In continual contact with suffering in its most demoralizing physical forms, often exhausted between my Vatican duties in the morning and the never-ending round of duty with the wounded during the rest of the day, some of the most harrowing experiences live on with the clear-cut lines of yesterday's events.

How could one ever forget the arrival of the first casualties from the Italian invasion of Greece? For days the wards of our hospital were filled with the stench of rotting flesh. Night and day, and day after day, the surgeons took turns in operating. Sometimes arms as well as legs had to be amputated in a last desperate attempt to save a human life. The thousands of amputees in the hospitals of Bari, Naples and Rome were not the victims of combat. They had been sent to Albania in the winter of 1940, clad in the light cotton uniforms provided for an African desert campaign. Their gangrenous toes and fingers were the inevitable result of exposure to the snow and ice on the wild mountain ranges.

How can there be any joy in remembering such tragic times? Only because it was then that I saw, as I had never done before, the heights that human courage can attain when sustained by faith. It was then that I discovered that even man's poor service can be used to comfort and console.

It was Gennaro who first asked me to accompany him into the operating theatre. He was just eighteen and far from home. He had no false pride; he wanted to have a familiar face close by when he went under the surgeon's knife. Once Gennaro had broken the ice, many of the other young soldiers asked me to be with them when the dread moment came. By the time the war ended I had stood through more than a thousand operations.

At the beginning I sometimes wondered whether the hours consumed in the operating theatre could not have been more profitably spent in other ways. Then I saw how much a presence and a smile can mean to any youngster, tough and self-reliant though he may be, when he is very much alone. There is no waste of time when one stands in companionship at the foot of the Cross.

My admiration for those simple soldiers increased. I admired the unassuming courage with which they had done their duty, even in a war they could not understand. I admired their lack of bitterness against the enemy, their fortitude under pain, their ability to smile when the future held nothing for them but black uncertainty.

It is not easy to be sound of body and to speak to men who are maimed of such things as patience and resignation and the love of God.

Sometimes, when my courage failed me, the thought of Father Welsby would come to me. The elderly Jesuit, with the ascetic face and the sharp eyes twinkling behind his steel-rimmed glasses, had been the English assistant to the Father General during my student days in Rome. He had been a living demonstration of what a joyous person an ascetic can be. When he sacrificed his one hour of relaxation to visit the sick, no one could feel that the long tramp through the streets in the stifling heat of a Roman summer gave him anything but pleasure.

In 1938, stricken with cancer, it was our turn to visit him. His pain was savage in its intensity, but he would not admit defeat: "Pray that I may get well. If only I could get well!" In a man so resigned to the Will of God this petulance puzzled me until one day, inadvertently, his secret was revealed. "Now I know what it is to suffer. If only I could get well! If only I could be on my feet again! Now I would know how to console the sick. Now I would know."

Veuillot has summed it up so simply: "Certain things cannot be seen except with eyes that have wept."

How can one walk into a ward and approach one of the sick—

he is reading the newspaper, he looks up with a smile, things are much better now, his wound is healing, soon he will go home—and say: "Battista, I have bad news for you: your only child, the five-year-old whom you have hardly seen, whose picture you have carried in your wallet from Trieste to the Ukraine, your little boy is dead"?

A mother is visiting her son for the first time since he bade her good-bye three years ago: "How well you look. Thank God, you are better! You haven't changed a bit. You will be home soon." One must take her aside as she leaves and tell her: "You did not notice when you entered the ward and saw Giorgio glowing with health, his blue eyes shining, his big grin welcoming you, that the covers on his bed were flat. He did not have the courage to tell you. . . . He has no legs."

These are the moments when the compassion that one feels, the welling-up of pity in one's heart, are stronger to console than any words that one may seek. Only they can open up to those who are afflicted, a feeble vision of the infinite compassion and loving mercy of God.

On Saturday evening they would call me to their bedsides and pour forth in Confession the little miseries of their lives. And I would lift up my hand in Christ's name and, in the beautiful words that follow the absolution, I would say with all my heart:

"May the good things you have done, and the evil things you have withstood, obtain for you the remission of your sins, an increase of grace and the prize of eternal life. Amen."

The evil things you have withstood! My eyes would rest upon their patient heads bowed in prayer and upon their pitiful stumps placed together as their mother had taught their tiny hands to pray, and my whole consciousness would be seared by this blinding thought: how great must God's compassion for these poor souls be if a man, and such an inadequate and unworthy one, can feel so much pity for them in his selfish heart!

It would be well past midnight when my day ended. Even at that late hour some of the wounded were still awake, staring in silence at the darkness of the ceiling.

"Gianni, not asleep yet?"

"Father, what will I do without arms? How will I live? What will happen to my family?"

The awe-inspiring mystery of pain and suffering and sorrow!

But the "Why?" of the evil let loose upon the world, that wreaked its toll of broken homes and mangled limbs and children that wept, troubled the sufferers less than it did the compassionate onlookers whose faith was not strong enough to answer the anguish of their hearts.

I think of Ottone. Here before me, as I write in my library, I see the cheap wooden rosary beads and the medal that Ottone bequeathed to me when he died.

I remember the day that he arrived in the hospital. He was in no pain as yet. It was not suffering that had twisted his mouth into a bitter sneer. He was hard and discourteous by long usage. Even his family had broken with him.

It was not easy to visit him. Each time that I reached his room, I paused for a moment with my hand on the door-knob before opening it, knowing that I would see the ironical eyes turn to watch me and the sarcastic smile betray his knowledge of my discomfort.

When the first signs of a dread disease manifested themselves, the irony turned to rage. From then on, Ottone's body went slowly but inexorably into dissolution. The rotting flesh fell piece by piece until the toes showed to the bone.

He sat there night and day, propped up by pillows, his feet dangling from the bed and, under them, two basins slowly filling with the droppings of his own physical corruption.

I do not know why it was that the doctors had hoped to arrest the disease without amputation. Even then, before the operation could be performed, he had to be transferred to a sanatorium on the outskirts of the city; X-rays had revealed that he was suffering from tuberculosis. All of a sudden he seemed very lonely as he was carried out to the ambulance.

Every day after that I tried to visit him, hurrying from the hospital to the tram, changing to a bus, staying with him sometimes only for a few minutes and hastening home again.

Now and then it seemed to me that he was changing, that he was less sarcastic, less bitter, more restrained in his tirades against the nurses. Soon there was no longer any doubt. Even his thin, tormented face was reflecting the inner peace that was taking possession of his soul.

As I entered the room, his patient eyes—deep, melancholy eyes —would turn towards the door and a wan smile soften the corners of his mouth. Sometimes I would find him asleep, worn out after the tormented sufferings of the night, a little metal crucifix lying abandoned on the quilt and his worn fingers resting gently on the figure of his Christ. I would place a note on his bed and creep out again to leave him undisturbed.

"Be careful, Father," the scrub-women would warn me as I descended the stairs and instinctively touched the handrails. 'Wash your hands carefully." They knew as I did that some of the embittered men in the wards spat on the handles of the doors, in dull hatred against society and against the people who were not sick.

One day I was leaving Ottone's room and the head nurse met me.

"Father, I cannot stand it any longer. Why does a God who is supposed to be merciful let a poor boy suffer so?"

I smiled, and yet I did not mean to smile.

"Nurse, if I had ever had any doubts about God and His goodness, Ottone alone would have given me the answer. You remember him when he first came to the sanatorium; he was filled with hatred. You can see him now—his serenity and his courage. What has wrought this change in him if not his acceptance of the means that God has offered him for his own redemption? Suffering is evil but the alchemy of divine grace and human courage can turn it into gold."

I had in mind the words of Salvaneschi: *There is no conquest without suffering . . . no rising without suffering . . . no reward without suffering. I ponder on the suffering in the world of today . . . it has a hundred faces, a hundred expressions; but springing forth from all this sorrow, all this pain, a great flame is rising toward the Almighty, a fire of burning hope that Love may come again. Love in sorrow, Love for sorrow.*

I saw him the day before I left for Lisbon and for home.

"Ottone, I am leaving now, but I will see you very soon. What would you like me to bring you from my country?"

He took my hands into his own diaphanous ones and the smile that he gave me was radiant with understanding and almost fatherly in its blessing—and he so much younger than I.

"When you return, Father, I shall not be here." His voice was gentle, almost inaudible.

A moment of suspense—an instant stretching into eternity—and he added, lower still, with the stupendous, earth-shattering confidence that love had given him: "When I am in Paradise, I shall always remember the Irish priest who came to visit me."

CHAPTER THREE

Attila in Rome

SEPTEMBER 8, 1943, began like any other day. Looking back, this seems strange. Surely some sixth sense should have told us, the very moment that we opened our eyes, that it would be a fateful date in history!

The morning was interrupted as usual by the sound of bombardments. Successive waves of Flying Fortresses circled over the city. Strangely enough, it was not on the railway yards, but on the hill towns south of Rome, that the fury of the Allied attack seemed to concentrate itself. At Frascati even the sixteenth-century villas, isolated in their princely gardens, went up in flames. When I reached the town, two hours later, only the shell of the cathedral where James Stuart, the Cardinal Duke of York, had been bishop was left standing—a gaunt skeleton in the midst of desolation.

Climbing over the debris into what had been the main square, I found the bishop, Monsignor Budelacci, toiling among the ruins. The silence of death had settled over the town but the desperate search continued, spurred on by an occasional moan from under the fallen masonry. Two venerable monks were digging among the rubble. Others were preparing the dead for burial. For the first time in centuries the Camaldolese hermits had left their tree-hidden monastery on the slopes of Mount Tusculum for this tragic contact with the outside world.

I saw the white figures again at nightfall, trudging back up the hill, their coarse white habits soiled with dirt and stained red with blood. The world would continue on its fratricidal course and they would resume their solitary life of toil and prayer and per-petual silence. The words of *Wisdom* came to my mind: *In the sight of the unwise they seemed to die: and their departure was taken for misery, and their going away from us, for utter destruction: but they are in peace.*

It was at seven forty-five that evening that we heard the news of the armistice over the radio. First, the declaration of General Eisenhower; then, the voice of Badoglio, Mussolini's successor as Head of the Government: "The Italian Armed Forces will suspend all hostilities against the Anglo-American Forces. They will resist if an attack comes from any other quarter."

The news caught the man in the street unprepared, even if the armistice was obviously the logical conclusion to the fall of Fascism.

"They bombed us when we were enemies. How is it, if an armistice has been signed, that they are bombing us worse than before?"

Perplexity soon gave way to relief. Excited groups formed at the street-corners to discuss the probable consequences of the new situation. "My boy is a prisoner of the English; now he can come home!"

The rumour spread that Hitler was dead—that he had been shot—that he had committed suicide. Near the Piazza di Spagna two German soldiers tore off their military tabs and danced a jig: "Hitler dead. The war is over."

Something, however, was missing. Joy did not come easily. It was not June 25, the day that Mussolini fell. There had been real joy then, the heady exultation of freedom. Now there was hope but dampened by fear. It was too easy. Three years of fighting, of bombardments and privations, to end with the announcement over the radio! And the Germans? They were everywhere in Italy. What would their reaction be?

As a matter of fact the few German soldiers who appeared in the streets next day had a subdued look. Smoke pouring from the chimneys of the German Embassy showed that documents were being burned. German trucks were seen heading north on the Via Cassia. The city was agog with optimistic rumours. "The Americans have landed at Ostia. They will be here before nightfall."

The Germans, more than anyone else, expected that the Allied invasion fleet, which had appeared off the coast of Naples on September 8, would head north to effect a landing close to Rome. In that case, with parachutists seizing the airfields and the Allies utilizing the five Italian divisions stationed near the city, the eight German divisions to the south would be isolated.[1] As it turned out, however, the Allies did not land near Rome. They disembarked at Salerno, even further south than Naples. More than a hundred and fifty miles of rugged mountains, stretching from coast to coast, cut them off from Rome. The dropping of parachutists on the Roman airports was definitely abandoned.[2]

Without Allied support, the Italian General Staff gave up all hope of defending Rome. Before daybreak a cortège of cars crept silently from the city and sped eastward through the mountains towards the distant port of Pescara. Fishing boats took the Royal Family, Badoglio and the General Staff south to Brindisi, to set up a new Government on Allied-occupied territory.

No-one in the city knew as yet of the flight of the King and his generals. By midday, however, most people had realized that the bombing from the west was not caused by the dismantling of the minefields, as had first been rumoured. It marked the outbreak of fighting between Italian troops and the Germans. "Here we go all over again."

In the afternoon the presentiment of imminent disaster increased. One after another the stores put up their shutters. The iron-studded doors of the Roman palaces were pulled to and bolted tight. Night fell and an uneasy silence enveloped the city. At ten o'clock the quiet was broken by the air-raid sirens. A solitary German plane flew over the houses, dropping bombs indiscriminately. The all-clear sounded and silence returned.

Another hour went by and the narrow street outside our hospital echoed to the thunder of caterpillar wheels. Startled faces appeared at the dark windows of the houses as tanks and army trucks crowded with wounded drove up in quick succession.

---

[1] Field Marshal Kesselring has since told us that Hitler himself had already given them up for lost and was making plans to set up a new defence line in the mountains farther north.

[2] Eisenhower points out in *Crusade in Europe*, p. 189, that after the capture of Sicily he had been instructed to send seven divisions to England to prepare for the Channel invasion. This left him short of troops. Captain Harry C. Butcher, Eisenhower's naval aide, states in *My Three Years with Eisenhower*, pp. 407-425, that there were too few landing craft available and that a landing near Rome would have had to be carried out without the protection of fighter-planes whose closest bases were in Sicily.

« Surely these victims of the War were destined to become the new messengers of peace and goodwill among men! ».

« What good are we doing keeping them alive when all they have to live for is to rot on the streets? ».

Most of the wounded came from a desperate battle being waged west of the city, on the Via Ostiense. The German Second Parachutist Division, 10,000 strong, had attacked the greatly outnumbered and hitherto untried Italian Grenadier Division. The Italian boys were fighting courageously but blindly; their attempts to get in touch with Army Headquarters had proved unavailing. Who was in charge of the Army? No-one knew. Such orders as did reach the commanders in the field were contradictory and it was not clear by whose authority they had been issued. It was already suspected that the Germans had captured the Italian Army cipher and were using it to create confusion.

The morning found us still feverishly at work. If we had left the hospital we would have been unable to understand the calm of the citizens going about their daily business. We had lived through a night of horror but the people outside were seemingly ignorant of the tragic events that were deciding the fate of Rome.

News had begun to trickle through of the successes scored by the Italians north of the city. The Piave Division had wiped out the German parachutists dropped at Monterotondo. The Ariete Division had routed the powerful German Third Infantry Division near Bracciano, destroying seventy tanks, a hundred trucks and two batteries. A radio announcement further reassured the citizens: Marshal Caviglia, the highest-ranking officer left in Rome, had assumed command. The seventy-year-old general was in high spirits: "Everything is under control. The Germans have agreed to leave. Rome is in no danger."

While this ingenuous wave of optimism was breaking over the city, the military situation on the Ostiense was growing steadily worse. Marshal Caviglia had allowed the Germans to cross the Magliana bridge but, instead of going north as they had promised, they had turned their guns eastwards. German shells were soon falling on the centre of Rome.

The flow of wounded increased. The wards in our hospital were filled to overflowing and the new arrivals had to be placed on stretchers in the corridors. In the mortuary the dead were already piled one on top of the other.

The situation, as we could see it, was growing desperate. Even the cadets from the Carabinieri school had been rushed into action. Hundreds of civilians, armed with guns of every description, had crossed the open fields to join the soldiers on the Via Laurentina. Would the reinforcements from Monterotondo never arrive?

In the hospital, a Carabiniere cadet lay on the operating table. The look of death was already in his eyes. "You know, Father, life is strange. Only today a friend of mine brought me a letter from mother. *I have no news from your two brothers in Russia. At least you, son, are out of danger in Rome.*

A young soldier, burning with fever, looked at me reproachfully as I restrained him from getting out of bed. In his delirium he imagined that he still had the little pressed-board valise that he had taken with him from home when he was called up to fight. "There are things I must send home. Father, let me get up! Father . . . !"

The news was becoming more and more disastrous. The victorious divisions north of the city, ignorant of the situation in Rome, had obeyed the orders left them by the fugitive General Staff and had withdrawn to Tivoli. The troops on the Ostiense had fallen back and the townspeople were erecting barricades in the streets between the Basilica of St. Paul and the gate of the city. Groups of young boys were taking part in the fighting. It was rumoured that the Germans were already in the Piazza Venezia, only five hundred yards from the hospital.

To have some idea of the truth, I took advantage of a lull to accompany one of the doctors on his motorcycle through the deserted streets. In Piazza Venezia, nothing! Half a mile away, near the Baths of Caracalla, where summer tourists used to listen to open-air opera, there were some signs of a recent conflict. At St. Paul's Gate a skirmish had just ended. Two boys, twelve or thirteen years old, lay dead in the roadway. The hand of one still clutched the "Molotov cocktail" that he had been ready to hurl under an enemy tank. A damaged tank had been abandoned near the pyramid of Caius Cestius. The contorted body of a child sprawled over the edge of the sidewalk into the gutter, his rigid fingers clawing a piece of leather belt, his long dark curls mercifully covering the bloody devastation of his face. Now all was quiet.

Earlier that afternoon there had been fighting in the heart of the city. In the Piazza dei Cinquecento, opposite the railway station, civilian snipers crouching behind overturned carts were trying to dislodge the Germans from the Hotel Continentale. One young boy, acting as a look-out, was hit as he rose to point out a German aiming from a window. Wilting gently on to his side, he stretched out his legs over so slowly and moved no more. Three teenagers staggered across the square with a machine gun, firing as they went.

At five o'clock a special edition of one of the newspapers was being sold in the streets. The blaring headlines occupied the entire front page: *The Allies are at Cisterna.* "Thank God! Cisterna is only thirty miles away. By nightfall they will be here."

At nightfall it was the Germans and not the Allies who entered Rome. They poured through the gates. Silently, implacably, they advanced along the Triumphal Way, past the Arch of Constantine and down Mussolini's Via dell'Impero. No civilians were in sight, but a hundred thousand eyes were watching from darkened windows. There was no indecision. Each officer knew where his men must go. They spread through the city like a spider weaving its web. When the whole army had been absorbed, there was silence. We had expected uproar, drunken singing, the thunder of armoured cars. The very absence of sound was more unnerving. Isolated shots throughout the night, momentary bursts from a sub-machine gun, then silence again.

When the new day dawned, Rome was a sad spectacle. Some of the stores had been sacked and gaped wide open; the rest were tightly shuttered. No-one went to work. Not a policeman was to be seen. Empty trams and buses stood in the streets where they had been abandoned the day before when the siren sounded. The roads were unswept, and in many places rust-coloured patches showed where blood had been shed.

During the morning the city came partially to life. There was shooting—where, we did not know—and armoured cars were patrolling the streets. Civilians who ventured abroad found themselves obliged to hand over their watches; bands of German soldiers began to loot the stores.

At one o'clock, instead of the usual news bulletin, a gutteral voice over the radio told us that an armistice had been signed.

In the afternoon the *Giornale d'Italia* and the *Avvenire* appeared in one-sheet editions. They carried the text of a proclamation signed by General Calvi di Bergolo, son-in-law of the King and now Italian Commander of the Open City of Rome. The German Army would respect Rome as an open city and would remain outside its limits. The only buildings to be occupied would be the German Embassy, the radio station and the German telephone exchange. Did Calvi really believe that they would keep their word, that they would give up the strategic places they had occupied during the night? Did he not suspect that they were only playing for time, waiting for an opportunity to disarm the rest of the Italian troops, carry off General Calvi himself to Germany and replace their own military commander with a more ruthless man?

In the evening a proclamation, signed by Field Marshal Kesselring, declared that the Italian territory under his command was subject to German martial law. Any crime committed against a member of the German Armed Forces would be punished accordingly.

Next day we heard that Mussolini had been liberated by German parachutists from his isolated cell on the Gran Sasso mountain.

The nine-month occupation of Rome had begun.

CHAPTER FOUR

Life Goes On

WITHIN THE first few days of the German occupation we made the astonishing discovery that even in an occupied city life must continue. The stores must open; the tram-cars must run; the population must be fed; each family must carry on its daily struggle for survival.

In the hospital, operations had to be performed, wounds had to be dressed. Never had the doctors been so glad to have their day occupied from morning until night.

For the wounded it was more difficult. To lie immobile day after day, staring up at the blank whiteness of the ceiling! Nine months would go by before they would receive news of their families. Late at night I found them still tossing and turning in tormented meditation: "This evening's bulletin said that the Allies are fighting near Pontecagnano. That is where my wife and kids are."

For the old-timers in the hospital, amputees from the African and Russian campaigns, the arrival of the newcomers, wounded in the recent fighting against the Germans, could not but cause new and even more painful reflections. They might not voice their feelings, but the bitter line of their mouth and the shame with which they hid their truncated limbs under the sheet revealed their anguish.

"Yesterday I could still believe that I lost these fighting for my country. I did not know why I had to fight, but I fought just the same. Who was it that said: *Their's not to reason why, Their's but to do and die?* But what am I now? A traitor, perhaps, for having fought alongside the Germans against the Allies? What will I be tomorrow? A mutilated trunk, a half-man who was mad enough to fight and fool enough to lose his limbs?"

What comfort could one give them except the truth? The truth that is so difficult to understand and still more difficult to accept when comfort and self-interest dominate our lives: the value of pain and sorrow, the value of even *useless* sacrifices when they are offered to God in atonement for our own sins and for the redemption of mankind.

"It has been so useless, Father." The words of the young amputee were a statement, but the heart-rending appeal in his eyes revealed his need to be contradicted.

"No sacrifice is ever wasted. You tried to do your duty and no one can ask for more. God certainly does not. Offer your mutilations to Him. Offer them for yourself and for your family: *Father, not my will but Thine be done.* He will unite them to the *useless* sacrifice of his Son in the same holocaust of love. It is your sacrifices that will help hasten for your country the day of redemption."

They were difficult words, but "the spent, exhausted, bitter, wholly dedicated soldier who had burnt out of him, by sorrow and suffering, any faint interest in getting ahead in the world"[1] could understand and accept them.

[1] A description of the fighting-man by Gretta Palmer in *The Sign Magazine*, 1947.

CHAPTER FIVE

The Houses are Blind

BLIND EYES do not see. Nor do they reveal. As I walked through the streets of Rome and looked up at the houses, it seemed to me that they, too, were blind: black and mysterious at night, expressionless by day, seeing nothing, revealing nothing.

There are two hundred thousand people hiding in these houses. They are living under false names, wearing disguises. They are huddled in holes under the roof. Where are they? The stolid front of the buildings gives us no clue. There is no indication of the secrets, the heroism and the terror, the misery and the horrors, inside these walls.

In Via Tasso three men take turns in peering through the shutters. There is a price on their head; they dare not walk abroad. They keep in touch with life, with a world of men and women who talk above a whisper, by squinting at them through the wooden cracks as they hurry by on the sidewalk. They squat round the radio at intervals during the day. The voice of the announcer is almost inaudible, but they dare not risk more. They sit with their ears pressed against the wooden box, waiting and not daring to hope. The sullen building across the street is also blind—and dumb. If it were not, it would cry vengeance, vomit hatred. The number of the house in the street is 145. There are carpet-lined rooms inside, shaded lamps, comfortable chairs, elegant figures of SS torturers tapping well-manicured fingers in emphasis on their mahogany desks. In the adjoining corridors and in the naked rooms below there are blood-spattered walls.[1]

Shots are heard in the night, bombs are thrown and there are

[1] Another infamous place of torture was the Pensione Jaccarino in Via Romagna under the control of the neo-Fascists of Lieutenant Koch.

feet running. A sudden scream, the grinding of brakes, shouts, guttural commands. Then there is silence and no-one knows, except the houses, what has occurred.

Clandestine newspapers are thrust into our hand as we pass by, are pushed through the mail slot, furtively, anonymously. There are thirty of them in Rome—thousands of copies being printed each day. By whom are they written? Where are they printed? There is the death penalty for distributing them. Presses are pounding, men are talking, and the noises are suffocated by the stone walls.

Heavy footsteps are heard after the curfew; it is the nightmare sound of German boots. A man opens the door of his apartment and closes it softly behind him. He runs up the dark steps to the roof. The rope which he carries is thrown over the iron hook firmly cemented into the wall. He slides down it to the terrace of the house next door. Another door, another staircase, and the way is free to the alley behind the house.

In every building men are hiding, army officers, Jews, Allied prisoners-of-war. Round each one a network of protection: women opening the door, answering the phone, searching the market despairingly for food; children running messages, sliding noiselessly through the shadows, wide-eyed, innocent, when a stranger stops them.

A young boy was carried into our hospital one night. He had been padding through the streets in the darkness, his bare feet silent on the cobble-stones. A German patrol turned the corner, unexpectedly noiseless, casting a light from left to right, from right to left. He tried to press into a doorway but the torch outlined him in the shadows. "Halt!" He was running desperately down the alley-way. A hand grenade exploded behind him, spattering him with metal fragments. Blood was trickling down his legs, but he ran, curving in and out of the passage-ways until he knew that the Germans, afraid of those dark alleys, had given up the chase. An old woman took him into her home and, later, brought him to the hospital.

Late one afternoon, a woman knocked at my door. Her anxious eyes were imploring even before she spoke. Her worn fingers were twining and untwining. A friend had suggested that she come to see me. She was sheltering a South African prisoner-of-war. He was just like her son; he was a prisoner, too, in India. The South African was sick—terrible pains, vomiting—it might be appendicitis. She could not take him to a hospital. He would be seized by the Germans; for her there would be the death penalty.

An hour later, a surgeon carrying his black bag slipped out of a doorway and made his way furtively through the dark streets. I met him outside the house. A moment's hesitation—it might be a snare. The surgeon shrugged his shoulders philosophically and knocked gently at the door. It swung open at once. Inside, the water was already boiling; the kitchen table was covered with a sheet. The operation took longer than usual. The table-lamp, held as near as was hygienically possible to the surgeon's knife, cast more shadows than light upon the incision. At last it was over; the patient was put to bed. The surgeon brushed aside the woman's thanks; one does not risk one's life for thanks or for a fee.

When the nine months of the occupation were over, many of us wondered why it was that we had never kept a diary.

Dangerous? Yes! But also humanly impossible to jot down each day's tragedies with the diligence of a housewife making out her daily budget.

So, these personal accounts of life under the occupation were never written, and the memory of many happenings has dulled with the passage of time. One thing remains: a sudden quickening of the pulse as the remembrance, not of events, but of human kindness, loyalty and courage, returns to send the blood coursing through one's veins.

An English prisoner-of war had found refuge in the home of a working man and his wife. His presence meant another mouth to feed, a daily living in fear, the certainty of death for them if he were caught. Perhaps it was this that began to prey upon his mind. He became taciturn, moody. To a friend, who visited him, he confessed the reason:

"I am going to leave here."

"Why? Where will you go?"

"I don't know. I don't care if I am caught. I won't stay here."

He was grateful to the family for the risks they had taken, for the food they had given him, but when he had asked to be allowed to sit with them at table they had refused.

"I do not want to stay where I am not welcome. They are kind to me because they feel it is their duty, but—inside—they still consider me an enemy."

The friend was puzzled; such an attitude was not typical of the Romans and certainly not of that particular family. He spoke to the woman of the house.

"Poor boy. He is so far from home. We are used to roughing it but he is accustomed to all kinds of things that we cannot afford. Even if we had the money, it would not be possible to find enough for all of us."

So, if there was an egg, he had it and they went without; if he found some little luxury on his plate, he took it for granted and did not know that the good people in their kitchen had the usual watery soup and their ration of poor bread.

His friend told him the reason for his banishment from table and he wept. When he did return to his country, he would not tell the fable of the Italian family that had saved him and had hated him, but the true story of kindness that had nearly ended in a tragedy of misunderstanding.

As the heavy weeks of the occupation lengthened into months, the Romans lost their quizzical calm.

Life became more difficult each day. Early in the morning well-dressed women were in the public gardens, searching among the grass for any edible herbs. Mothers waited in line for hours in the hope of obtaining half a glass of watered-down milk. Men trudged thirty miles into the country to seek a small bag of flour. The spectre of famine hovered over the city.

Fear had become a normal ingredient of living. Especially after the removal of German Air Force General Stahel as Commander of Rome and his replacement by brutal General Maeltzer, man-hunts were the order of the day. When the menfolk were a few minutes late in the evening, the women were inconsolable. The round-ups were not limited to escaped prisoners or deserters; the Germans needed men—any men—to work on their military defences. The Romans had refused to collaborate; they must be corralled by force.

A young man was hastening home from his office when a German patrol stopped him. He and sixteen other captives were taken by truck to a labour camp at Palidoro, twenty miles north of Rome. That night, under cover of darkness, three of them managed to escape. The reaction of the Germans was senselessly cruel. Three of the remaining prisoners must die because their companions had escaped. They were made to dig three graves in the sand and to stand round them in a circle. A soldier handed them a lighted match. The prisoner left with the spent match in his hand would be killed.

The game began. The match passed in haste from one to the other. It stopped. The young man holding it was looking in horror at his younger brother only four places away. The soldiers motioned threateningly with their guns and forced him to continue, but the flame was now spent. The loser was shot at the base of the skull and his companions had to lower him into a grave.

The game continued. This time the young man had managed to place his brother next to him. The burning match was again nearing its end. His brother tugged frantically at his arm, but he held it until the flame died. He was thrown into the ditch and the boy— tears running down his cheeks—must help fill in the grave.

How could one live, how must one act in such a sadistic and terror-stricken world?

When the war had first broken out, it had seemed wrong that I should be strolling so pleasantly in the evening under the cool shade of the linden trees while people elsewhere were dying. When Italy had gone to war, my work for the wounded had brought me some comfort, but it was so little compared to the great torrent of human sorrow. All that I could do was to resolve that whoever might come to me for help would find an open door.

I had reason to thank God many times for this simple decision. There was no room for diplomatic reflection: Is it prudent? Can I really help? Shall I compromise myself? All that one had to do was to open in God's name and leave the rest to Him.

How many there were, during the Nazi occupation, who needed help! Jewish mothers and their children; the wives of men in jail; Italian officers and political men in hiding; mothers seeking news of their sons in far-off prison camps; children searching for their parents; escaped Allied prisoners-of-war; men and women caught up in the dilemmas of everyday survival.

How hopeless most of their problems were and how little one could do to help! The disappointments were many, and the wanton cruelty that one encountered engendered a feeling akin to despair.

For three days in succession I had gone to the SS Headquarters to enquire about an aged general whom they had arrested. On the third day, a clean-cut young officer had come out to speak to me.

"I have good news for you. You can assure the relatives of General X that he will soon be released."

I had thanked him, a little hesitantly. Something in his eyes, a certain quality in his suavity, had disconcerted me.

The daughter had wept for joy when I had given her the news. For four days more she had taken a flask of black coffee to the Regina Coeli prison:[1] "Please give this to my father. He has a weak heart." The fifth day, the flask had been refused and a package handed to her; it contained her father's belongings. "He was executed a week ago!"

Sometimes, thank God, we encountered kindness to help re-adjust our vision. Kindness hidden, perhaps, under a cold exterior but all the more admirable when one realized how dangerous it was for a German official—soldier or diplomat—to show leniency. They themselves were under constant surveillance.

I was a luncheon guest at the Finnish Legation.

"Do you know Mr. and Mrs. Z?" It was a young German diplomat who smiled at me across the table. "What charming people they are and how *hospitable*."

I could not miss the emphasis on the last word. That same afternoon I called at my friends' house to warn them to transfer elsewhere the Jewish lady whom they were hiding.

"The Vatican has been bombed!"

It was eight o'clock in the evening and the four explosions had startled us as we sat down to supper. The damage was serious but not irreparable. Only a few yards to the left, however, and one of the bombs would have demolished the dome of St. Peter's.

Although the bombs were British, it was soon rumoured that the small plane that had dropped them had been piloted by the secretary of a leading Fascist. It was no secret that the neo-Fascists

[1] The old prison of Rome.

were furious at the Vatican for refusing to recognize the new Republic of Salo. To drop bombs that might destroy the Basilica of the Apostle was one way for a fanatic to express his resentment.

The German authorities were more circumspect. It is true that on September 13, only three days after they entered Rome, the German Command had placed paratroopers in full battledress along the broad white lines outside St. Peter's Square. They had been careful to explain, however, with perhaps unconscious irony, that they were there to "protect" the Vatican.

The Vatican authorities had replied by arming the Swiss Guards at the gates with rifles instead of the usual ceremonial pikes and by increasing the volunteer enrolment of the Palatine Guards. These token defence measures would have had little practical value in case of an attack, but they indicated that the Holy See would resist any attempt to interfere with the neutrality and integrity of the Vatican State.

As far as the safety of his own person was concerned, Pius XII had no illusions. He knew the long-standing resentments the Nazis had against him. They had rightly attributed to him a large share in the drafting of the Encyclical "Mit Brennender Sorge", Pius XI's scathing denunciation of Nazism. Between 1933 and 1939, as Cardinal Secretary of State, he had addressed more than fifty-five protests to the Nazi Government. His election as Pope had drawn bitter comments: "The Nuncio and Secretary of State Pacelli had little understanding of us: we have few hopes for him: we do not believe that Pius XII will follow a different course. . . ." (*Schwarze Korps*, March 9, 1939.) The Nazis had not let pass unnoticed that the official weekly of the Communist International had praised the College of Cardinals for putting at the head of the Church "a representative of the Catholic resistance movement" (*La Correspondence Internationale*, Paris, March 11, 1939). When the German army had invaded Poland, Pius XII had had the audacity to side with the conquered against the conqueror, to publicly invoke the "resurrection" of Poland at the very moment that Hitler was celebrating his victory. He had stigmatized the invader again when the Germans entered the Low Countries. Within a few hours he had despatched telegrams to the rulers of Belgium, Holland and Luxembourg in vibrant protest against the aggression that had "exposed [each one of them] to the

cruelty of war . . . against its will and against its right". On
this occasion, the Italian Ambassador to the Vatican had told
the Pope how angry Mussolini had been at this interference.
Pius XII had not minced words: "We are not afraid to go to
a concentration camp." If, in fact, the Nazis expected that,
because the Vatican City-State now lay practically at the mercy of
their army, the Holy Father would cautiously avoid offending
them, they were sadly mistaken. The persecuted would be helped
no matter what the consequences might be.

Tens of thousands of hunted men were supplied with Vatican
identification cards to save them from the German round-ups.
The religious houses of Rome opened their doors to more than
forty-one thousand hunted people without distinction of religion
or political belief. The Vatican itself set the example; in the extra-
territorial buildings of the Holy See, Communist leaders such as
Roveda and Negarville, Socialists such as Nenni and Saragat,
Democrats of Labour such as Bonomi and Ruini, Christian Democrats like De Gasperi, were all given shelter. The personal
prestige and the indomitable courage of the Pope were their only
guarantee of safety.

This action of the Vatican followed the line taken by the
Church in all the occupied countries. In Bulgaria Monsignor
Roncalli, the future Pope John XXIII, had succeeded in saving
practically the entire Jewish community. In Rumania, as Dr.
Safran the Chief Rabbi in Bucharest has told us, the Nuncio had
been able to prevent the deportation of large numbers of Jews. In
Slovakia, the Holy See had overcome its reluctance to deal with
Monsignor Tiso, the head of the puppet State, in order to save the
Jewish population. In Hungary the Nuncio, Monsignor Rotta,
gave as many as five hundred personal documents a day to the
Jews, certifying that they "worked" for the Vatican. When the
situation grew worse, he gave shelter to all he could in his bombed
residence and to a host of others in the network of tunnels,
excavated centuries before by the Turks, that led from the cellars
of the Nunciature under the hill of Buda.

Should the Pope, in addition to the principles enunciated in his
famous Christmas messages which were a clear denunciation of
war crimes, and his open support of the local Hierarchies in their
denunciation of racism, the deportation of the Jews, the steriliza-

tion of the unfit, have come out with his own explicit condemnation of Nazi and Russian crimes? It is a question that has been warmly debated.

Strange, how little attention has been paid in these discussions to the point of view of the people who were most directly involved. Nothing easier than for Pius XII, at a distance, to have made a clamourous protest against the German—and, of course, the Russian—war crimes, if he had been willing to ignore the inevitable consequences for millions of already tortured people.

Monsignor Jean Bernard of Luxembourg, an inmate of Dachau from February, 1941, to August, 1942, has told us how the thousands of priests interned there trembled as soon as they heard that another protest had been made by the Church. As for the Protestant ministers, they were convinced that the worsening of the treatment of the prisoners was due "to that great ingenue that the Pope is and to those good men, the bishops, who open their mouths too much. . . . They should get it into their heads, once and for all, and keep quiet!!! They put up a fine show; but we have to suffer the consequences."

The negative consequences of some of the protests made by the bishops were a clear indication of the danger. The action of the Dutch bishops in publishing the telegram of protest that they and the Protestant Churches had sent to the Reichskommissar, Seys Inquart, had resulted in all the Christians of Jewish ancestry being sent to the concentration camps. The Synod of the Reformed Churches had strongly disapproved of this insistence of the Catholic bishops. Was the Synod right?

"If the Pope had spoken," said Dr. Marcus Melchior, the Chief Rabbi of Denmark, "Hitler would probably have assassinated more than six million Jews and perhaps ten times the ten million Catholics. . . ."

No-one who knew Hitler can doubt that, with the last brake removed, his maniacal frenzy would have pushed him into even more tremendous reprisals. The Gauleiters in the occupied countries would have been compelled, for their own safety, to intensify their repressive measures. No-one in an official position would have dared any longer to close an eye to the rescue work being carried on by the Catholics.

As the Pope told the Sacred College on June 12, 1943: "All our words . . . must be seriously weighed and measured by us in the interests of the victims, lest we render their situation more unbearable."[1]

Never, in those tragic days, could I have foreseen, even in my wildest imaginings, that the man who, more than any other, had tried to alleviate human suffering, had spent himself day by day in his unceasing efforts for peace, would—twenty years later—be made the scapegoat for men trying to free themselves from their own responsibilities and from the collective guilt that obviously weighs so heavily upon them.

Not that I overlooked, even then, the possibility of misunderstandings, suspicion and even of malice. When I went to the SS Commands and to the concentration camps in an often vain attempt to help those who were persecuted, I realized that, apart from the danger to myself, my actions might be misinterpreted.

My mind jumps to the year 1947. I was seated in a Club car on the train between Washington and New York. The man opposite me put down his Scotch and soda to ask a question.

"Tell me, Reverend, what do you think of that clergyman over there in Europe?"

"You mean Cardinal Stepinac?" Up to recently the newspapers had been carrying reports of his trial and condemnation. "What can I think, except that after suffering under the Nazis in defence of liberty and of human dignity, he is now being crucified by the Communists for the same reason?"

"Well, I don't know. He must have done something wrong. I have a principle: there is no smoke without fire."

I was conscious of the fact that every newspaper in the Club car had been lowered, and that many pairs of ears were following the conversation.

"That is very interesting. I find it particularly so for a very personal reason. I, too, lived for a time under the Nazi terror. I tried to save as many lives as I could. One thing always consoled

[1] When, in the latter part of 1942, Pius XII had finally managed to communicate with Archbishop Sapieha of Cracow and two other Polish bishops, they had confirmed the enormity of the crimes committed by the Nazis against the civilian population, but had begged him not to make public his letters to them, lest they make matters worse.

me —a very human consideration, I must admit—that if I myself
were to be taken, tortured and killed, everyone would say: Monsignor Carroll died trying to help his fellow-men. It never dawned
on me that some people might say: He must have done something wrong; there is no smoke without fire."

Each long day, seemingly interminable with its anxieties, its
sorrows and its alarms, came inevitably to a close. The shadows
fell. Upstairs, in my tiny room, shutters tightly closed, a little
group gathered. It was an ever-changing group: men with a price
on their heads seeking a moment of spiritual repose; future
members of the Government in a free and democratic Italy;
young police officers who changed their hiding place each day.
We talked and we dreamed. And, while we talked, a kettle boiled
on the stove. It was not a convivial drink, and yet, when the
steaming tea was poured, we joked and we laughed. We laughed
softly, for the consciousness of the dread patrols that lurked outside was ever with us. Some of us joked, perhaps, so as not to cry.
   Laughter and tears! Two safety-valves for human sanity! How
can men laugh in the midst of tragedies? We did, and the jokes
and the laughter seem to have remained, at least on the surface of
our memory. Now and then, however, even today the tears of
yesterday make themselves felt—a vast pool of unquietness in the
depths of our being—with a gnawing fear lest other tears like
them should ever return.

> Shall we go back to Via Monserrato? It is sad perhaps,
> but it is holy, that little room on a top floor!
> Let us close our eyes and rest a little.
> The tea is boiling on the stove;
> the dead are listening to us;
> the living, heavy with thought, remember.[1]

It was usually very late before I got to bed. No matter how
advanced the hour was, I could look across the roof-tops and
know that a light was still shining behind the heavy curtains on a

---

[1] From a speech pronounced by Senator Mario Cingolani for the 25th
Anniversary of the Priesthood of Monsignor Carroll, recalling the part he
played in uniting the forces of liberty under the Nazi occupation.

third-floor window of the Vatican. A lonely figure sitting at his desk, papers dealing with a thousand human problems piled neatly in front of him; a lonely figure bearing upon his fragile shoulders the weight of a suffering world; a figure to inspire and to lead, not by violence, but by the unswerving gentleness of the strong.

CHAPTER SIX

The Humiliation of Rome

ON THE evening of Friday, October 15, a strange-looking woman in shabby black, her draggled hair drenched by the rain, ran across the Mazzini bridge over the Tiber. She headed for the ancient Ghetto, the area round the Synagogue where many of the Jews still lived. When they opened to her, she was breathless. She tried to explain that a lady for whom she worked as a charwoman was the wife of a police officer; he had seen a list of two hundred Roman Jews who were to be deported to Germany.

The Jews knew her; she had relatives in the neighbourhood. She was also a terrible gossip, and that evening her rambling speech was even more incoherent than usual. Angrily she sensed their unbelief; she swore by her children that she was telling the truth. "If only I were a lady," she protested peevishly, "you would believe me."

They told her that the story of the two hundred Jews was old news; a ransom had been paid and the matter was closed. Now all that they and their families wanted was to be left alone and allowed to stay out of the public eye. It was late. Tomorrow was the Sabbath. They shut their doors in her face.

Yes, the Roman Jews had already paid a ransom in gold.

On September 26, the President of the Jewish Community in Rome and the President of the Union of Italian Jewish Communities had been summoned to the German Embassy. They had been received with exaggerated politeness by young Major Herbert Kappler, the Obersturmbannführer of the dreaded SD.[1] He had

[1] *Sicherheitsdienst*, the security service of the SS (the *Schutzstaffeln*, or Nazi party troops, of Heinrich Himmler), commanded by Richard Heydrich.

lolled elegantly against his desk and spoken lightly of this and that, while the two elders sat uneasily in their chairs wondering what was to come. Suddenly his attitude had changed.

The Jews in Rome, he told them, were doubly guilty. As Italians they were traitors. As Jews they were the eternal enemies of the Reich. Unless they delivered a ransom of fifty kilograms of gold before eleven o'clock on the morning of September 28, two hundred Jews would be deported to Germany.

They did not think they would be able to accomplish this in forty hours? Would they like him to assign some of his security troops to help them? No? Sorry! He was only trying to be helpful. To show them how reasonable he was he would give them an extra hour to accomplish their task. His watchful calm was that of a cat toying with a mouse.

By the time the leaders of the Jewish community had been able to meet, little more than a day was left for what seemed an impossible task. Fifty kilograms of gold! Ever since the Ethiopian War the private possession of gold had dwindled to insignificance.

At this psychologically important moment word had come from the Vatican that Pope Pius XII had made available fifteen kilograms of gold by having some sacred vessels melted down. Next day it had not only been the Jews who had flocked to the collecting centre next to the Synagogue. Many of their neighbours had also come—timidly, afraid of offending—to contribute a gold ring or a piece of jewellery. So the ransom had been paid and the Jews had felt safe at last.

Two weeks later, they had refused to listen to poor Celeste. Disconsolate, she had retraced her steps across the Tiber, still mumbling to herself: "If only I looked like a lady they would have believed me."

At midnight the Jews in the old Ghetto were sleeping soundly when shots were heard. Nothing unusual; it was now a nightly occurrence in Rome.

The firing continued. They got up to peer through the slats of the shutters; there were German soldiers out there in the rain, firing their guns into the air, throwing hand grenades purposelessly at the sidewalks. Had they gone mad? Now they were screaming, shouting unintelligibly, laughing raucously. The children began to cry; they clung to the grown-ups, huddled as far back as possible from the windows. Hour after hour the infernal uproar continued. Would they never tire? Why didn't they do something, anything—knock down a door—break into a house— and not just stand there screaming diabolically and shooting, shooting, shooting?

Four o'clock in the morning: the firing stopped. The soldiers were leaving. Thank God! Frozen to the bone, exhausted, the Jews crept back into bed.

Another hour, and a young woman was crying hysterically: "The police!" Nothing could disguise the fearsome metallic tread of soldiers marching to block off the street. A whole family—a father, mother and six children—were the first to be dragged from their home. Hoping against hope, the word went round that the Germans were only going to take away the men, that this was just one of the usual round-ups for the labour corps. An old woman dressed in haste and hobbled downstairs. Two young SS men were at the door.

"We are taking away all the Jews," they informed her.

"I have a broken leg," said she, pointing to her cast.

The two young soldiers motioned to her to escape while she could, an incredible act of clemency when one considers that either of them might have reported the other for his leniency.

Whole groups of families were now beginning to emerge from the streets round the Synagogue. Steel-helmeted guards marched on both sides of them. The grown-ups, frozen into stupefied silence, had already bowed to the inevitable. The children were clinging to them, whimpering, bewildered, looking up into their faces for some sign of reassurance. An old man, with patriarchal gesture, placed his hand upon the head of his little grandson and left it there as though in benediction. And the "Gentile" neigh- bours flocked to their doors and accompanied the sad procession down the street towards the Theatre of Marcellus. The Roman women wept openly and threw their aprons over their heads in an age-old gesture of sorrow and shame. Then they, too, were threatened by the pointed guns and brought to a helpless halt. Their neighbours, the people with whom they and their ancestors had lived for centuries, were being taken away and no-one would ever see them again.

The old woman with the broken leg did not have the heart to stay away from her apartment house. The same two SS men were still at the door. Others were inside. Four children—nephews visiting their uncle and aunt in the apartment next to hers—ran on to the landing as she came limping up the stairs.

"These are my children," she said to the Germans and—incredibly again—they let them go.

Another woman succeeded in escaping with her children. She hurried them across the Garibaldi bridge. A military truck drove by; her husband was on it. She screamed. The truck screeched to a halt. The SS men jumped down and seized her. A passer-by placed a protective arm round one of the children. "This is my child." But the little girl pulled away, her arms stretched towards the woman: "I want my Mummy."

As soon as the dreadful news reached the Vatican, Monsignor Hudal was sent to the German Embassy, and saintly Father Pfeiffer, who had succeeded in obtaining the release of many people arrested by the Nazis, was sent in the name of the Holy Father to the military headquarters. All to no avail. The cattle-cars at the Tiburtino Station were sealed and the train, with more than fifteen hundred men, women and children aboard, started its journey north.[1]

On that fatal morning I was in my office, in the ancient Palace of San Calisto. At ten o'clock I sprang to my feet and ran to the window. I had heard the only too familiar grinding of brakes. The SS had already surrounded a house across the tiny square. A few yards up the street was the restaurant where pre-war tourists had enjoyed the home-made noodles and listened to the twang of Roman guitars. This was Trastevere, the homely quarter of old Rome, transformed into another theatre of savagery. There was nothing that one could do, except watch in futile anger as men, women and children were dragged from their homes.

What would happen to them? To what humiliating and forced labour programmes would they be consigned? Not for a moment did I think of anything worse. The Allied radio bulletins that

---

[1] Altogether 2,091 Jews were deported from Rome by the Germans. The remaining 4,000 found refuge, mostly in the religious houses, and were saved.

reached us daily gave no hint of the existence of extermination camps. Even the energetic protests made by the Hierarchy in the northern countries made no allusion to the existence of any such programme.[1]

There had been rumours aplenty, even in Italy, of Nazi atrocities. The Italian soldiers coming back from Russia spoke of trainloads of seriously wounded German soldiers being halted in railway tunnels by the SS, so that they were killed by the fumes. Some people believed these stories just as firmly as they believed the widely-spread reports of Allied atrocities, that American planes had dropped fountain-pens over towns such as Leghorn, which had exploded in the hands of the children who ran to collect them. "What do you mean, you don't believe it? A friend of mine saw three of the children who had had their hands blown off."

After the war it was still often difficult to learn the truth. There were conflicting reports even on such established events as the Katyn massacre of Polish officers, attributed by the Germans to the Russians, and by the Russians to the Germans. Eventually, of course, it was known that it was the Russians who had been responsible.

I went back to my desk that October morning and wondered why my colleague, Monsignor Vitucci, had not yet put in an appearance. It was one o'clock before he did arrive and he was visibly agitated.

On entering the convent of Our Lady of Sion that morning to say Mass he had found the place in an uproar. A crowd of Jewish women and their children had sought refuge there from the round-up and were in a state bordering on hysteria. Some of them had had their menfolk taken away; others did not know where their husbands and sons had gone to seek a hiding-place.

Almost immediately word came from the Vatican that, because

---

[1] Not even those of the Dutch bishops who had made some of the most outspoken protests against the sterilization of the unfit, the killing of hostages and the brutal treatment of the men and women taken to Germany for forced labour. Why? As the Secretariat of the International Committee of the Red Cross has told us, even the Red Cross "during the war, knew nothing of what was really happening in the concentration camps, which were really extermination camps" (*Communiqué at the XVIII International Conference*).

of the emergency, nuns would be allowed to give hospitality in their convents to Jewish men as well as their families. Soon after. a document arrived from Cardinal Maglione, Secretary of State of Pius XII, to be affixed to the front door, stating that the convent was under the special protection of the Holy See and could not be entered without its consent. The Vatican had been able to have it countersigned by General Stahel.

Going back to the hospital that day, I noticed that a similar document had been affixed to the door of the Franciscan Monastery of St. Bartholomew on the Tiber Island. Little did I know that behind that sleepy façade another four hundred Jews were in hiding.

With each day that passed, Monsignor Vitucci and I found ourselves becoming increasingly involved in the problems of the hideaways. The word had passed from one good sister to another. from one convent to another. Soon we were in touch with many of the more than a hundred and fifty religious institutions that were sheltering the Jews.

Our task would have been made easier if we had known at once of the existence of such organizations as that of the Pallottine Father Weber, which enabled two thousand Jews to leave the country, and that of the saintly Capuchin, Father Benedict de Bourg d'Iré.

In the summer of 1940, a flood of Jews, escaping from the German occupation of the Low Countries, had made their way to the south of France. Father Benedict, from his convent in Marseilles, had furnished them with food, money, identity cards and safe-conducts to take them to Spain or Switzerland. When Marshal Petain agreed to deliver fifty thousand Jews to the SS, Father Benedict appealed successfully to the Italian Army stationed in Southern France to take them under its protection.

"The God of the Jews is also the God of the Christians," the good Father told the soldiers.

After the fall of Fascism, Father Benedict left for Rome. On July 16 he was received in private audience by Pius XII and explained his plan. As the Italian soldiers were withdrawn from France, he would try to have twenty thousand to thirty thousand Jews move with them. Once in Italy, a way would be found to take them by sea to North Africa. The Pope promised his full support.

Contact was established with the American and British diplomats in the Vatican, who in turn informed their Governments of what was being planned. Unfortunately the announcement of the armistice made further steps in that direction impossible. Father Benedict himself was obliged to remain in Rome, now under German rule.

He did not remain idle. With the permission of the Father General, he housed a Jewish refugee organization in the Capuchin Generalate on Via Sicilia, only a stone's throw from the headquarters of the Germans. It soon became the meeting-place for thousands of Jews. Why the good friar was never arrested during the long months that followed, only his Guardian Angel can possibly know.

A block away from the monastery of Father Benedict was a convent of English nuns. The lay-sister opened one day to a visitor.

"Did you hear, Sister? Hitler has committed suicide."[1]

The little nun, who had just suffered a grievous bereavement in the German bombardment of London, grew pale as death.

"Dear Lord, have mercy on his soul!"

Why do I think of her now? Because her sublime charity gives me the courage to remember what one's horror and indignation would have one forget. If peace and love are ever to reign in the world, the chain of hatred must be broken. We must unite ourselves spiritually to those who suffered and join them in forgiving, and share in the common guilt of those who tortured and implore forgiveness.

We must reflect on a truth, which our smug respectability finds it difficult to accept: when the madness born of lust and pride takes hold of a man, shutting out the image of God and stilling the voice of conscience, the door to all wickedness is opened, none excluded. Too easy to dissociate oneself verbally from evil, imagining it to be impossible in one's own circle of life! A shocked father looks at his killer son; a town recognizes the citizens who have tortured sadistically; a nation studies in the newspapers the distorted faces of a hate-ridden mob. Fearful uncertainty enters the heart. A maniac slashes a defenceless girl and grown men look

---

[1] One of the false rumours that frequently circulated in Rome.

down passively from the safety of their living-room windows. A demented soul stands on a roof-top, and the crowd below incites him to jump, to smash himself on the sidewalk, in a sudden, incredible lust for blood.

Band them together: the killers, the sadists, the criminally insane who mask their madness. Surround them with cowards who crave to lord it over their fellow-men. Give them licence and encourage them to corrupt and recruit the young. A vast and terrible army will have sprung up in any land.

Nations, as well as individuals, can cry with the voice of Peter: "Not I, Lord." But there is not one that cannot truthfully confess: "There, but for the grace of God, go I."

It is one thing, however, to try to sort out responsibilities. It is something abysmally different to try to obliterate these monstrous events from history, to act as though more than eleven million human beings—six million of them Jews—did not die by execution squad, in concentration camp and gas chamber, were not sadistically tortured and barbarously massacred by their fellowmen, with every refinement of cruelty that the distorted brains of madmen could devise. We must not forget that it was possible for hundreds of thousands of men in one nation to participate actively in such unspeakable crimes against humanity.

We must remember these things, not to foster hatred, but out of justice to those who died. Remembering their holocaust, we may strive, perhaps with new courage, to prevent, not only the prejudices and the satanical pride in which such savagery can breed, but also the tolerance of lesser evils which prepare the way for it.

It is historically impossible to assess the responsibility of the common individual—the German man in the street—for allowing the Nazi monster to grow. It is probable that few, if any, of them even remotely foresaw the horrors that would eventually result. However that may be, it is consoling to remember the men who need no defence, the men who were not passive, the bravest of the Germans, who suffered persecution and lost their lives because of their courageous fight against Nazism.

Hitler had come to power in January, 1933. By September, 29,780 of his countrymen had been sent to concentration camps. How humiliating for us to recall today the general indifference of the world to their plight, an indifference that lasted right up to and even beyond the outbreak of war.[1]

Between 1933 and 1945 more than one million Germans, non-Jews, were arrested by Hitler's police; more than two hundred thousand of them were executed or met their death in prison and concentration camp.

Even in death these martyrs were not honoured. Churchill, speaking of the German resistance movement, called it "the noblest and greatest that has ever been produced in the political history of any people. . . . We hope for the time in which this heroic chapter of German domestic history will find its just valuation."[2] Only recently has the pall of silence been lifted—and even now only partially—from the story of the gallant men and women who suffered and died for the true honour of their country.

My mind goes back to a sunny day in the early summer of 1934. I had stopped for a moment at the ancient Benedictine abbey at Ettal in Southern Bavaria. An old lay-brother was carefully arranging the religious books on a stand in the vestibule of the church. He told us that he had just been released from prison. He had been guilty of the crime of selling Cardinal Faulhaber's sermons condemning the Nazi persecution of the Jews. As we talked I noticed that several copies of the Cardinal's book were prominently displayed on his bookstand.

"Won't they arrest you again?"

"Probably." A gentle smile played round his mouth and a tiny gesture seemed to say that all of us are in the hands of God.

Was this old monk one of the 2,579 Catholic bishops and priests imprisoned in one horror camp alone? Did he, too, die in the gas chamber? Or did he emerge, a living skeleton, on the day of liberation, to plead for his people as one priest did: "Many people will say: *As these torturers were, so are all Germans.* Please, not all were."

---

[1] When, in 1933, the "Brown Book of the Hitler Terror" was published in New York, an ex-Ambassador of the U.S. to Germany wrote a spirited defence of Hitler in the *New York Times*: Hitler had unified the Germans, created a Spartan State animated by patriotism, put a limit to parliamentary government, which was so unsuited to the German character, etc. (October 15, 1933).

[2] Speech in the House of Commons, 1946.

CHAPTER SEVEN

Peace on Earth

JUST BEFORE Christmas I left the hospital late one afternoon and drove to a village at the foot of the mountains, east of Tivoli. There were men up there in the caves, Italians, Americans, British, hiding like hunted beasts, cut off from every material and spiritual comfort.

When night fell I set out on foot with a young boy as my guide, and headed up the steep mountain paths. After an hour's climb we passed over the shoulder of the mountain and reached a small plateau. My guide left me there and disappeared into the night. After ten minutes there was the sound of feet approaching. One by one, the deeper shadows in the dark revealed each man kneeling before me.

"Padre, perdonami, perché ho peccato."[1]

They asked God confidently for forgiveness because they for their part had already forgiven their fellow-men in their hearts: "Forgive us our trespasses as we forgive them that trespass against us." When Christmas morning dawned they would venture down into the villages for Mass. Or the brave priests of the countryside would come up into the mountains to bring them the Sacred Host, the Christ who came into the world a Child to love all men and Who died, forgiving them, on the scaffold of the Cross.

"Thank you." Dawn would soon be breaking and I was saying good-bye to my little guide. How had he managed to scramble up those stony slopes with his bare feet exposed to the cold? I offered him a small gift: "For your Christmas present."

He turned his head away and looked at the ground.

"I didn't do it for money."

[1] "Father, forgive me for I have sinned."

"I know you didn't. But take this for your mother; she must need it."

His little hand grasped the note. The sleep disappeared from his eyes and one could sense his joy. The local peasants had stripped themselves of their meagre resources to feed the hundreds of Allied prisoners-of-war concealed in the mountains.

"Buon Natale!"[1] Like an arrow released from a bow, he shot towards the group of stone cottages. I pulled my scarf higher on the nape of my neck and sat down on a rock from which I could watch the highway without being seen. Three German trucks passed at break-neck speed. It would be some time before my car appeared; it had to respect the curfew laws.

"Buon Natale!" What unconscious irony! Millions of people were mourning, millions in deadly terror.

I thought of the men in the hills who would not bow to the oppressor, of the people starving themselves to help them, of my little guide risking his life for a cause. Men were making choices this Christmas; not easy choices based on self-interest; their consciences were discerning the right from the wrong. Was not this the real message of Christmas? Might they not find in this war-time Christmas the happiness that is peace, the peace of which the angels sang, which comes on earth to men of goodwill?

[1] "Happy Christmas!"

CHAPTER EIGHT

The Landing

SINCE NOVEMBER there had been little good news from the Fifth Army. A six-week offensive against the Winter Line, sixty miles north of Naples, had cost the Allies 15,864 casualties: American, British, French and Italian. They had advanced a mere eight miles to the hills overlooking the Garigliano river. When they gazed north towards Cassino, they could see an even more formidable mountain range blocking their way.The weary soldiers were sick of the mud and the rain, depressed and frustrated by the bloody, inconclusive fighting.

There was only one meagre consolation for them in that dismal mid-January of 1944: now that they had fought to complete exhaustion there would have to be a pause for reorganization. There would be nothing for them to do in the ruined villages on the bleak mountainside, but there would at least be hours for sleep and a chance to wash themselves clean of the mud.

The troops were stunned—incredulous and then bitter—when their orders came. There would be no halt in the fighting. All available forces were to be thrown into an immediate all-out offensive against the Gustav Line. The British Tenth Corps attacked at once at the lower Garigliano. The American 36th Division struck across the Rapido river, backed up by the XII Air Support Command. The French forces launched a violent attack on the right flank. It seemed as though the Allies had been seized by collective madness. The Germans were amazed at this futile action, but, as a precautionary measure, they rushed up reinforcements from Rome.

The grey dawn was breaking over the little fishing village of Anzio a few mornings later—January 22, to be exact—when the Allied VI Corps went ashore. At last the reason for the incredible offensive became apparent. Less than a thousand Germans were on hand to greet them when the fifty thousand American and British troops and their five thousand two hundred vehicles landed.

The news spread through the capital like a brush fire. There was wild exultation. The Germans whom I met seemed on the verge of panic. Within twenty-four hours´the Allies would be in Rome.

If we could have seen General Alexander's dispatch that day to Winston Churchill we would have been even more encouraged: "We appear to have got almost complete surprise. I have stressed the importance of strong-hitting mobile patrols being boldly pushed out to gain contact with the enemy."

Mr. Churchill had replied: "Am very glad you are pegging out claims rather than digging in beachheads."

That evening, as soon as our duties in the wards were over, we climbed into the old clock-tower on the roof of the hospital. What we could hope to see from there I do not know; any direct view towards Anzio was blocked by the Janiculum and Aventine hills. In any case it was thrilling to stand there, on the open platform of the belfry, looking out over the seemingly sleeping city and knowing that tens of thousands of people like ourselves had thronged to the roofs to await the dawning of a new day.

Next morning I was faced with a dilemma. I had promised to visit the children in an orphanage on Monte Mario. If the Allies arrived in the early afternoon, the bridges over the Tiber would probably be destroyed and I would find myself cut off on the other side. I decided to take the risk, but I was uneasy. As soon as I could, I said good-bye to the children and hurried back to the bus stop. An unending column of trucks and ambulances passed me on the Via Aurelia. It was a precipitous retreat.

A city policeman crossed over to speak to me. "The buses stopped running an hour ago. By now the Allies have reached Rome."

I went down the hill on foot and headed for the Tiber. German soldiers with sub-machine guns were guarding the approaches to the bridges, congested with military vehicles. I was almost running from one bridge to another. Only when I reached the narrow Ponte Sisto was I allowed to cross.

That evening we were impatient to climb the iron ladder into the tower. It was delightful up there. The air was mild and the sky star-studded. The domes of the Chiesa Nuova, of St. Andrew, St. John of the Florentines, St. Charles of the Chainmakers were bathed in moonlight. A little farther off, the beautiful dome of Michelangelo rose majestically from the shadows. In the direction of the sea, all was still; not a sound, not a sign of activity.

For several nights we climbed the ladder, each time more despondently. On Wednesday there was a change. All night long we could hear the dull thunder of German tanks and troop-laden trucks rushing through the streets towards the south.

On Friday I dined at one of the Embassies. A German Secretary sat next to me. "This inactivity is incredible. The Americans must be planning another landing farther north."

The incredible had indeed happened. The commanding general had been unwilling to change his defensive plan, even after it became evident that the landing was a success and that the expected German counter-attack had not materialized. The first twenty-four hours of Allied inaction gave Field Marshal Kesselring time to rush his anti-aircraft guns to the new front and hem in the invaders on the beachhead. Another twenty-four hours and he had pulled out every unit that could be spared from eight different divisions at Cassino and dispatched them to Anzio in what he himself described as "a higgledy-piggledy jumble". Twelve hours more and he had brought in staff officers from the First Parachute Corps and the Seventy-sixth Panzer Corps stationed at far-away Pescara, to weld the heterogeneous mass into an efficient fighting force. It was a masterly show of action. In assigning the command of the Anzio front to General von Mackensen, Kesselring could already say: "I regard our position of defence as consolidated and we no longer have to fear any major reverse."

In Rome we knew nothing of these dramatic developments. We were too bitterly disappointed by the non-arrival of the Allies even to wonder what had gone wrong. We climbed the steps to the roof no longer. Four interminable months would go by before the Allies would enter Rome.

Across the desolate, rain-sogged fields on the Anzio beach-

« There was gentle dignity in their resignation and a deep well of sadness. If they should every return home they would find their cottage destroyed ».

« A ration of dark bread ».

head, the Allies could see a circle of volcanic hills rising in the distance. The grey basalt rock peeped out among the naked chestnut groves, and the bare rows of vines traced a dull pattern across their lower slopes.

I wonder whether any of those weary soldiers had visited the Castelli Romani before the war. If they had, how tantalizing to remember the peace of the little towns whose names are associated with the light, golden wines in the straw-encased flasks: Frascati and Velletri, Marino and Albano. They are the historic sites of ancient Tusculum, founded—so legend says—by Telemachus, the son of Ulysses; of Albanum, where Pompey sojourned and the Emperor Domitian built his palace; of Castrimoenium and of Velitrae, the city of the Volsci, who were the sworn enemies of Rome. In a much later century these villages became the fortresses —the *castelli*—of the great Roman princes, perpetually feuding with each other.

In my student days I liked to visit the Castelli, riding from Rome on one of the little blue trams which rattled noisily through the cobbled streets. Women gossiped as they filled their copper jars at the fountains; old men sat in the sun, and sturdy-legged children with strong white teeth and radiant smiles—startlingly reminiscent of the cherubs of the Renaissance painters—played merrily on their way to school. Life bubbled with the innocent, fresh, lazy effervescence of the local wine. There was poverty but not misery.

"This is to become a battlefield?" Impossible! Where will the armies come from to devastate this unimportant, under-developed land? To the south there are only bare mountains, stretching across the peninsula from sea to sea. Only Africa lies to the south. No army would ever come from there.

And yet, in the month of January, 1944, an army did come from the south. The soldiers were in their dug-outs at Anzio, and the Castelli Romani, the Alban hills and the great plain stretching below them to the sea had become a bloody theatre of war.

I was walking up the main street of Albano on February 1. It was about one o'clock in the afternoon. The town was less animated than usual, but there were children playing and old men sitting in the doorways.

We heard the planes overhead and the children clapped their hands with the unconscious cruelty of the young. They were beautiful, those Flying Fortresses, glistening like silver in the morning sun. Fifteen, thirty, forty-five, sixty: the children were counting them as they flew by in perfect formation like flocks of wild geese. Every morning at that same hour they passed over the Castelli on their way to bomb the railway farther north.

The people gazed up at them as they did every morning, the women apprehensively, the old men grumbling toothlessly to themselves. This morning there was a difference. Even as we watched, black things were detaching themselves from the silvery planes like grapes from the bunch on the vine. There was a scream that was one long lament, and people were running madly in all directions.

An arm pulled me violently into a store and out of the store into a room in the rear. At that moment the bomb fell in front of the cottage. For an interminable second we watched the ceiling bending towards us, before we were buried in a deluge of plaster and splintered wood and baked-earth tiles. The beams held firm at one end and formed an arch over us as we crawled out, cut and bruised and covered with plaster, but otherwise unhurt.

I was unconscious of everything except that I was alive. I must have been leaning against a part of the ruin; I cannot believe that it was my legs that held me erect. Then I began to see things: the sky and the beautiful tower of a church. I had never seen that church before; it had been hidden by the houses. Where were the houses?

A little boy was sitting on what had been a house, his house, his home. He was not weeping; he was only trying to understand. Five minutes ago he had had a home. He was playing in the yard in front of it. Surely in a few more minutes his mother would appear at the door and call him: "Gianni, come in and wash your hands. Your dinner is ready."

And he would go inside and the table would be set near the window and in the corner would be the rough little cot where he would lie down in the evening, before his mother would come to tuck him in and kiss him good-night.

His mother! Still the tears would not come. How could they come? How could an eight-year-old understand that five minutes ago he had had all that and now . . . no table near the window, no little cot in the corner, no home . . . no mother . . . any more . . . for ever and ever . . . never any more.

I did not speak to the child. Other hands must have led him away from the ruins. But the memory of him and of all the things he said in the vacant misery of his eyes remained with me.

As events had precipitated on the battlefield, the Allies had bombed one small Castelli town after another, probably in the mistaken belief that the Germans were using them to billet their troops. The poorly built cottages had crumbled under the bombs and the death-roll had lengthened into the thousands.

The survivors were in a dilemma. If they left the area, where could they go and how could they take their household goods with them? Most of them sought refuge in the wine cellars under their ruined homes or in the caves on the outskirts of the towns.

After the bombardment, Pope Pius XII gave orders for the Papal Villa at Castel Gandolfo to be opened immediately for the evacuees.

When I drove up to Castel Gandolfo that afternoon the towns-people were discussing it in the street: the "Albanesi" had moved into the palace of the Pope. *Albanesi!* I was puzzled. Then it dawned on me: the Albanians whose presence was so offensive to the good people of the town were not from the country across the Adriatic; they were old rivals from next-door Albano. "Just like their nerve!"

The main staircase inside the palace had become a public dormitory; on each wide step someone was sleeping. In the Hall of the Swiss Guards, where the Pope usually granted audience to larger groups of summer pilgrims, there was a sea of beds and mattresses. People were eating and mothers were washing their babies. The marble floor, the red damask walls and the gilded ceilings added an incongruous note, but the great Pietà at the end of the hall—the dead Christ being lowered from the Cross—was singularly at home in the pathetic gathering.

The gardens presented a bizarre spectacle. Round the massive trunk of each centuries-old tree a family had erected a makeshift canopy of wooden slats and tarpaulins as a shelter for themselves, their donkey and their goat, their table and cots and chairs. The formal Italian garden was bordered by rows of improvised huts and tents that turned it into a down-at-heel country fair. The underground hall of the Emperor Domitian gave a refuge to hundreds of people who only a few days before had had a home of their own and were now penniless.

When night fell I looked down from the terrace of the villa and tried to piece together the puzzle of the battle being fought on the plain before my eyes. There was gunfire far out to the left. How could I know that it marked the attempted advance of the American 3rd Division towards Cisterna, or that it had brought them three thousand casualties in the past five days? How could I have believed—even if someone had told me—that the fierce fire to the right, towards Campoleone, meant that the very flower of British regiments—the Irish Guards, the Scots Guards, the 2nd Sherwood Foresters, the 1st Duke of Wellington's Regiment, the 1st King's Shropshire Light Infantry—were engaged in a desperate fight for survival? They were names enshrined in history; they had no place in the confusion of that desolate expanse of land.

How could I know, as I gazed in helpless fascination at the battlefield spread before me like a map, that it was thus, perhaps, that history was made, not by the brilliant execution of military master-plans, but by the indomitable, unquestioning courage of tired soldiers bogged down in the mud?

A day or two later I received a call from the Vatican Secretariate of State asking me to go to Genzano, to arrange for the evacuation of two communities of sisters to Castel Gandolfo. Setting out from Rome that afternoon, I could not foresee that this excursion was to lead to the Anzio battleground and its caves becoming my home for the next five months.

It did not take me long to complete my task and see the sisters safely on their way. There had been no interference from the German gendarmes posted on the outskirts of the town. I walked up the main street of Genzano to the square and waited by the fountain for my car to appear. As I stood, melancholically contemplating the ruins, a countryman came running down the hill. He implored me to wait a little longer: his little boy, only two years old, was deathly sick and should be taken to a hospital.

I accompanied him down the road that leads to the lake. Soon there were no more houses and I began to wonder where we were going. It was growing dark and the waters of the lake were black and strangely menacing. We had almost reached the bottom of the descent when the man motioned me to follow him down a path leading directly to the water. Still no one in sight. A few more yards and he was sliding down into the mouth of what looked like an enormous drainpipe. That, in fact, was what it was: an ancient Roman tunnel, built to control the water level of the lake.

I slid down the muddy slope and entered the drain. A man held up a lantern, and the light shining into my eyes made it difficult for me to see. Stumbling over outstretched feet, banging my head against wooden slats in the wall above me, I followed my guides. With outstretched hands I could easily touch the damp walls of the tunnel; overhead, on a trellis made of branches, old people and children were lying; along the sides of the gallery, men, women and children were squatting with their backs to the wall. They looked up, startled, as I squeezed by. Their first thought was of a death; a priest, at that hour! The women crossed themselves, and the lurking terror of a pestilence showed itself in their eyes.

The child was feverish, his tiny face burning to my touch. The mother was bending over him in anguish.

One of the men took the child into his arms and our little procession made its way back, down the drain, past the three thousand people crammed into that unspeakably foul refuge. The clean air outside was laden with all the fragrance of the countryside; honeysuckle, damp grass, moist rich earth.

Even before I reached the top of the mound, the tunnel seemed like a far-off nightmare. There was silence round us, the reverent silence of nature, accentuated by the gentle lapping of the waters.

There was silence, but my guide told me that nine thousand people were living in the vicinity of the lake, herded together in caves all round us and in the cellars under the ruins of the houses. They were asleep now, most of them, or trying to sleep. Before long the fireworks would start and then no-one would sleep. As if to confirm his words, the guns roared for a few brief moments on the battlefield; then they, too, were silent. The sick child was delirious during the drive back to Rome. He kicked incessantly at the blanket in which we had wrapped him. It seemed an eternity before we reached the children's hospital on the Janiculum hill.

For the next few days my mind kept reverting to the plight of the people in Genzano. From what I heard, I suspected that similar if not worse conditions prevailed in the other areas, from the lower Anzio beachhead all the way across the hills to the valley leading up from Cassino. Surely it should be possible to provide some help, organize at least some medical aid, for these abandoned populations. I spoke to Cardinal Pizzardo and it was he who told the Holy Father of my wish to go into the battle areas. What did I hope to do? I would have been embarrassed to have had to give a reply. To my surprise, Pope Pius XII accepted it as a natural request and gave his approval at once.

Count Nasalli Rocca, the director of the hospital, gave me permission to use two of the ambulances to transport the sick from the Castelli to Rome. He also allowed me to ask for volunteers among the young recruits of the Italian Association of the Order of Malta. The response was overwhelming. I gave our little group the pretentious title of "Medical Aid to the Battle Areas". We loaded up an ambulance with supplies, and, with no permit from the military and a great deal of mournful head-shaking from our friends, we headed for the Front.

CHAPTER NINE

Civilians on the Battlefront

WE WERE lying in a ditch by the side of the road. The giant planes were veering in the direction of the south. The air-raid was drawing to a close but bombs were still falling; it would be a waste for the airmen to take any of them home unused. Perhaps one of those last bombs would devastate our tiny plot of ground.

The last one had fallen; other people might be dead, but we were still alive. The thirty thousand human beings who were crouching in caves or lying in ditches breathed their own selfish sigh of relief.

We did not leave our hole yet; it was always prudent to wait a few minutes after a bombardment. It was then that fighter planes liked to swoop down from nowhere and strafe the roads with machine-gun fire.

Giacomo and Marcello were talking. They were two of my volunteer helpers from the Order of Malta. Giacomo was tall, slender, with a boyish face and expressive eyes. Marcello was smaller, of more stocky build, with a wide, humorous mouth. Today, Giacomo is a lawyer; Marcello, a doctor. Then, they were eighteen years old and they were discussing fashions.

"Great heavens! Here we are lying in a trench and these two are arguing about the masculine mode." Marcello was for the loose, sporty coat; Giacomo, for the more sophisticated attire.

The past weeks had been filled with intense activity; groups of volunteers had been formed in the different localities; the caves had been disinfected; medical dispensaries had been organized; the dangerously sick were being transported twice a week to Rome.

When each day ended we were so tired that, even though we slept fully clothed on the floor of a cave, we fell asleep at once.

The boys who accompanied me had never known anything but
the luxuries of a comfortable home; an appeal to their generosity
and the inspiration of an ideal had transformed them overnight
into self-reliant and self-sacrificing men.

Prince Enrico Barberini had come to ask me to allow his boy
to accompany me to the battlefields.

"He is your only son." If anything should happen to him, I
thought, this family would be extinguished after centuries of illus-
trious history.

"He wants to go with you and I am proud that he does."

Early one night there was a brief bombardment. I lay in the
dark of the cellar listening with strange detachment to the muffled
sound of the explosions; they must be at the lower end of the
village. My three helpers had been dead tired that evening; as soon
as they had stretched out, they had dropped off to sleep. When the
bombardment ended, I crept out alone to make a brief tour of the
streets. Before I had reached the bottom of the hill, the three boys
were already by my side.

There seemed to have been no casualties. The people underground had not even bothered to come outside to assess the
damage. In a town already destroyed, a few houses more or less
. . . ! Then, in the middle of the Via Appia, we saw him, the
man whom the one chance in a thousand had killed, struck
between the eyes by a tiny scrap of shrapnel. We detached a
wooden shutter from a ruined house and carried him to the nearby
graveyard. The isolated German trucks, dashing at break-neck
speed towards the front, swerved in fright as the shaded head-
lights caught the funeral procession briefly in their glare.

Afterwards we sat for a while by the roadside, looking down
into the darkness that was the Anzio plain. There was contentment for us in the silent tranquillity of the night.

"We must get some sleep. At six o'clock we must be on our
way to Velletri and I must say Mass before that."

I knew that there was no sacrifice that I could not ask of these
boys. They knew that there was no hardship that I would refuse to
share.

The tiny lamp burning before the Blessed Sacrament threw a
flickering light on to the rough ceiling. If I had stretched my arm

beyond the white sheet separating the sleeping area from the improvised altar, I could have touched the door of the tabernacle.

An old man was snoring. An old woman was mumbling in her sleep, repeating a name over and over again: "Sandro! . . . Sandro! . . . Sandro! . . . Sandro!" Marcello and the other boys slept soundly close to the wall. Down the centre, on malodorous mattresses, pieces of sacking and rough boards, were the old folk from the battlefields. Without a home, without a family, their nights were filled with dreams of yesterday, of stalwart sons now dead or far away, and of grandchildren scattered through the caves and cellars of a desolate land.

When morning came, Christ would emerge from the cellar. He would return to His little church on the street above. Tonight He was with us in the cellar, vigilant while we slept, another refugee in a world where hatred walked boldly abroad.

"Chi è?"[1]

I had awakened with a sense of shock. A hand had grasped my shoulder.

"Chi è?"

This time it was the voice of Don Giua, the local Salesian superior, that softly echoed my words. He, too, was awake.

"Sono Mario."[2]

It was the local Communist leader, arrested three days previously by the SS, news of whose execution had already spread through the town.

"I was to have been shot today. I managed to escape."

By now the SS would be searching everywhere for him. They would leave no stone unturned.

The whispering seemed to echo against the low roof of the cellar, as loud as the blood pounding in one's ears. Would the Germans sleeping in the next room hear it?

"Go into the woods, as far as the fountain. Tomorrow, after the curfew ends, I will meet you and try to get you through the German block-posts into Rome."

The shadowy figure melted into the darkness. Several minutes of suspense. By now he must have passed the sleeping Germans;

[1] "Who is it?" [2] "I am Mario."

now he must have reached the top of the stairs. Would there be a sudden outcry, a burst of fire from a sub-machine gun? The silence was unbroken. He must have evaded the sentry and vanished into the night.

I struck a match. Two o'clock. Still three hours left to get some sleep.

Once a week I returned to the city to search for the medical supplies and food that would enable our hospitals to carry on for another eight days. I had to make a report, too, to the Commission of Cardinals for the Vatican City on the situation of the refugees in the Papal Villa.

What a luxury it was to take a shower and to sleep in a real bed! Wonderful, too, to walk through the streets of a city that was not a mass of debris, where men still lived in houses, where they had beds and a kitchen in which to cook and a door to keep out people and windows to protect them against the dust and the cold.

I brought a piece of bread with me one day from the Front. In consistency and general appearance it resembled a door-knob. It was made of the ground-up pulp of a young poplar tree, mixed with crushed lupins. When it was moist and still warm from the ashes of the fire it could be eaten. When it grew cold it became a piece of wood again.

What excitement the day that a mule dropped dead on the dusty path leading from the pine-grove near Nemi! The owner sold the meat on the spot to the first-comers. We were among the lucky ones to eat it for supper.

The only real food to be found in those areas—a food that undoubtedly kept many people alive—was the wine. The enormous wooden casks were stored, as they had been for centuries, in cool grottoes carved deep into the soft stone of the hillside. The Germans had found most of these cellars and requisitioned the wine, but some of the smaller deposits had gone undetected. Every now and then a German patrol would stumble on to one of them; they would generally take away what wine they could carry and let the rest run to waste. When I heard of an act of vandalism I knew that it probably would not be long before I would have to accompany the owner to the German military police to lodge a protest.

When I had first entered the battle area I had had several sharp encounters with the German gendarmes. They had even wanted to confiscate our ambulances on the grounds that they were not allowed to circulate outside the city limits of Rome. Very soon, however, they had become accustomed to seeing us on the roads near the Front and we were not interfered with any further.

It was lucky for all of us that we did not have any SS troops stationed permanently in the Castelli area. The regular German soldiers were dour and resentful towards the Italians but they were usually well behaved. When they were drunk—and in the evenings they often were—it was better to keep out of their way. Apart from that, they were good, bad or indifferent as are soldiers in any army.

In my dealings with the local German commanders I soon found that, if I had any requests to make, the most effective way was to present them as simply and confidently as possible, no matter how improbable it might seem that they would be granted. This direct human approach was surprisingly effective.

In Genzano we needed two large ground-floor rooms for an emergency hospital; the only suitable ones were in the Salesian Institute and they were being used by a detachment of soldiers as a kitchen. Accompanied by a Dutch Salesian student, I visited the head surgeon at the German military hospital to ask for his help. The colonel received us in his operating theatre, a medieval hall of the Sforza Cesarini Palace with ornate ceilings and frescoed walls. He had thrown his rubber gloves on to a metal tray and was removing his white smock. His face was lined with fatigue and in his eyes was the look of spiritual weariness I knew so well. On a golden table with a marble top lay the limbs he had amputated.

I explained to him how badly the local population needed an emergency hospital. Only two days previously I had watched a country doctor operating by the light of an oil lamp in one of the caves. The surgical instruments had had to be fished, one at a time, out of a pan of boiling water.

"I should be shot for operating under such conditions," the doctor had growled as we scrambled back up the hillside.

The German colonel was sympathetic but said that in his position he could not help us; only the gendarmes had any jurisdiction over civilian affairs in the town.

In the military police barracks the hard eyes of the sergeant never left my face as I made my request.

"Do I understand that you are asking me to move *German* soldiers for the convenience of *Italian* civilians?"

"No, I am asking you to help me prevent an epidemic that would not make any distinction between soldiers and civilians."

He stood for a moment, a man hacked out of granite.

"All right!"

He turned on his heel. That was that. The soldiers might curse me as they dismantled their kitchen, but the sergeant's word was law and would brook no appeal.

"Will you hear my confession, Father?"

The young German soldier slipped into the outhouse where I had spent the night and knelt on the dirt floor. He would have to be careful not to be seen when he slipped out again; otherwise no one could foretell what the consequences might be.

Karl, an older soldier, looked rigidly in front of him each time we met in the yard. As we drew abreast, however, he invariably indulged in a prodigious wink. One day I ran into him in the woods above the town.

"Are you still here, Karl? I don't know how you have succeeded in keeping out of the fighting."

"Carlo malato"—his gutteral pronunciation of Italian was atrocious—*"molto malato."*[1] He rolled his eyes comically and clutched first at his stomach and then at his chest in a mock search for his ailment.

Karl was one of the many Poles on the Anzio Front who had been forcibly enrolled into the German Army. He was determined not to die in it. "My old woman is waiting for me in Warsaw."

The fighting on the Anzio Front was terrible in its intensity. "It is worse than Russia," said one of the veterans of the Russian campaign, when more than two thousand Germans were killed in a single day. Yet, once the firing stopped, the countryside looked

———
[1] "Charles is sick . . . very sick."

as peaceful as ever. The brown land rolled luxuriantly towards the blue horizon. There was the scent of violets in the air and, now and then, the wild song of the meadow larks. From afar one could not see the ruins of the cottages nor the stunted limbs of the trees. The massive tanks, waiting menacingly in the hollows, were camouflaged by nets intertwined with leaves.

I found myself on the battlefield on one such peaceful evening. I was taking advantage of the lull to visit an aged couple and bring them some flour. They had refused to leave the dark cellar under their farm and were now completely isolated in that desolate no-man's-land. It was a joy to walk through the soft darkness and inhale the heady scents of the countryside. I made my way noiselessly along the rural lanes. There was still a mile to go when, suddenly, the sky burst into light and the Front was alive.

I threw myself to the ground and crept under an overhanging boulder. The shells were exploding some distance away and yet the noise was deafening. There was the vicious chatter of machine guns and heavy tanks were coming up on the left. If this was to be an all-out attack it would probably continue until dawn.

Unexpectedly the firing began to diminish. Soon it stopped altogether, except for a few sporadic bursts of machine-gun fire. It was one of those mysterious actions for which the outsider could find no logical explanation. There might be silence now for the rest of the night.

I made my way through the ruins to the cellar where the old people lived. They were shaken by the recent uproar, but it was an everyday occurrence and they accepted it philosophically.

"It is strange, Father," said the old woman. "Before the war we had everything, our farm, our family . . . everything. We were not bad but we never seemed to find time to pray. God was so far away. Now everything has been taken from us and He is so near. The whole world seems to be full of Him. . . ."

As I made my way through the devastated fields in the darkness I, too, felt the presence of God. When meditation fails, it is only sorrow that can silence the clamour of life and let us hear His voice.

It is strange to walk through a battlefield in the dead of night and know that two armies are facing each other in the blackness. Tens of thousands of young men are looking up at the stars and wondering whether those same stars are shining over their homes. Young men are poised to kill and to be killed, and yet their hearts are not filled with hatred. There is only bitterness and fatigue and an unspoken longing for home.

The night had its moods, as did the day. When the fields were bathed in the magic light of the moon, even the ruins stood out from the shadows with a savage beauty of their own. But, sometimes, the sad wind moaned across the desolate plain and the abandoned villages were spectral in their solitude. Then, loneliness weighed heavily and a nostalgic longing for peace welled up inside us. On some evenings we ate and there were cots on which to rest. On other nights there was no food and very little to shelter us from the cold.

One evening we were lucky. Marcello and Giacomo and I found ourselves close to the old monastery of Palazzolo on the slopes above Lake Albano. The joyful prospect made us hasten our steps. At Palazzolo we were sure to find a bed.[1]

When we arrived, Anita, the caretaker's wife, was taking a steaming bucket of wine off the fire. The German sergeant, who had brought it in to be heated, was standing by the door. Obviously the villa had been occupied by the army. Before carrying the wine outside the sergeant threw a piece of meat and a loaf of bread on to the kitchen table.

As soon as the songs from the refuge told her that the soldiers were settled for the night—they were sleeping in a two-thousand-year-old Roman tomb for safety—Anita pushed aside a loose board in the ceiling and brought out some ham and cheese. Eaten with the black German bread, it was the most delectable meal we had tasted in months. While we ate, Anita sat by the fireside with her children. She was a tiny woman, with toil-worn hands and hair prematurely grey.

"If I did not ask them for food twice a day, they would know that I had some. One fine day they would start searching for it. As it is . . . !" She shrugged her shoulders.

[1] Palazzolo was the empty summer home of the Venerable English College, my own Alma Mater.

"As it is, you are more than a match for them," I thought.

We slept that night in an outhouse, on a pile of mattresses thrown on top of a mountain of furniture. Even the restless goat tied to the door-knob could not keep us awake.

Rising early, I strayed as far as the Via dei Laghi, where army trucks were unloading the German dead from the previous day's fighting. Their usefulness had ended and they were being piled unceremoniously into a common ditch. I stood for a moment in silence, not unconscious of the resentful glances that some of the soldiers were launching at me. When I raised my hand in a last blessing, one blond youngster picked up his gun and shouted hysterically: "Our dead don't need any prayers."

I returned to Palazzolo. A German captain was standing in front of the house. He asked me to wait for a moment. When he returned he brought with him a pile of crucifixes, probably removed from the students' rooms.

"You had better have these."

I thanked him and asked him whether he was a Catholic.

"No, but . . ." He saluted without completing the phrase and went back into the house.

Before I left Palazzolo, Luigi, the caretaker, took me aside with a conspiratorial air. The local partisan leader wanted to see me. An Allied prisoner-of-war, whom they were hiding, was sick. I sent Marcello and Giacomo off to Castel Gandolfo; no use having them run a needless risk.

Down by the lake, I found a young countryman leaning nonchalantly against a rock. He seemed to know me, for without more ado he led me to a clearing at the foot of the cliff.

"Lupo!" He was looking up at the rock face.

The leafy branches of a small bush growing out of a crevice parted, and the partisan leader squinted down at us. Instead of the stern face I had expected, I found myself gazing at the rubicund countenance of an old acquaintance.

"Monsignore!"

A rope-ladder came hurtling down and I clambered up into the cave. We first discussed the matter of the Allied soldier. I did not ask where he was but I did agree to find a doctor for him.

A straw-encased flask and two glasses appeared as if by magic.

"How is your wife?" I inquired, a trifle maliciously.

"Eh! Eh!" He closed one eye in a ponderous wink and smacked his lips with relish as he tasted the wine.

In the peaceful pre-war days the last thing that I would have expected of so hen-pecked a husband was that he would blossom into a hero. At that time he could not have drunk a glass of wine without a nagging from his buxom Maria.

Anita, Luigi, "Lupo". Perhaps not one of those stolid country people had ever been to school. They understood little of the remote causes of the turmoil round them. They had no desire to be heroes. Nevertheless they had the same quiet strength, the resourcefulness, the wry humour, that had enabled the Italian people at large to adapt themselves uncomplainingly to the abnormal situations of war. It was this amazing resilience more than anything else that made me hopeful that Italy would rise again when, at long last, the savage war ended.

In the meantime the destruction and the bloodshed continued. When March ended, the Allies on the Cassino and Anzio Fronts had a casualty list for the past two and a half months of more than fifty thousand men.

At the beginning of February, General von Mackensen had launched an all-out offensive to throw the Fifth Army back into the sea.

They had been days of unbearable suspense. From the hills we were looking down upon the battlefield where the fate of Rome and perhaps of Western Europe was being decided. During the day it was difficult to tell how the fighting was going, but, when night came, even a superficial observer could see that the line of Allied fire was being pushed back slowly but surely towards the sea.

On February 17, the Fifth Army was only seven miles from the water, fighting desperately to hold the positions it had reached the very first day of the landing. Von Mackensen threw in every available man and, next day, the German tanks and artillery moved forward for the final thrust down the Albano-Anzio road.

The Italians in the Castelli were despondent. The Germans were jubilant.

"Tomorrow the Americans will be in the water."

We stood all night in the darkness of the hills, seeing what we

1946: The Boys' Court in the first Boys' Town of Italy.

« To inspire, one cannot set oneself up on high ».

feared was the worst and hardly daring to hope. Yet, even before the next nightfall, the German High Command knew that its massive offensive had failed. The Allied artillery had poured an avalanche of shells into the path of the attack. It had been touch and go. Could the Germans break through the deadly fire that covered the last one thousand yards? The Allied units, isolated on the flanks, were fighting desperately. In the centre the shells were falling mercilessly, relentlessly, upon the mass of grey-clad soldiers pressing forward, wave upon wave, in the concentrated assault that Hitler himself had ordered. Once again the issue had hung in the balance. Though the fields were covered with their dead, the Germans had still found the strength to make one tremendous last push. It had seemed impossible that the Allies could hold on to that tiny strip of land. They had, and the titanic onslaught of the enemy had spent itself.

On the Cassino front it was the Allies who were making a gigantic effort to break the stalemate that had developed after the petering out of their January offensive. They hoped to do so by the sheer weight of bombardment.

On February 15, 576 tons of explosives were dropped on the Monastery of Monte Cassino, causing its almost complete destruction. A month later, the town of Cassino was bombed. This time more than 1,320 tons of explosive were dropped, followed by an artillery barrage in which two hundred thousand rounds were fired in two hours. The favourable results that had been confidently expected were not forthcoming. After the two offensives, the Germans were more firmly entrenched than ever.

When the second bombardment took place I was eight miles away, on the outskirts of Pontecorvo, sufficiently far to dull the terrific impact of sound but not to rob the experience of its apocalyptic character. Strange, therefore, that the day should have left so small an impression on my mind. Perhaps great cataclysms surpass our human powers of absorption. It is not the mass catastrophe as such that can strike most deeply into the soul. It is the tragedy of each lonely soldier who dies, multiplied—if you will— a million times, the tragedy of each little child crawling pathetically through life with its mutilated limb.

When the guns had been silenced and dusk had begun to fall, I ventured forth from the cellars of Pontecorvo to drive away from

Cassino. Along the deeply rutted road, that once passed through rich farmlands and now traversed a barren waste dotted with craters and barbed wire and the gnarled stumps of trees, came two small figures. At first they were two specks in the distance, but as they drew near I saw that they were children: a boy and a girl, holding each other by the hand as little children do. Their clothes were filthy; their faces and legs fouled by mud; their eyes swollen by excessive tears. Now they smiled, a vacant smile that put a chill into one's heart. Seemingly unconscious of my presence, they meekly took their place beside me in the car.

I saw them again in the months to come, well looked after by the good sisters in an orphanage. They continued to smile, heart-rendingly, upon a world whose cruelty had caused their tiny minds to break. Whose children were they? No-one's. They were the children of the war.

"Whose boy is it?" an old woman asked me one day as I extracted a child from the ruins where his parents lay buried. Then she saw the uselessness of her question. "Just one more child alone in the world."

It was only now that I began to notice the presence of children in the war. I had seen them in the hospitals after bombardments; crushed limbs, sightless eyes, fragile little bodies hideously burned. I had seen them running madly through the streets, screaming pitifully as the bombs fell. I had seen them huddled in damp caves and cellars, shut out miserably from the fresh air and the sun. Yet their sorrow had been too unobtrusive. I had accepted it as a part of the one, great, tragic panorama of the war. Their natural resilience, so far superior to that of an older person, had reassured me. I had been blind to the effects of the terrible loneliness that war had planted corrosively in their souls.

My awakening started in Albano the day that I saw the little boy sitting on the ruins of his home. He was trying to realize that his whole world, past, present and future, had dissolved into nothing. I began to wonder: what happens to the heart of a child when he suddenly discovers he is alone? What would I have felt if, in one dreadful moment, I had lost my mother and my father and my home?

I had come a long way, but not far enough. Once again the uncomplaining voices of the children were too weak to be heard. If I wondered about their future, I reassured myself with the vague thought of relatives who would provide, of orphanages that would give them shelter. How unquestioning we can be in our calm acceptance of another's sorrow! We do not see ourselves in the garb of the man whom Christ condemns, who rudely asks: "Am I my brother's keeper?" Yet our placid assurance that in our well-ordered society some organization will provide is often equivalent in its practical results to a blunt rejection of our brother's grief.

A few months later the Liberation would dawn and a hundred thousand homeless children would emerge from the caves. They would invade the cities. Their hungry faces and bitter eyes would greet us on every pavement. In the late winter of 1943-44 that moment had not yet come.

CHAPTER TEN

Hope Dies

DURING MARCH the situation of Rome deteriorated rapidly. Every day thousands of refugees reached the city from the bombed-out towns to the south. They came furtively, using the back roads to avoid the German block-posts on the highways. When they had passed through the medieval gates of Rome and were able to lose themselves in the anonymity of the city's teeming population, they heaved a sigh of relief. Not to attract attention, not to fear the cold eye watching, wondering, suspecting: this was worth enduring the squalor, the uncertainty, the degradation of a refugee's life in Rome.

Some of the newcomers had relatives in the city. They crowded into tiny apartments, content to sleep on the bare floor. If they had no other place to go, they searched for a few square yards of space in one of the malodorous refugee camps.

A million refugees—completely destitute—in a city of a million and a half people, mostly unemployed! What employment could there be in an encircled city?

Starvation lurked at the door. Each day the furnishing of flour from outside hung by a thread. The actual reserves could only have provided one small roll of bread per person for two days. When, as a child, I had read of the siege of Paris and of the desperate people hunting for rats, I had never realized how easily a modern city could be reduced to a similar plight.

To save Rome from starvation, the Holy Father took it upon himself to send one convoy of borrowed trucks after another northwards in search of flour. Only when the trucks had been loaded did they return to Rome, seeking to slip through the tortuous mountain passes in the safer hours of dusk. There were casualties among the drivers; even the neutral white and yellow flags of the Vatican could not protect them when the planes were strafing the roads that led to Rome.

I was returning late one evening from Terni, the steel city seventy miles north of Rome. As I approached the next town, a medieval citadel perched high on the rock above the highway, the sky behind me was red with the flames that had suddenly cut into the night. Terni was under bombardment.

The slope towards the pass that cuts through the mountains was partially blocked by a long line of trucks. They had pulled in as close as possible to the towering rock, hoping that no flare from the planes would suddenly reveal their presence. The drivers had scrambled off the narrow highway and were clinging to the stone face of the cliff below the road. There was no place for them to seek shelter, no cave into which they could crawl.

With all lights extinguished, I edged past the trucks, hugging their black outline to avoid the unseen drop into the ravine.

"Buona fortuna!"[1]

A stolid young face had peered into my car; now the leader of the Vatican convoy recognized my voice.

"Iddio ce la mandi buono!"[2]

I reached the top of the hill, my eyes still straining to discern the white stones that bordered the highway. My mouth was dry. Pulling into a space overhung by trees I got out of the car. The voices of the truck drivers calling to each other came faint but clear from the hollow.

Now a gruff voice was making caustic remarks in the Roman dialect. Laughter greeted his quips. The fear was passing. The raid was ending and each one was conscious that once again he had faced death and had survived.

With a strange feeling of detachment I watched the city burn· ing in the distance—a monstrous funeral pyre in the blackness of the night. Were the men who joked and I who observed indifferent to the human beings caught in that inferno? It was not callousness; it was the human mind saying no to the insanity of too much suffering.

In Rome the Allied bombardments continued. Each morning at the same hour the far-off thunder reached us from the outlying

---

[1] "Good luck!"   [2] "May God have mercy on us!"

sections of the city. If our ambulances were available, they hastened to the scene to assist in the removal of the wounded. A hundred visions of horror: a wrecked hospital and the patients dragging themselves painfully out of the ruins; a burning home and a young mother—right eye dangling on cheek—running in a frenzy with her dead child in her arms. All about them, the life of a great city going on dully, methodically, with hardly a glance at the tragedy in the house next door. When we headed south again, for the more dangerous, perhaps, but more breathable atmosphere of the battlefield, we heaved a sigh of relief.

The terrors of the occupation continued, but the embers of the Resistance were growing cold. The brilliant invective of an Italian commentator from London exhilarated us for a moment, but many of the Italian language broadcasts from America were disheartening. *"This is the American way of life."* One does not risk one's life to listen to platitudes. "If that is all the Americans understand of our plight there is no hope left."

It appeared as though time was standing still and the whole future was to be frozen into the stagnant present: the Allies permanently facing the Germans at Anzio and Cassino, the population living for ever in the grey hopelessness of the occupation.

March 12 came and, with it, the first of two dramatic events that were to break through the apathy: the audience granted by Pius XII in St. Peter's Square to the refugees in Rome.

I marvelled at the courage needed to call such a meeting in an occupied city. The dangers were obvious, as some of his closest advisers did not hesitate to point out, but Pius XII was not to be deterred; to encourage fear was not the answer to human problems. He was the Bishop of Rome; he had a right to speak to his people.

In the morning it rained and, even though the showers stopped, the sky was menacing. There was a heavy air raid, and rumours were circulating that there would be German reprisals for the Fascists killed in a recent ambush. The streets were silent as usual —there was little traffic in occupied Rome—but, as the afternoon hours advanced, an eerie sound was heard in continuous crescendo: the patter of tens of thousands of feet converging on St. Peter's.

When the lonely figure in white appeared on the balcony, clearly outlined against the sombre grey stone of the basilica, half a million people had gathered in the square. Pius XII spoke to them not of war but of peace, not of hatred but of love. He spoke of their sufferings, of trust in God, of prayer and penance. He appealed to men of all nations to safeguard the universal patrimony of Rome. The very calm of his measured tones inspired confidence. As his last words faded into the air, the vast multitude shouted itself hoarse.

On March 23 tragedy struck: an ambush and—in reprisal—the massacre of the Ardeatine Caves.

At six-thirty that evening I was returning home from the Irish Legation to the Holy See. It was after the curfew and there was no-one on the streets. I hurried through Piazza Esedra and down the hill to Piazza Barberini. "Halt!" A German soldier had emerged from the darkness and poked his gun into my ribs. He peered closer and saw that I was a priest.

"Get away! Quickly, quickly! Go, go!" He was wildly agitated and his alarm communicated itself to me. Something terrible must have happened. I ran into the narrow Via della Purificazione. Avoiding the main streets and keeping close to the wall in the dark alleys, I made my way home.

Rumours were already spreading as to what had taken place in Via Rasella.

Every day, about the same time, German SS trucks drove up the narrow street leading from the tunnel under the Quirinal hill. No-one had paid any attention to the street-cleaner's cart standing there that particular afternoon nor to the street-cleaner himself—a Communist partisan—sweeping the road with his characteristic broom. As the column drew near, he had lit the fuse to the explosives in the cart. Thirty-three SS men had been killed.

The German reaction was ferocious. General Maelzer was beside himself with rage. There must be a mass execution. The whole district must be razed to the ground. Finally word arrived from Berlin that ten political prisoners must be shot for every German killed.

The names of the victims trickled through, one at a time. One did not know what fresh shock the next morning's whispered

news might bring. Several days went by before I learned that
Lieutenant Maurizio Giglio, one of the first wounded to enter our
hospital in the early days of 1941, was among the dead. He had
often wondered vaguely what he would do after the war, not
knowing that, in the end, it would be his own young enthusiasm
to open and close the way to his future. With the Nazi occupation
he had thrown himself passionately into the struggle for freedom.
On March 17 he had been arrested. After seven days in the torture
chambers, the SS had transferred him to the Regina Coeli prison.
From there, bound hand and foot, he and the three hundred and
forty-four other hostages had been taken to a lonely spot outside
Rome. The regular army had refused to carry out the massacre,
so it was left to the dreaded SD to shoot them and throw their
bodies, dead or alive, into the nearby caves.

"This is the day which the Lord hath made; let us be glad and
rejoice therein."

It was Easter Sunday. There was open-air Mass in the refugee
camp at Cesano. An immense crowd, made up of old men, women
and children, had gathered round the makeshift altar.

The peace of the Easter morn was rudely shattered. After the
consecration, and before the tinkle of the server's bell had died
away, the skies were filled with the drone of Allied bombers. The
terrified people threw themselves prostrate as the earth shook
under the tremendous impact of the bombs. The crackle of
machine-guns and the screech of gyrating planes told us that
German fighters had also made their appearance in the sky. A
Messerschmidt fell in flames; three others took to flight. The
Flying Fortresses, their mission accomplished, headed back towards the south.

When I returned to Rome there was a distraught woman in the
back of my car. Her parents and the one child remaining to her
from a former bombardment had perished in the morning raid.

"Where will I stay tonight?" She repeated the question over
and over again with frightening monotony. There was no-one to
provide for any more, except herself. One can weep and weep and,
suddenly, there are no tears left and one must carry on as before.

I left her in Rome and drove on to Velletri. The unploughed
fields, stretching as far as the eye could see, were verdant with the

spring. Not a tank could be seen on that strange battlefield. Not a sound disturbed the quiet of that Easter afternoon.

I halted at the Capuchin monastery. A venerable white-bearded monk showed me the ugly wounds on his head where a drunken soldier had just beaten him with the butt of a gun. He had tried in vain to prevent the tabernacle from being desecrated. Now, not a single soldier was anywhere in sight.

Velletri itself was a ghost city. There was a death penalty for anyone venturing inside its walls. As I passed, a cloud of swifts rose from the mute bell-tower of a church and circled tumultuously overhead. Even in the lanes outside the town only two or three country people were abroad. On Tuesday Giacomo, Marcello and Giuseppe would join me to start our rounds of the medical stations. That evening I had only one small mission to accomplish.

I must find someone who could direct me to the villa of Countess Z.; for more than two months her relatives in Rome had received no news of her. The first countrymen I stopped could be of no assistance; they were all fugitives from other towns. Finally I espied an old woman in ragged clothing coming slowly down the lane.

"Excuse me, Granny. Do you know where Countess Z. is living?"

The old woman trembled; my sudden appearance had frightened her. I repeated my question. To my astonishment she let fall her two pails of water and burst into hysterical sobs.

"Sono io la Contessa Z! Sono io la Contessa Z!"[1]

She screamed the words, beating her breast frantically to emphasize her identity.

I accompanied her to the cellar of an outlying farm and left her with a peasant family until I could return to take her to Rome.

I went on towards Cisterna where I intended to spend the night. I received a cordial welcome. It seemed as though that eventful Easter Sunday was to close on a note of peace.

The first gigantic explosion brought us to the door in alarm. There was no mistaking the fearsome whine of the shell piercing the air, the earth-shattering force of its exploding. Only the guns of the Allied battleships off the Anzio coast twenty miles away could produce such an intensity of sound.

[1] "I am Countess Z."

We sat in the cellar for an hour, well knowing the uselessness of it; the first shell to hit the cottage would bury us alive. With chronometrical precision, with absolute regularity of pattern, the shells fell upon the empty town, the explosion of one mingling with the screech of the next one on its way. Only when dusk came did the guns out at sea cease to vomit their fire upon the land. The sudden silence was painful, almost more difficult for the mind to bear than the ear-splitting sound that had preceded it. We sat, saying nothing, until it was time to eat our plate of soup and lie down to rest.

I was tired, more with the mental stress than with the physical exertions of the day. I feared that I would not sleep.

I dreaded the thought of lying awake and thinking of a war that dragged on, of brutality that showed no sign of diminishing, of the heavy weight of human hopelessness that oppressed us.

But sleep I did, and in the blessed oblivion of unconsciousness peace came.

CHAPTER ELEVEN

Exodus

SEATED ON top of an antique bureau, each jolt of the swaying bus threatened to bounce my head against the roof. The leg of a chair poked me in the back and a goat sniffed at my shoe. I could not pull up my foot, so I contented myself with giving the inquisitive animal a discouraging poke on the nose. Chickens fluttered excitedly under the furniture, disturbing an old man in his slumbers. His fat wife, enthroned on a table-top, with Marcello and Giacomo on either side, fanned herself dramatically, raising her hands from time to time in abundant gestures of despair.

The motor began to splutter; the bus bucked like a bad-tempered mule and stopped dead in the middle of the road.

"Che cosa faccio adesso?"[1] The householder, who was carrying his belongings to Rome, threw up his arms in exasperation.

"That is none of my business," retorted the driver. "You'd better unload your junk at once. If the Germans found me carrying civilians on a requisitioned bus they would shoot me." He opened the hood and took a pessimistic look at the motor.

Giacomo and Marcello and I had been lucky to get a lift that far. We continued towards Rome on foot, leaving the man and his wife sitting disconsolately by the roadside. The chickens were pecking contentedly among the grass and Billy the goat was sniffing the ancient milestone with a far-away expression in his eyes.

The exodus of refugees from the Castelli had begun early in February, immediately following the Anzio landing. As soon as the bombardments ceased, the flight, too, had come to a halt.

Towards the middle of April it was the Germans who decided

---

[1] "Now what must I do?"

that the towns of Genzano, Ariccia and Albano should be evacuated. Anyone who remained after April 30 would be interned in the refugee camps at Cesano or Torre Gaia.[1]

On the afternoon of the fatal day I drove through the abandoned towns with Signor Bonomelli, the director of the Papal Villa at Castel Gandolfo, to make sure that everyone had left before the four o'clock deadline. For several days trucks from the Papal Villa had been helping the poorer people move their belongings. Thanks to this, the evacuation had been an orderly one.

Ariccia, a village of three thousand inhabitants, was our last stop. We followed the parish priest into the church and knelt for a moment in front of the bare altar. The old man tugged at the ropes and the bells rang out the Angelus for the last time. Bells inviting to prayer and no-one there to pray! We did not dare to catch his eye. We were wondering—as he undoubtedly was— whether he would ever return to his beloved parish and to the people whom he had baptized and married, exhorted and scolded for over half a century. It was the first time that I had seen a town abandoned. It was illogical, inhuman. Homes without people; the uprooting of families; the disintegration of a community that had dwelt in the same place for a thousand years.

A solitary shutter was banging in melancholy fashion as our car drove slowly over the bridge.

At Genzano there was a delicate problem to be faced. A shelter for old people and homeless children had been set up in the cellars of the Salesian Institute and time was needed to find a new refuge for them. I drove over to Lanuvio to see the colonel who was the area commander. He received me with the icy correctness to which I had become well accustomed. As soon as he heard what my mission was, he cut me short. The evacuation order had come from General Headquarters and he had no authority to extend the deadline.

I insisted, hinting that if he could not grant permission for the

---

[1] On April 18 the status of our organization had changed. It had become an integral part of the Pontifical Refugee Commission, officially founded that day by Pope Pius XII. Monsignor Ferdinando Baldelli was appointed President; Father Faller, S.J., Father Carlo Egger and Monsignor Carroll-Abbing, the other members.

old people to stay he could at least ignore their presence for a few days.

He looked at me quizzically. "You tell me—pff—like that . . . so simple . . . *ignore their presence*. What makes you think there is any probability of my saying Yes?"

"Why should you say No? These poor people can harm no-one. They are alone in the world."

"Ah! Then you believe that I, a German officer, can be a human being and actually do kind things? I am afraid that few people round here would agree with you."

I kept silent. Whatever comment I might have added would not have helped matters.

The colonel stood at the window, as though admiring the perfect symmetry of the tiny square. The buildings round it were gems of rural architecture. In the fifteenth-century palace Prince Marcantonio Colonna, the victor of Lepanto, had been born. I studied the ramrod rigidity of the colonel's back. He turned suddenly.

"Very well. I don't want to disillusion you. Keep the old people inside the Institute, but—I warn you—if they are found straying outside, my soldiers will have to do their duty and arrest them."

One difficulty had been overcome; another one—and a seemingly insurmountable one—remained: how were we to feed our charges in the lapse of time before their transfer? We were completely cut off from Rome; no truck was allowed to bring provisions into the evacuated areas; our present supplies could not possibly last more than a day or two. That very evening the solution arrived and from a wholly unexpected source. The German cook came to tell us that the soldiers who were billeted in the same building were going to forgo a portion of their daily ration to feed the old folk and the children.

I wondered what the colonel at Lanuvio would have thought of this act of human solidarity on the part of his own rough soldiers. In their simple gesture there was no calculation, no finesse, only compassion.

We were never really able to express our gratitude to the soldiers for their kindness; outwardly they maintained their surly attitude and went about their daily duties as unsmilingly as ever.

When the time came, however, for the old people and children to leave, it was the soldiers who, in their own undemonstrative way, seemed to regret their departure most.

They stood in knots in the yard, watching the Little Sisters of the Assumption fluttering busily among their charges. The old people were too confused to grasp the significance of their journey. If they felt a wrench, it seemed to be more than compensated for by the prospect of a ride in the buses, for many of them the first automobile ride of their lives. The children were more matter-of-fact, looking out of the windows with indifferent eyes and munching stolidly on their hard piece of bread.

The soldiers loaded the pots and pans and the mattresses on to the roofs of the buses and tied them expertly with rope. When the doors slammed to, they walked as far as the gate to watch the cumbersome vehicle trundle heavily down the hill. I hesitated for a moment before going over to offer them my hand. I was surprised at the warmth of their grasp. Karl, the middle-aged Pole, held my hand a trifle longer than the rest. A young Czech soldier seemed close to tears. There was a dreadful feeling of finality about our farewell.

I drove away along the Olmata, under the trees now green with spring. The next time that I would come up that avenue, less than a month later, I would have to stop my car and walk on the bodies of the German dead before I could reach the top of the hill. The stench of death would be everywhere, the terrible sickly-sweet smell of corpses in decay under the sun.

As the Allied pressure against the enemy lines increased, the probability grew that the Germans might soon have to withdraw to a new defence line along the crest of the hills. In such an event the presence of thousands of hostile civilians in the caves would constitute a grave danger for them.

It was no surprise, therefore, to hear from a good source in Rome that the High Command was preparing an evacuation order for the rural area round Velletri. It will not be an easy task, I thought, to dislodge more than thirty thousand people by force in a zone exposed to enemy fire. This was the argument that I used to convince the local German commanders to act with moderation in interpreting the new evacuation orders that began to reach them. The whole burden of a rooting-out action would fall on their shoulders.

Time worked favourably for us. As far as Velletri and Castel Gandolfo were concerned, the policy of procrastination was so successful that the Liberation came before an evacuation was carried into effect. In Lanuvio, however, we were taken by surprise; without warning, the entire population was rounded up, placed under an armed escort and marched sixteen miles to the refugee camp at Torre Gaia.

I met them by chance at Frattocchie, near the Ciampino airport. I had stopped my car to stare at the effects of a recent bombardment, when the sad procession came into view. The women broke into a chorus of supplications. "My sister lives at 62 Via Nomentana. The name is Morrone." "Let my daughter know where they are taking me. You remember me? I have the little store at the corner." *"Padre, padre, che ci fanno? O Dio mio buono!"*[1]

An old man threw down his bundle in feeble protest. The SS men strode up and down the line, shouting unintelligible commands. One of them motioned me away angrily with a gun.

The long line wended its way slowly, like a sluggish serpent, along the curving road. The one young man in the group had helped the old man to rise and had taken his bundle upon his own shoulders.

They were going to Torre Gaia—the Gay Tower!—to what had been a steel works and was now a camp. They would find two women in charge, in addition to the military commander and his staff. One, a middle-aged Bavarian, hard-faced, hard-voiced, a disciplinarian but not cruel. The other, young, elegant, neither German nor Italian. What was she? Spanish? Yugoslav? She was charming and informative whenever I or any of the other members of the Pontifical Refugee Commission visited the camp. One day, however, after leaving, I had turned back unexpectedly. I had found her, as I had been told that I would, presiding over the distribution of the soup ration with a horsewhip in her hand. When the Allies arrived in Rome, they told me that Rosina was one of the people whom they were most anxious to catch.

[1] "Father, Father, what are they doing to us? O my dear God!"

I could picture the arrival of this new group of evacuees at the refugee camp. I had been at the Cesano camp one morning when the German trucks unloaded several hundred of them at the gate. It was early and the camp commander was still asleep in his villa. The womenfolk seated themselves on the grassy bank by the roadside, pulling their woollen shawls tightly over their shoulders to conceal the meagre bundles of linen that they clasped to their knees.

There was gentle dignity in their resignation and a deep well of sadness. Their lives had been emptied of every significance. If they should ever return home they would find their cottages destroyed. Their only trust lay in God; their only link with life was the presence of their children. One of the women kissed a religious medal, while her arm instinctively pressed closer the child huddled sleepily at her side.

Thousands of people were already living in the vast sheds herded together in demoralizing promiscuity. The newcomers would be given a few square feet of bare floor; they would stretch out there at night and remain immobile throughout the endless day. There was nothing to do in the camp, nowhere to go, no shady spot where they might enjoy the open air. They would take their place in line at the taps each morning to wash in the feeble trickle of water. They would line up again at midday to receive their ration of dark bread and watery soup. The children would play listlessly in the dusty desolation of the stockade, accepting even the depressing monotony of survival as just another aspect of the mad world into which they had been born.

A column of German trucks going north for supplies stopped at the Cesano camp one day. The sergeant in charge brought orders to transfer five hundred refugees to another camp further north. Names were called in alphabetical order and, as each one responded, he or she was pushed on to a truck.

"Gianni, Gianni." A woman was hanging over the dashboard, desperately calling the name of her child. The boy could not hear her; he would not know that he was without a mother until later that day, when he had searched frantically in every nook and corner and finally found someone able to tell him that she had gone. He would continue to stay in the camp, listlessly, hopelessly. There was nothing else that he could do. When the Liberation came he would leave. He would head for the city and join the army of homeless children searching for food.

In the battle area itself there were many orphaned children, stunned, emaciated little creatures whose predicament only became known when hunger drove them forth in desperation from under the ruins. I met one in the woods, late one afternoon. He had fallen to the ground from exhaustion. There was an instinctive tremor in his body when I felt his pulse. He could not have run; his matchstick legs were not strong enough to carry even the negligible weight of his skeleton body. After that first shudder of fear he seemed to lose consciousness of my presence. His eyes, deeply sunken and ringed with black, contained the premature knowledge of all suffering. They were too tired to look out upon the world, now that the spirit had already relinquished its hold upon life. They gazed vacantly inwards, passing effortlessly beyond the wall of death into eternity.

I carried him in my arms for several miles. With the fingers of one hand I could have encircled the muscleless, fleshless bones of his leg.

As a small boy I had picked up a baby bird that had fallen from its nest and held it on the palm of my hand. I had been moved to pity as I felt the feeble pulsation of its tiny heartbeat. Now I held a starving child in my arms. The heartbeat was as feeble as that of a bird; the pinched nostrils struggled desperately for air, as they do when death is near.

In a cave a peasant woman and her husband found a spoonful of sugar. Dissolved in warm water, we fed it through the purple lips and the lowered barrier of the teeth. There was a sudden contraction of the ribs as though the liquid would be rejected, but it stayed down. The limbs relaxed, the head sagged and the eyelids closed mercifully in sleep.

The woman's fingers touched the silky eyelashes, the only beautiful—stupendously beautiful—feature left in that pitiful death's head of a child. She handled him as I had done, afraid that a rough gesture might break the eggshell fragility of his body. She laid him on a folded blanket; fluffing it up at the sides so that he lay cradled in its warmth.

I slept in the open that night, a hole in the ground for my hip and my coat folded over a root for my pillow. Tomorrow I would carry the child to Velletri and wait for the ambulance to take us to Rome and to the Hospital of the Child Jesus on the Janiculum hill. I looked at the stars and listened to the far-off thunder of the guns. War! Heroic war!

What was I to do with the other homeless children I had gathered from the battlefield? I had placed most of them in temporary shelters until such time as it might be possible to transfer them elsewhere. With the bombardments increasing day by day it was dangerous to leave them there any longer.

The solution came when Father Carlo Egger, a member of the Pontifical Refugee Commission, returned from a trip to Umbria. He had found two medieval communities, Gubbio and Citta' di Castello, which were far off the beaten track and were willing to give hospitality to the children.

Buses had still to be found, and petrol, and the necessary travel permits. A week went by before everything had been arranged.

I came that morning from Cisterna, a little town down on the plain, at the extreme limit of the German front line. The day had begun in lively fashion with a naval bombardment by the American ships off the coast. Shellfire followed me all the way to Velletri. I stayed there for an hour, discussing with Father Laracca if there was anything more that could be done for the people in the caves. Flight was now impossible. We could only hope that, when the Allied advance did come, it would roll over them rapidly enough to give them a chance of survival.

When I reached the Via dei Laghi, the panoramic motor-road of which Mussolini had been so proud, an Allied plane swept low over the car, its machine-guns spitting flames. It was dangerous to continue, but an unusual sense of urgency made me prefer the risk to waiting in a ditch for the firing to cease.

As I approached the villa where most of the children were housed the Flying Fortresses were already overhead and the bombs had begun to fall. The car came to a halt in the shadow of the trees. At that very moment a bomb hit the house to which my eyes had instinctively been drawn. A great sickness twisted agonizingly inside me. One minute the building had been there, an ugly three-storey structure. Sixty seconds later it had already settled into a compact pile of ruins. My heart pounding violently, I clambered over the debris into the garden overlooking the lake. There was only one hope left. Yes, the outhouse where the kitchen was situated was still intact! Inside, huddled under the tables, speechless with terror but physically unharmed, were the children. They had been waiting for the distribution of their morning piece of bread when the bombing started. Some boys were missing but the women in charge told me that a few children had run off into the woods. We would not be able to know until later whether any had been buried under the ruins.

At four o'clock that afternoon the buses—dilapidated military vehicles—arrived from Rome. We led the children on to the road. As each name was called, a child scrambled on board. Against three names I traced a cross; three bodies had already been found under the debris.

From overhead, indistinct at first, then louder, came the heavy drone of Allied planes. The children froze; terror flared into their eyes. Screaming, they fled into the woods and huddled under the bushes and fell into the ditches. The ones in the buses threw themselves out of the windows or crushed their way out of the doors, running blindly like maddened creatures, not seeing, not caring, where they went or how.

The bombs were falling again. A tree, only a hundred yards away, was torn from the ground and hurled into the thicket. I crouched by the side of the road with a child in my arms—the only one left—and the beat of her heart pulsating madly against my arm mingled with the uncontrollable quivering of her thin little body. At last it was over and only then did the girl begin to cry; sobs like vomiting tore at her sides and strange gurglings strangled in her throat. It was better, however, than the terrible stillness of shock that I had seen tearing at a child's mind.

It was a long time before the children found their way back to the road. We hastened our roll-call. The doors of the buses were closed, and the new pilgrimage began.

There was a halt in the Vatican. It was not safe to venture on to the Via Flaminia until nightfall. Tables had been set up in the courtyard near the Hospice of Santa Marta and hot food had been prepared. The Allied diplomats who lived in the adjoining buildings[1] came out of their apartments to gaze in horror at the emaciated faces of the children and at the black rings that still circled their eyes.

When darkness came, the buses began their four-hour journey northwards to Gubbio and Citta' di Castello. On their return journey—luckily empty—they were machine-gunned from the air and destroyed.

---

[1] When war broke out, the diplomatic representatives of four countries entered the Vatican City: France, Great Britain, Poland, U.S.A. Later, the representatives of eleven others: Brazil, Chile, China, Colombia, Cuba, Ecuador, Italy, Yugoslavia, Peru, Uruguay, Venezuela. After the Liberation the former left and others entered: Japan, Germany, Hungary, Rumania, Finland, Slovakia.

CHAPTER TWELVE

Liberation

DURING THE night of May 11 the Allied offensive exploded into action.

We had stayed up as usual after our meagre supper, sitting round the rough wooden table in our underground refuge. The flickering light from the solitary candle cast grotesque shadows on the vaulted ceiling but could not penetrate the dark recesses of the cellar. We were waiting for eleven o'clock to come, the hour when the Allies usually launched their last bombs. Useless trying to sleep before the planes had withdrawn for the night.

At eleven o'clock sharp, instead of the aerial bombardment, came the unexpected thunder of Allied heavy artillery. We did not know it then, but it was the beginning of a general offensive that would culminate a week later in the storming of Monte Cassino by General Anders's Polish troops. All the way along the line, from Cassino to the sea, and including the Anzio Front, a thousand guns opened fire simultaneously, smashing into carefully identified enemy positions. While the Germans were still reeling under the shock, the airforce followed up with more than fifteen hundred sorties. The French crossed the Garigliano river and penetrated deep into the Gustav Line.

On May 13, two days after this offensive on the Cassino Front began, Signor Bonomelli, the director of the Papal Villa, and I called on the German general in command of the Castelli area. An edict had just been posted in Castel Gandolfo ordering the entire population to leave within forty-eight hours. The inclusion of the Papal Villa in the evacuation order called for a formal protest, but this was not the only reason for our call. We hoped to persuade the commander to extend the evacuation deadline for all the people in the town. If they were obliged to abandon their belongings, they would never see them again.

The general had his headquarters in a tree-encircled villa on the side of Monte Cavo. In pre-war days it had been a country house like any other, with a dog barking at the gate and children playing in the garden.

The general was icily polite but told us quite bluntly that the presence of extra-territorial properties in the immediate vicinity of the battle-line created an intolerable situation for the German Command.

I ventured to point out that the extra-territorial properties had been there to start with and that the Vatican was not responsible for the High Command's choice of a battle-line.

The general bowed stiffly to acknowledge my observation and went on unperturbed: " . . . and the presence of escaped Britishers inside the Villa is certainly not helpful to us."

"I can assure you," I replied, "that there are no *English* prisoners-of-war in the Villa or its grounds."

For the first time a thin smile cracked his lips. He bowed ironically.

"English, no, but South African, yes."

He was referring to a South African prisoner-of-war who had broken his leg down by the lake and had been carried to the infirmary in the Pope's Villa.

The commander had thawed considerably. He ended by promising that the wording of the order would be rectified and the evacuation date for the people in the town extended to May 30.

As we left the Villa, I remembered the last time I had been there, on April 20. I had paused to watch a soldier placing flowers and ribbons on the top of a pole in the garden.

"Was ist der fest-tag?"[1] I had asked.

"The birthday of Hitler."

"Happy feast," I had said ironically.

The soldier had turned on me ferociously and spat out the words: "Would that he had never been born!"

[1] "What feast-day is it?"

Something new was definitely in the air. There was a perceptible note of discouragement among the Germans, a sense of expectancy, a new tension during the Allied bombardments. I found myself moving rapidly from one part of the Front to the other, trying to contact the isolated groups of civilians before the situation changed.

I called upon the German colonel commanding the western area of the Castelli. I told him that a rumour was circulating that his troops were planning to destroy what was left of the little town of Lanuvio before they withdrew. The colonel did not deny the rumour nor express surprise. He did not even deny the possibility of an imminent retreat, which was significant in itself.

"I will do what I can," he said quietly.

"You are in command."

He looked at me for a moment reflectively, as though undecided whether to speak. Then, bitterly: "You do not seem to realize that we are living again in an age of vandals and barbarians."

In nearby Genzano I picked up another rumour. The caretaker of the museum down by the Lake of Nemi had heard a sergeant speaking of "burning the boats". The boats were obviously the two large galleys contained in the museum, that had been used by the Roman Emperors as floating palaces and had been salvaged only a few years before by partially draining the lake. I informed the Fine Arts authorities in Rome of the danger and they took up the matter with the German Embassy. One of the Secretaries at the Embassy was indignant with me for giving credit to an idle rumour: "Do you really think we are such barbarians?" When the Allies arrived a week later, the historic boats had already gone up in smoke and all that was left were a few ashes and the bronze nails that had held the boards together for nineteen hundred years.

Although Signor Bonomelli and I had protested, as in duty bound, against the inclusion of the Papal Villa in the evacuation edict, we were worried about the fate of the thousands of people who had found shelter there. If Castel Gandolfo were evacuated, the Papal Villa would become an island cut off from the outside world. If the Germans so wished, they could prevent any food supplies reaching it from Rome and destroy the pipe that brought water up from the lake. The evacuees themselves had no such worries; they were on Papal territory, which, as far as they were concerned, meant that no-one could touch them.

Luckily, when the Allied advance on the Anzio Front did come, it was so rapid as to upset any German plans for resistance.

Looking down from the hills early on the morning of May 23, the plain could be seen swathed in an unusually dense haze. It was under the cover of this mist that, at that very moment, the Allied tanks were silently penetrating the German positions. This surprise attack was to be the beginning of the end. On May 24 Cisterna—long considered the key to the Anzio Front—was isolated. On May 25 the American forces farther south entered Terracina, and the 85th Division, which had already broken into Fondi, crossed the hills to take Mount Monsicardi. The Adolph Hitler Line finally collapsed and the Germans hastily withdrew up the valley towards Frosinone.

Instead of sending all the Anzio forces towards Valmontone to cut off the Germans retreating from Cassino, General Mark Clark ordered the 34th and 45th Divisions to climb the hills east and north of Lanuvio and so cut into the Via Appia, south of Albano. The German resistance had not weakened in this sector and it seemed for a while that they might decide to hold the heights.

What would be the fate of Rome? In a rapid visit to the capital I had been amazed to see people sitting peacefully outside a café. The contrast was shocking. Had we permitted our imagination to run away with us, or was it that the Romans had already been submitted to too many alarms to allow themselves to be panicked?

On May 26 Tivoli was bombed. When I reached there the town was a shambles. Volunteer rescue squads were digging frantically among the ruins. More than a thousand people had been killed and the moans of others could still be heard from under the debris. The Allied bombs had spared the giant hydro-electric plants that supplied Rome with power and light, but our great worry was that the Germans would destroy them before withdrawing. The partisans were on the alert, but in the end it was a caretaker who saved the dynamos by opening the valves and flooding them.

The Republican Fascists were in a frenzy. Admiral Campioni and Admiral Mascherpa were dragged out of prison and executed.

The *Messaggero* hysterically attacked the Vatican newspaper for protesting against the shooting of patriots. The rumour was rife that a house-to-house search would be made and all the men who had not reported for duty with the Fascists would be shot.

The Germans were more realistic; they began to exercise a new restraint. A popular uprising at the moment would have been a disaster. There was even a free distribution of flour in the poorer quarters of Rome. General Maeltzer could not refrain even now from having the photographers there, but this time he did not have the soldiers retrieve the food after the photographs had been taken. The madman, who had ruled Rome like a Nero, was nearing the end of his reign of terror.

There were many signs that a retreat was imminent. The General Headquarters for Transportation left the Hotel de la Ville. A strange fire broke out in the Pensione Jaccarino, the torture house of the Italian SS Battalion. Were they destroying their equipment? The installations at the Ciampino and Urbe airfields were mined and blown sky-high. The German wounded were evacuated from the hospitals, and German diplomats and journalists took advantage of the safer evening hours to leave the city and drive away to the north.

The Allied radio introduced a new feature into its programme, broadcasting the names and addresses of the spies and informers in Rome. The delusion under which some abject creatures had been labouring, that they would be able to continue business as usual when the Allies arrived, was dashed to the ground.

On June 1 Castel Gandolfo was a besieged citadel in the midst of the battlefield. An Allied column had reached the Nemi crossroads, only seven miles distant, and a second force was emerging from behind the hills in an encircling movement. The thunder of German batteries on Monte Cavo and at Genzano, Albano, Fratocchie and Ciampino continued day and night.

On June 2 the Germans blew up the military radio station at Santa Palomba and set fire to a granary. It was a hopeful sign, but we were still not sure that they did intend to withdraw from Rome. The evacuation of the wounded might be only a preliminary to the all-out defence of the city. Twice that day I tried to get through to Rocca di Papa. My second attempt failed like the first. Groups of German soldiers were retreating through the woods towards

Marino, and the Allied fire was following them. Farther ahead it
became so intense that it was impossible to continue. A German
despatch-rider, a few yards in front of me, received a direct hit,
and his dismembered body was catapulted from his motor-cycle
down the slope towards the lake.

That afternoon a shower of silver foil told us that another
aerial bombardment was imminent. A minute or two more and
the bombers were overhead, majestically aloof as usual. Houses
crumbled and spouts of water rose high on the lake. Dead fish in
silver-grey clusters floated on the surface.

A part of the hillside towards Marino collapsed, burying more
than thirty people in a cave. I left the Papal Villa with a Vatican
engineer and scrambled down to where the mass of stones and
earth had settled. The blonde tresses of a woman, protruding
from what looked like a solid wall of rock, provided a clue as to
where the opening had been. We needed light to enter the adjoining caves, and I sent a young man to search for a candle. Three
German soldiers appeared just as he entered an empty cottage.
They pulled him into the open. Only by a miracle did I prevent
them from shooting him on the spot as a pillager.

"Our comrades were in that cave! You damned traitors!"

They were hysterical. The slightest mistake on our part and
they would completely lose control of themselves. I had seen them
that way once before, in Albano, the morning after a massive
Allied bombardment of Berlin. They had roamed through the
deserted town, smashing everything breakable, hacking furniture
to pieces, shouting incoherently: *"Berlin kaput! Alles kaput!"*[1]

Events were precipitating. It was obviously only a question of
a day or two before the Allies would enter Castel Gandolfo. I
had better pay a flying visit to Rome, to receive any instructions
that might be given me, before I found myself definitely cut off
behind the Allied lines.

As soon as I had concluded my business in Rome, I called the
Vatican garage to ask for a car to take me back to the Castelli.
There was a long wait. "It is too late. The Americans entered
Castel Gandolfo an hour ago; it is now on the other side of the
lines."

Early next morning I went to see His Eminence Cardinal

[1] "Berlin is done for! Everything is done for!"

Canali, President of the Commission of Cardinals for the Government of the Vatican City. His Eminence regretted as much as I did that I had not been able to return to Castel Gandolfo. There was still no definite idea as to what the Germans would do: withdraw peacefully from Rome or blow up the bridges and hold the northern bank of the Tiber? From the Janiculum and the Monte Mario hills their guns could dominate the rest of the city. It was a moment when my presence in the area south of Rome might have been useful. I did not mention to the Cardinal what my plans were, but I felt sure that, in some way or other, I could get through the German lines even during the day-time and return to the Castelli.

I managed to find a car to drive me as far as the big tree—"the Alberone"—on the Via Appia Nuova. Allied planes were over-head. Near Via Mondovi the planes swooped down to strafe the road, and my driver refused point-blank to take me any farther. I could not blame him. I paid him and he sped back at full speed towards the city. On the far side of the street a German soldier was seating himself on a mule cart and picking up the reins. The dispossessed countryman was standing by disconsolately.

"Do you promise faithfully to bring it back?"

"Sure," said the German, waving his whip, "you just keep on waiting there."

I headed south. There were not many Germans on the Appia Nuova, but those that I did meet glowered at me with doubt in their eyes. German tanks and guns were concealed under the viaducts. There was heavy firing from the direction of the Acqua Santa.

A German soldier called out to me from the doorway of a house, but I could not make out what he was saying and I did not wait to listen. I continued on my way, expecting to feel a bullet in my back at any moment. I was too conspicuous a figure on the highway. I decided to leave the road and cut through fields. It was rough going and I soon realized that I had made a bad mistake. On the road I might reasonably have been thought to be heading for some nearby hamlet. Pushing through the fields, where groups of Germans were ensconced in trenches, I was un-doubtedly suspect. I made my course an erratic one. Instead of walking due south, I proceeded diagonally, heading towards any

farmhouse in sight as though that were my destination. Two hours
went by. The summer sun was hot, but I could not lose time by
halting to rest.

Suddenly it dawned on me that, when I did reach the cross-
roads at the Frattocchie, it would be absolutely impossible for
me to continue. If I tried to cross the highway, as I would have to
do, I would be caught in a trap. It would be better for me to
cut back to the highway now and edge my way round the demolished airport of Ciampino and so approach Castel Gandolfo
from below.

I scrambled up the bank on to the road, turned the corner by a
group of houses and—to my dismay—found myself facing a long
line of tanks heading towards Rome. At that very moment the
leading tank wheeled round and rumbled back in the direction of
the south. "The Germans are starting a counter-attack!" I ran
back into the fields. A hundred yards away, a group of peasants
was coming towards me. They were waving their arms but I could
not hear what they were shouting. They were the first civilians I
had seen in the past two hours.

"*Sono arrivati,*" they were calling.

"*Chi?*"

"*Gli Americani,*"[1] they replied, pointing to the road and to the
tanks.

Sure enough, they were American boys sitting wearily on those
monster tanks. They looked at me without curiosity as I approached.

"*Sacerdote cattolico?*"[2] asked one.

"Yes," I replied.

"American?"

"No, Irish."

"Where have you come from?"

"From Rome."

Only then did they seem to realize how near Rome was. They
probably knew by heart the distance in miles but here was someone who had actually been there, only three hours before. All of a
sudden it was a real place and not merely a mirage that had
taunted them for months on the bloody battlefield.

[1] "They have arrived." "Who?" "The Americans."
[2] "Catholic priest?"

"Will you bless us, Father?" A G.I. had removed his helmet and knelt on the road. Others followed suit.

My hand was raised in blessing over the bowed heads of the soldiers and my unspoken prayer came from the heart: "Dear God, bring these boys safely back to their families. Amen."

One tall boy was leaning against a tank, oblivious of everything that was happening round him. In his arms he held a child and his hand was caressing it gently, monotonously. He was the first of hundreds of other soldiers whom I was to know, who would lavish on the children of the war their nostalgic feelings of tenderness for their own children and for their younger brothers back home.

After a brief meeting with a staff officer, a jeep was placed at my disposal and I left for Castel Gandolfo. As I arrived triumphantly in the village square, an over-enthusiastic citizen ran into the church to ring the bells. The excited townsfolk surrounded me and shouted exultantly but prematurely: *"Roma e' liberata."*[1]

I called the Vatican over the radio-telephone and spoke to Cardinal Canali.

"Where are you speaking from?" His Eminence inquired.

"From Castel Gandolfo. The Allies will enter Rome late this afternoon."

That is how I missed being in Rome when the Germans left and the Allies arrived.

I did not see the defeated army leave the Eternal City, the crowds lining the sidewalks and the dominators of yesterday retreating in disorder across the Tiber. Every vehicle, whether motor car or horse cart, had been seized, but most of the soldiers left on foot, dragging themselves wearily along, unkempt, unshaven, with a look of numb despair in their eyes.

I did not see the tumultuous, triumphant entry of the Allied troops into Rome, the boys waving from the tanks and the exultant crowds welcoming them at every street corner, flowers thrown from windows, tens of thousands of people cheering and children running, mothers weeping with joy and old women kissing the hands of their liberators.

They were historic scenes but I do not regret not having witnessed them.

[1] "Rome has been liberated."

Now that the uglier passions have died and resentments have been dulled by the passage of time, if I think of that dramatic and blessed day, I like to remember two little episodes of which I heard, delicate gestures which inserted themselves significantly into the vast, chaotic turmoil of the Liberation.

As the German soldiers retreated on foot through St. John's Gate, the younger ones threw themselves, exhausted, on the grass in front of the Basilica. The women from the nearby houses, forgetful of their months of anguished torment, came down into the street with jugs of water to refresh their enemies.

As night fell, and the tumult of welcome increased instead of diminishing, a soldier knelt alone on the steps of the Church of the Gesù his head bowed in prayer against the closed doors.

How many of us look back with something like nostalgia to those tragic, eventful months! In spite of the agony, the tension and the starvation, it was a glorious time, a time when men were united in suffering and rediscovered for one splendid moment that they were brothers.

PART TWO

Germany's Withdrawal and Surrender, 1944–45

CHAPTER THIRTEEN

Disillusionment

ROME HAD been liberated. The German troops had retreated rapidly to a line south of Leghorn and Florence. The bombardments and manhunts might continue farther north but, for us, they had ended.

For the first few days the heady novelty of freedom absorbed us. The luxury of being able to walk abroad without fear was so novel as to exclude every other thought. Then, inevitably, each one was engulfed again in the daily cares of living. The burden, by contrast, seemed heavier than before. Long lines of women waited hopelessly for food. A million homeless people fretted in enforced idleness. The repatriation of the menfolk, from Africa and India, from the prison-camps of Germany and Poland, seemed to have drawn no closer.

Italy had a Government at last, presided over by Ivanoe Bonomi, a respected old-time Socialist. For the purposes of practical living, however, it was powerless. It could not feed anyone unless the Allies provided the flour. It could not distribute medicines or re-open schools or repatriate the refugees. The Allies were still fighting a war; everything else must take second place. Even to provide the population with eighty grams of bread a day, liberty ships had to be diverted from military purposes and used for the transportation of flour.

One high officer in the Allied Military Government advocated the reduction of the bread ration. Others opposed it. "Can we give the people less bread than they had under the Germans?"

"We should prevent civilians from bringing in food for the black market?"

"Why? We need more food in Rome, not less, black market or no black market!"

Perhaps the Liberation had been too eagerly awaited. We had been like ingenuous children longing for graduation day, the day that should bring perfect joy and, instead, only opens the door to more difficult goals. Once the excitement of the Liberation had passed and the realization had come that, after all, freedom is only the normal setting for life, disillusionment had set in. After the struggle to survive oppression, there was no other immediate objective on which we could focus our attention. The drab hope-lessness of the situation was too great to make a normal life seem even remotely attainable.

After the exuberance of the first few days, the attitude of the Allies, too, seemed to have changed. The fighting boys had moved on. The military who remained were icily efficient. A war had to be won; an administrative job of government had to be done; there was no room for sentiment.

In this watchful pause, the news of the excesses being com-mitted by the North African troops in the villages leading up from Cassino burst with the impact of a bomb. "The men had to run from the German round-ups; now we must hide our womenfolk from the Liberators."

I was on my way to Cassino when I stopped at Palestrina and found the townspeople in a ferment. The Goums had threatened to burn down the town unless the women were made available to them before nightfall.

I had first visited Palestrina as a student, curious to see the birthplace of the composer Giovanni Pierluigi da Palestrina. I had sat on a vine-covered terrace, trying to pick out by name the grey-stone medieval towns perched roundly on the hillocks across the plain. It had been there that the police had stopped me in May, 1938, on my way back from Cassino. Hitler was paying his first State visit to Mussolini and everyone entering Rome was being halted for interrogation.

The Allied bombs had not spared Palestrina during the fight for Cassino, and Allied guns had come to threaten its complete destruction even after the Germans had withdrawn. The city fathers had walked several miles to persuade the military that the Germans had really left. They had been difficult to convince; the Germans might not be there, but a barrage of fire, breaking open the ancient houses, would be an added precaution. After all, what did a hundred or more shells cost?

I drove back to the highway and waited for the first army jeep to come into sight. The young English officer at the wheel listened sympathetically to what I had to say but was reluctant to get involved. "This is the French zone. We cannot interfere . . ."

He was a decent boy and ended up by taking me to the nearest French post. The major in charge listened impatiently, fumbling with the pens on his desk and looking daggers at the young lieutenant standing in the background.

"Who have these troops been fighting for, for five bloody months? Do you realize how many of them have died just to liberate you . . . ?" The tone of the major's voice grouped me contemptuously with three million other worthless people.

"I fully appreciate their heroism and we are all grateful to them. But, as you yourself say, *c'est une guerre de liberation,*[1] a fight to free people from fear . . . !"

At last, after a telephone conversation in which the major did the persuading, he assured me that the troops would be withdrawn from the vicinity of Palestrina. I thanked him; I thanked the lieutenant, and continued on my way.

I said Mass next morning in the hospital chapel at Pontecorvo. When the time for Communion came, I found a line of young girls in hospital garb kneeling at the rail. I did not realize who they were until after Mass, when the young peasant who had been my server turned to me in the sacristy: "And they called this the Liberation!"

The gentle voice of an old lay-sister, bringing in my surrogate coffee,[2] interrupted him: "That is the evil of war. Violence begets violence." Sister Felicia had been a hospital cook for almost forty years. When the Germans had made the sisters evacuate their hospital, she had dismantled her enormous kitchen stove and carried it piece by piece on her head up to a hiding-place on the mountain. When the Allies arrived, she had carried it back again. She had no time for useless recriminations: "There is already too much hatred in the world."

---

[1] "It is a war of liberation."   [2] Made from roasted barley.

There was no doubt, however, that the warmth with which the people had greeted the Allies was diminishing. They sensed that there was little real cordiality in the way many of the officers of the Military Government regarded them. The British, in particular, seemed to brush off resentfully any overtures of friendship.

"Yesterday, these damned Italians were our enemies. Now, because the Germans are losing, they want to be our friends."

The military could not be expected to understand the deep-rooted distaste the majority of the Italian people had had for the Nazi-Fascist alliance imposed by Mussolini, or their inability, after so many years of dictatorship, to do much about it. They did not know that for months past, during the Nazi occupation, the Allied broadcasts had been persistently assuring the Italian people of the warmth of their friendship. "We have no quarrel with the people of Italy." The little folk had ingenuously accepted this as a fact. Now they were being sadly disillusioned.

Of course they, too, generalized. When they saw how Allied officers frequented the homes that until recently had lavished hospitality on German officers, they did not try to understand that this was only the indiscretion of a few. When respected political men, who had suffered for their unbending opposition to Fascism, found themselves treated with discourtesy, they did not pause to reflect that it was natural for the Allies to be suspicious of proclaimed anti-Fascism in a country where, all of a sudden, no-one seemed to have belonged to the Fascist party. They only remembered the long years in which they had suffered for their principles, the dangers they had faced to help the Allied cause. Was it for this they had worked and suffered?

"They seem to be convinced there is no room for democracy in Italy. Either Fascists or Communists! That is what Major X told me the other day."

Language was one of the great barriers. Officers speaking no Italian were at the mercy of their interpreters, whose personal likes and dislikes often became the supreme arbiters of a situation.

Knowing this, I agreed one day to accompany the mayor of a little hill village east of Rome to the nearest A.M.G. Office.[1] His people were literally starving; they had used up their meagre supplies to feed more than a hundred Allied prisoners-of-war. As a

[1] Allied Military Government Office.

consequence, many inhabitants of the village had been shot by the SS.

The major in charge refused to be moved: "If they did all that you say, it was only because they hoped for a reward. Or, most likely, to get themselves pardoned for their treachery in the past. Why did they go to war in the first place if they didn't want to put up with the consequences?"

Perhaps this particular officer did not know that towns such as Francavilla al Mare had been razed to the ground and all the men shot for harbouring American and British soldiers. Or that more than a hundred thousand Italian families had risked their lives to protect Allied prisoner-of-war.

Useless, after an incident such as this, trying to tell the population that they had been unlucky, that the great majority of Allied officers were kindly disposed!

Luckily, things began to change. More complete reports of Italian heroism began to reach Allied General Headquarters and have their effect. It was the Italian garrison that had prevented the Germans from seizing the port of Bari. It was the people of Naples who, by their four days of splendid rebellion, had prepared the way for the triumphant entry of the Allied troops. It was the Italian Navy that had taken their ships to Allied ports or sunk them rather than let a single vessel fall into enemy hands. It was the Italian Army that had lost seven hundred officers and six thousand men on the tiny Island of Cefalonia, that had captured the German garrison in Sardinia, that had lost 2,397 men in the victorious fight for the island of Corsica, that was still fighting victoriously in Montenegro, that had joined the partisans in Albania with two more divisions, that had given six hundred and forty thousand men to the German concentration camps rather than fight against the Allies. It was the everyday folk of the hill villages and of the cities that had risked their lives to save more than thirty thousand Allied prisoners-of-war.

Was it right to continue to treat these people as enemies? To ignore the fact that for months Italian boys had been fighting alongside Allied soldiers, shedding their blood, too, for the common cause of freedom? To remember only Mussolini's empty words and not see what the men and women of Italy had been capable of doing once they had been free to act?

I had expected that, once the Liberation came, my relief activities would diminish and that I would soon return to my normal work for the Holy See. Instead, I found that, in the tragic situation in which millions of people lived, they had a greater need than ever of help and encouragement. The Liberation had brought freedom from fear but not from hunger, misery, sickness and discouragement.

Instead of operating first-aid stations in the battle areas, medical dispensaries for displaced persons were needed in the cities. Pharmacies had to be set up for the free distribution of medicines to the poor, as well as specialized clinics for sufferers from diabetes, pernicious anaemia and serious vitamin deficiencies. In Rome alone, more than a hundred doctors volunteered to collaborate with us in visiting the sick poor in their homes.

From now on, an increasingly large portion of my time must be spent on the road. Medical relief centres must be established farther and farther north as new territories were liberated. The evacuees from the south would soon be returning to their devastated areas. They must be given a helping hand before they succumbed to desperation in the living martyrdom that lay ahead.

CHAPTER FOURTEEN

Through the Lines

I SPREAD the map of Central Italy on my desk. My finger found Spoleto and followed the highway northwards to Assisi, Umbertide, Gubbio.

After the withdrawal of the German troops to a new defence-line on the hills below Florence, Gubbio, eighty miles to the south, was left within a bulge still held by the enemy. At the beginning of July word came through the British Command that there had been bloodshed in the town and that seventy boys and girls had been seized as hostages. My thoughts flew immediately to the children whom I had gathered from the battlefield and who had been sent to Gubbio, in the belief that they would be safe from further harm.

After a day of painful indecision, I took out my map. I still did not know what useful purpose might be served by my going to Gubbio. Even if I did succeed in getting through the lines, it would obviously be impossible for me to go to German Headquarters to plead the cause of the children. The military would never believe that a mission that had brought me through their lines was a purely charitable one.

I left Rome by car, intending to drive as far north into Umbria as I could and then go over the hills on foot. Being familiar with the open nature of the country, I knew that this would only be feasible at night.

I stopped for a moment, half an hour beyond Assisi, to ask the name of the ruined hamlet through which we were passing. It seemed to me that the countryman blushed.

"*Casa del Diavolo,*"[1] he replied.

"*Salute!*"[2] said my driver dolefully, under his breath.

[1] "The House of the Devil."   [2] "Here's health!"

It was a British sentinel who stopped us as we drove up the road leading to the heights. My papers were in order but, even so, I was surprised that he allowed us to continue. He obviously took for granted that we were going to follow the road along the ridge, all of which was in Allied hands.

"Where are you going?" he asked me.

"To Gubbio," I replied truthfully but jocularly.

He laughed: "Let us know when you get there. We have been trying for six weeks."

We stopped for a moment at the top of the rise and looked intently across the valley at the medieval city. It was an enchanting sight, with its grey-stone houses and red-tile roofs warmed by the glow of the setting sun. The citadel of St. Ubaldo rose peacefully on the summit of Mount Ingino. Dante had called it "the mount chosen by Blessed Ubaldo". We were in a land blessed by the poets, the painters and builders of the early Renaissance. From where we stood, the noble Palace of the Consuls, the Ducal Palace and the twelfth-century cathedral were clearly visible. The guns planted on the hills were silent and there was no sign of military activity. In such a tranquil atmosphere it was not difficult to recall that this was the place where St. Francis had spoken amiably to the wolf. Dusk was falling; the enchantment was giving way to the vigilant menace of the night. It was imperative that I enter the town before the curfew.

I looked at my driver. "If you like, you can stay here."

His grimace said as plainly as words: "I think you are crazy, but I can't let you go alone."

We drove slowly down the incline, conscious of the citadel and of the guns that must surely be covering us. On the upward slope we gained confidence and drove more rapidly until we were entering the narrow, stone-paved streets of the town. We concealed the car in an ancient courtyard and I set out to find the bishop. Monsignor Ubaldi was amazed to see me and gave me the good news at once that our children were safe. None of them were among the hostages being held by the Germans.

It was true that there had been bloodshed in the town: two Austrian officers had been shot and—in reprisal—forty citizens had been executed. The German soldiers in the first execution squad had refused to fire: "We don't shoot unarmed people." A second squad had been picked. Perhaps they, too, were half-hearted; many of the victims were still alive when they were thrown into the grave. Two hundred and thirty other townspeople, including seventy children, were being held as hostages in the Basilica of St. Ubaldo.[1]

So far, the boys and girls we had brought from the battlefield were unharmed. Impossible, however, to predict the future. The town might be destroyed by Allied bombs or razed to the ground by the Germans. Better that the children leave while there was still time. Where could they go? There was only one place in those bare mountains where they might be safe: an abandoned sanctuary farther up the valley.

The children left under cover of darkness. They proceeded in Indian file, each child obediently holding on to the shirt-tail or dress of the child in front. They were subdued but unafraid, unquestioningly accepting this new development. This place of strange happenings was the topsy-turvy world into which they had been born.

I, too, left in the half-darkness. A group of young men pushed my car to the end of the street and we coasted silently down the hill. The driver deliberately delayed the moment when the splutter of the motor would sound like thunder in our ears.

I had been deeply moved by the kindness of the Bishop of Gubbio. I might have foreseen that it would be his charity that would finally save the town from destruction. Only the granaries were burned by the Germans and, before destroying them, the officer in charge, as a token of his admiration for the bishop, presented him with a quintal of wheat for every person in his diocese.

Soon after re-entering the Allied lines that early morning, I saw a far different and, unfortunately, a far more familiar aspect of the Nazi occupation.

Beyond the cross-roads to the right of Perugia, a man standing in the middle of the road brought my car to a halt.

"Can you give these young people a lift to Umbertide?"

He pointed to a couple sitting rigidly by the roadside and explained in a hoarse whisper that they had escaped across the

[1] The hostages were not released until July 24, the day when the Germans suddenly retreated.

hills during the night and were now trying to reach their relatives up the valley. The previous day the SS had set their cottage on fire along with several others in reprisal for the shooting of a German soldier. When their children had tried to escape, they had been thrown back into the flames. The frantic parents had come running from the fields, only to stand by helplessly as the blazing roof collapsed.

Like automata the couple entered the car; the frozen faces, excruciatingly young, betrayed no emotion; four dead eyes gazed unseeingly ahead. There was complete silence between us as we drove on our way. What could I say to them? What could they say to me?

In Citta' di Castello a great sorrow awaited me: two of the children whom I had sent there for safety were dead.

Citta' di Castello, like Gubbio, had unexpectedly found itself encompassed by the war. Until three days before my arrival, it had been occupied by the Germans. Allied shells and Allied bombs had poured destruction into the built-up areas. To the refugees it must have seemed as though they were back on the battlefield. For forty days they had huddled in the cellars, listening to the thunder of the guns and dreading the fall of each successive bomb. Then there had been a lull. The Germans had pulled back their batteries. The children had emerged from underground and gone with the sisters to a convent farther from the line of fire. They had been safer there, so safe, in fact, that at certain times during the day they could even play in the garden. It was on the terrace that a stray shell had found them, leaving the bodies of two little girls and that of a dead sister beside them.

If I had left them on the battlefield perhaps they would have still been alive! Or perhaps all the children, and not two only, would have died! Who could say?

That evening, in Citta' di Castello, I expected to be given a cot in the basement of the seminary. For once, however, protocol must take precedence over safety. The Rector led me up the dark staircase and along the deserted corridors to a room reserved for distinguished visitors. There was no light and I needed none as I undressed. The flashes from the German guns lit up the purple and gold wallpaper and gave me fleeting glimpses of an austere eighteenth-century bishop in an ornate frame. If I were to die I could not ask for a more correct ecclesiastical setting.

I closed my eyes and listened to the rumble of the guns. I had no fear that I would stay awake; for too many months the sound of cannon-fire had lulled me to sleep. Strange! I had a feeling of contentment as though the noise was evoking some pleasant memory. Life had been simpler in those days of physical danger than in the two months since the Liberation. One had never seemed to hesitate; one had known immediately what one should do. People had been simpler: courageous, patient, less critical, more generous. What was the answer to it all? Perhaps there was no other answer than to do the best one could day by day. That is all that God asks of any man, whether he be in peace or in war.

CHAPTER FIFTEEN

Beasts of Prey

ON AUGUST 11 the Germans withdrew from the centre of Florence. That same evening I left Rome for Tuscany. August 11, my birthday! Had a whole year gone by since I returned from Ireland?

After its rapid exodus from Rome, the German Army had retreated to a temporary defence-line strung loosely across the mountains south of Leghorn and Florence. Kesselring needed time to complete the massive fortifications of the Gothic Line farther north.

Leghorn had fallen to the American troops on July 19. Three-quarters of the city had been mined; even the corpses had booby traps concealed under them ready to explode.

What would be the fate of Florence? At first only the art treasures had been carried off to Germany. Then the pillaging had become more general; the scientific instruments had been stolen from the University clinics; even the beds had been taken from under the sick in the hospitals. Would the city itself be spared? The telephone exchange was demolished, then the power stations, then the flour mills. A word from Kesselring could lead to its total destruction. The hot August days dragged on. The hostages languished in jail. No-one even dared to hope.

On August 11 the dull thunder of explosions was heard: the bridges over the Arno were being blown up, one by one. Was this the beginning of the end? Was the city to be destroyed piece by piece? Towards noon the incredible rumour began to spread like wildfire: *The Germans are retreating across the Mugnone!* Could it be true? Yes! They were withdrawing and the city was still practically intact.

It took me seven hours to reach the outskirts of Florence, on roads congested with army vehicles. As my car crawled down the winding road past Galluzzo, a Fascist sniper fired from one of the houses. It reminded me that the Germans themselves were only four miles away, still dominating the city from the heights of Fiesole.

At the bottom of the hill the Arno brought us to a halt. Over the houses on the other bank we could see Giotto's Tower and the dome of Santa Maria del Fiore. People were waving to us and we waved back. We could not cross the river, even though one bridge was still standing; the Germans had spared the Ponte Vecchio but had effectively blocked all access to it by blowing up the palaces at both ends. The army engineers were already ploughing a way through the debris and others were throwing a metal bridge from pylon to pylon across the river.

After three days of conferences in the Palazzo Vecchio with the officers of the Welfare Branch and the heads of the children's agencies in Florence, I left for Pisa.

The Germans were entrenched in the mountains to the right of the highway leading towards the sea, and the Allied batteries were firing over our heads from hollows south of the road. The abundant vegetation masked a great deal of the destruction, but, as we reached one little village after another, we realized that all of them had been levelled to the ground. Even the bell-towers had been mined, so that the churches themselves were involved in their ruin.

In Pisa, the first impression was of complete devastation. The stately palaces along the Arno had been reduced to mere skeletons, their bones licked bare by the flames. The graceful bridges were now formless piles of stone. Field Marshal Kesselring had kept his promise not to repeat in Pisa the mistake he had made in Rome.

The streets leading up to the embankment were jammed with American tanks. It would be several hours before we would be able to cross the solitary pontoon bridge. From the sound of the firing it appeared that the advance forces of General Mark Clark's army had already reached the farthest outskirts of the town. The first man we did see after reaching the north bank was the general himself, flashing by in a jeep. He gesticulated angrily at the sight of a civilian car with a Rome number-plate calmly advancing towards his battle-line.

Dusk was already falling by the time we reached the cathedral square. It was delightfully cool; a soft breeze blowing in from the sea had dispelled the heat of the day.

Never had the nine-hundred-year-old cathedral and its baptistery appeared more beautiful than that evening, their pure white marble delicately tinted by the last, lingering rose-light of the sun, their graceful bulk outlined dramatically by the sinister glare to the north. I breathed in the beauty of it, enhanced by the solitude of the place and by the cool, slender elegance of the tower. How serenely aloof it was from the vulgar vandalism of war!

It was a shock to enter the cathedral and find the thousands of people encamped there. In the flickering light of the shaded lanterns it was only gradually that one's eyes distinguished the spectral multitude. The marble masterpieces of Giovanni Pisano were hidden by brickwork and camouflaged by piles of household goods. A girl was washing a few rags of clothing. A young mother was suckling her child.

I stopped to speak to an aged couple sitting on a wooden chest near the pulpit. Their two grandchildren, five or six years old, lay on their tiny mattress and looked at me with dull, incurious gaze.

"Their home was near Pisa. It was burned down by the SS. Their mother was shot as she tried to escape with their baby sister. Mariuccia, the baby, was thrown back into the flames."

She nodded towards the children.

"They were in the street. They saw it all."

I must have shown my embarrassment at her remarks, for she hastened to reassure me.

"Don't worry. They don't understand anything any more."

Savagery! Reprisals! Massacres!

After the retreat from Rome, that only by some strange miracle had not been turned into a rout, the dank chill of despair had sunk deep into the German soul. Even in this new failure to follow up a victory with a smashing blow lurked the spectre of American imperturbability. It was unnerving, this unquestioning certainty that their giant war-machine must continue to grow, must press forward relentlessly until, finally, inevitably, every opposition would be crushed.

Thoughts of the Russian disaster, of the German cities dis-integrating under the bombs, of the German boys, ever younger, ever younger, putting on uniforms to replace the millions who had died: these were the nightmares that returned to haunt them with terrifying insistency.

On June 6 the Allied landing in Normandy had begun. Thousands of planes, thousands of boats, hundreds of thousands of troops and many times that number ready to follow them! By August 7 the Canadians would have taken Falaise, and twelve more German divisions would have been lost.

Fear must be banished; sanity must be maintained. Each commander must concentrate on his own sector of the front, to the exclusion of all else. If other armies, other commanders, could hold their sectors against the Allied thrusts to the east and west, out of general exhaustion some hope might come. In the meantime every threat to army security must be ruthlessly suppressed.

In Italy Field Marshal Kesselring issued a public manifesto:

"Every village, where it is proved there are partisans or in which German or Italian[1] soldiers have been attacked or where attempts have been made to sabotage military supplies, *will be burned to the ground*. In addition, all male inhabitants of such a village over eighteen years of age *will be shot*. The women and children will be interned in labour camps."

The moment had arrived for the SS to come into its own. From now on, not even the remotest village would be safe.

A few days before my arrival in Pisa it had been the turn of the little town of Sant'Anna. Within a few minutes the whole place was ablaze. The women threw themselves out of the windows but were mowed down by machine-guns. Some of the infants were brained; others were hung on the house-doors, burning like torches; seven were thrown into the baker's oven. Altogether, five hundred and sixty innocent people died.

The massacres spread over Tuscany like a forest fire. The village of Farneta was set on fire and one hundred and seventy inhabitants were slaughtered. When the parish priest pleaded for the children to be spared, the SS men dangled three of them by the legs and hurled them into the flames. At Civitella Val Chiana all the males—two hundred and fifty old men and boys—were

[1] The neo-Fascist forces.

butchered. At Certosa di Farneta the Capuchin monks, who had been giving shelter to the Jews, were taken to Massa to be shot. At Mileto the bodies of the pastor and a hundred of his parishioners were burned in the public square. At Castelnuovo dei Sabbioni seventy people were killed with their priest. At Pioppe, after all the men had been rounded up by the SS, the houses were set on fire and the women and children slaughtered as they fled through the streets. Hundreds of other villages were ravaged; hundreds of similar massacres took place; tens of thousands of civilians were shot, burned alive, hung and tortured to death.[1]

At a later date we would meet some of the children who had survived these massacres, whose mothers and brothers and sisters had been killed. We would try to heal the wounds in their minds. We would try to erase, not the memory of these things, but the torment, the bitterness, the horrible confusion that the revelation of hell in men's souls had burned into their own.

There was confusion in the minds of the people in all the occupied countries. How could one reconcile the double personality of the German: the sadism of the torturer and the humaneness that revealed itself in unexpected acts of kindness? Many came to see that it was not a question of a double personality. There were two classes of people essentially poles apart. On the one hand, the rank and file of German soldiers, good, bad and indifferent. On the other, the real Nazis, the callous and fanatical men enrolled in such special forces as the SS, the SD, the SIPO and the Gestapo,[2] who had been completely dehumanized by the training they had received.

Hitler had deliberately set out to brutalize his young Nazis. He had done a diabolically thorough job. From six to ten the boys had marched and sung. At ten they had entered the *Jungvolk*, put on their brown shirt, worn their dagger, drilled, fought and

---

[1] This number does not include the civilians who joined the partisans and died fighting against the Germans.

[2] SIPO: the *Sicherheitspolizei*, a security police under the control of Himmler.

Gestapo: the *Geheime Staatspolizei*, a political police force set up by Herman Göring to suppress independent political thought.

learned to be physically hard. At fourteen, if they passed the test, they had become full members of the *Hitlerjugend* with their swastika armbands. Up to this point the appeal had been to many of the more generous instincts of youth. They had learned the supreme lesson of absolute devotion to the Reich and of blind obedience to their Führer. From then on, their training had been specifically intended to make them callous. Duelling, pagan rituals, Jew-baiting and sexual indulgence had become important elements in their curriculum.

The formation of the rank and file members had been thorough, but the training of the future leaders had been even more exacting. The strongest, the most ruthless, the most fanatically obedient youngsters had been picked at an early age to undergo a special probationary period of one or two years. Only those that passed every test had been admitted to the Adolf Hitler schools of leadership, where they had been segregated from every religious or family influence until the age of eighteen. During their years of service in the labour corps and in the army they had been closely watched; at each step only the toughest and the most promising young men had been retained. Finally, at the age of twenty-five, the cream—the élite of the élite—had been chosen for the supreme schools of Nazi training, the *Ordensburgen*—the Castles of the Order—where they had become the tough, pitiless men that the Führer had planned.

"My magnificent youngsters," he had said. "In my *Ordensburgen* a youth will grow up before which the world will shrink back. A violently active, dominating, intrepid, brutal youth— that is what I am after. Youth must be all these things. It must be indifferent to pain. There must be no weakness or tenderness in it. I want to see once more in its eyes the gleam of pride and independence of the beast of prey."[1]

The beasts of prey had been let loose, first upon their own countrymen and then among the subjugated peoples of Europe. As Lord Russell has said: "That the German people did not all yield easily, or willingly accept the Nazi doctrine and programme, is not disputed. Had they done so there would have been no SS, no SD and no Gestapo. *It was only by fear, torture, starvation and*

[1] Herman Rauschning: *Hitler Speaks* (Thornton Butterworth, London, 1939).

death that the Nazis eliminated at home the opponents of their régime, and it was in this way that these organizations of oppression gained the experience and the training, later put into practice abroad with such thoroughness and brutality, that made them the nightmare and the scourge of occupied Europe."[1]

They had manned the torture chambers; they had massacred harmless citizens; they had gassed and cremated millions of their fellow human beings. Through it all, their handsome, clean-cut young faces had shown the unbelievably cool indifference of men who knew no compassion.[2]

How miserable their victims must have seemed to them! How weak and contemptible, those despised Jews, those pale priests, those defenceless women and children! Yet, today, it is the writing of a little Jewish girl that has survived. It is the memory of indomitable men and women that comes to comfort us. Physically they succumbed. Very soon, perhaps, even their names will have been forgotten. But the knowledge that they existed, that they dared to resist and were not afraid to die, will never perish.

[1] *The Scourge of the Swastika*, p. 4 (Gollancz, London, 1956).
[2] In Italy their imitators were luckily few. Such as they were—men like Lt. Koch and Major Carità, the torturers of Rome and Florence—they were not inferior in cruelty to their masters.

CHAPTER SIXTEEN

The Return

THE FIERCE sun of mid-August beat down on Rome. This year there were no mass excursions to the sea and to the hills, no *scampagnate*[1] with picnic baskets in the chestnut woods, no crowds in Trastevere in the cool of the evening. The population, swelled to two and a half million by almost a million refugees, remained inside the city and sweltered. Even in the houses there was little respite. Gone were the days when one could close the heavy wooden jalousies on the windows and enjoy the cool, dark quiet inside. Each home was jammed with destitute relatives; their odds and ends of furniture blocked the narrow corridors and cluttered up the balconies. Tempers were short and nerves on edge.

In the improvised refugee camps tens of thousands of displaced persons languished. Herded together like cattle, the stench of unwashed flesh, the heat, the lack of air, of shade, of cool water, of quiet, the flies buzzing, the people arguing, the feverish children crying—it was more than human fortitude could stand.

Why did they stay? They were not idle drifters. They had been hard-working country people with homes of their own. It was not by deliberate choice that they continued to live week after week in the degrading promiscuity and demoralizing inactivity of the refugee camps.

For the old people there was no alternative. They were too feeble to begin life all over again. I had seen an old man some months before, dumped from a German truck at Cesano. He had stood in the middle of the road, uncertain which way to turn, until I had taken him by the hand as one would a child. He was a doctor, he had told me. Until a few hours before he had still been practising, even though he was seventy years old.

[1] Excursions to the country.

"Che faccio adesso?"[1] He had looked at his hands, pathetically, trying to realize that, without his instruments, without his dispensary, without his bicycle, without a home or the bare necessities of life, even the skill of his long, delicate fingers had deserted him. What good is a college degree in a refugee camp, especially when one is old? All that one wants is a piece of bread, a plate of soup, a place to lie down and to try not to think.

The bowl of soup! The piece of bread for their children! These two good certainties in a world of desolation bound thousands of mothers to the dank, malodorous places in which they had found refuge. They knew that when they did return home—ironic word!—they would be shocked at the spectacle that awaited them: the trees levelled by cannon fire, the vineyards destroyed, the cattle slaughtered, the fields mined. They were stolidly prepared for the worst. They would find no roof to shelter them. Even this would not have deterred them. It was the knowledge that in the wilderness there would be no bread for their children, no bowl of soup to keep body and soul together, that sapped their courage and turned the marrow of their bones to water.

As time went on even this dreadful prospect ceased to frighten them. "Better to die there quickly than to waste away slowly day by day."

It was now the Allies who hindered their return. The Army knew by experience the dangers that lurked in those hundreds of miles of desolate wasteland, where only the weird, terrifying beauty of ruined villages groped blindly towards the sky. With mines and discarded shells, with contaminated water and disease, death would reap its victims. There would be no shelter for the reckless people who might try to return to their native soil, no water, no light, no heat, no stores where even the most basic commodities might be purchased.

Yet some of the hardier peasants had already succeeded in returning to their land, had dug out caves for themselves under the ruins, and so far had managed to survive. The Pontifical Refugee Commission had brought them flour and, wherever it was possible, had set up a soup kitchen—sometimes only an iron pot on an open fire among the ruins—to distribute a bowl of thick

[1] "What can I do now?"

soup once a day. Once they had overcome the initial period of discouragement, these courageous pioneers had thrown themselves with fanatical determination into the task of reconstruction. They had crawled over their plots of ground, delicately removing the mines by hand. They had cleared the debris from the foundations of their cottages, sorted out the stones that could be utilized again and laboriously started to rebuild.

The Allied officers listened, not unsympathetically but sceptically, when Monsignor Baldelli and I pleaded with them to lift their ban, to go even further and provide us with trucks to facilitate the return of more people to their native countryside.

"How can you want them to go back to such unspeakable misery?"

How could I explain that it was the very immensity of their misery, the sheer human improbability of survival, that had convinced me that these people must return to their land? Within their fierce determination to go back, to fight death, if need be, but on their native soil, were the seeds of something greater than misery, something more tenacious and more durable than even the cold and sickness and hunger, than the black, deep, viscid waves of discouragement.

There were some areas, however, where even I could not envisage the possibility of a return: the reclaimed Pontine marshes, where the Germans had blown up the dikes, and Cassino, where the banks of the Rapido river had been destroyed. Pestilential waters stagnated where lush pasture lands had been, and frogs croaked gloomily in the darkness. Myriads of parasite-carrying anopheline mosquitoes filled the night with their obsessive drone.

The evacuees should not, must not return to the swamp areas until winter had brought a halt to the danger of malarial infection. Should not? Must not return? Useless! No human power could restrain them. Staggering along under their household goods, pushing their old folks and their children ahead of them on makeshift handcarts, they returned home in their thousands. They found a situation which, even in their most pessimistic moments, they had never imagined could exist.

Without warning, a man would collapse in the fields, first shivering pitifully with the cold and then delirious and burning with fever. Small children, with emaciated bodies and hideously bloated bellies, would be heard crying in a hovel while their stricken mother lay helplessly on her bed of rags.

How many people were involved? The team of doctors I sent to the Provinces of Latina and Frosinone covered the territory inch by inch. With the help of the few local physicians, the statistics were compiled: more than fifty thousand people were suffering from malaria!

We knew what remedies were needed but where could they be found? When every source had been tapped, we had still not found sufficient quinine for more than a thousand people. What we had must be kept for the most serious cases, but how could they be reliably determined and how could a fair distribution be arranged in the chaotic situation that prevailed?

One thing was certain: nothing could be done from a distance. At the end of August I moved my headquarters to the Cassino and Latina areas.

As I drove down the Via Casilina I found myself looking forward to the weeks ahead. It would be a return, I thought, to the days of the Anzio beachhead and the battle for Cassino. How mistaken I was!

During the day there was little time for reflection. Moving on rapidly from one group of families to another, the daylight hours passed all too quickly. Then night came. Stretching out as best I could inside my car, I tried to sleep. It was a rainy period, unusual for September, and many a night the wind howled and the lash of the rain became a mournful lament. The car sank deeper and deeper into the mire. One was alone, abandoned in a world where all were dead. Useless to try to recall that less than a hundred miles away there was a great city, where there was light and food and houses. Useless to try to realize that there were other human beings scattered among the ruins. Difficult even to pray, to reconcile the presence of God with such inhuman desolation. What was it the countrywoman had said to me that night on the battlefield near Aprilia? "The whole world seems to be full of Him." How easy that night to feel the presence of God in the dark fields, fragrant with the violets and soft with the spring! How difficult now, in the cold of this desolate land, where hope was dying and sick men in their misery no longer had the will to struggle.

Misery! Before those nightmare weeks in the malaria swamps, I had thought that I knew a great deal about misery. Now I knew the contrary. I had not yet seen how it can curdle the very sap of man's existence, destroy the roots of his integrity, breed suspicion and resentments, and push man in his fight for survival, to unbelievable depths of malice.

My rounds took me one day to the little village of X. Before the war, that is, it had been a village; now it was a couple of hundred sick people squatting hopelessly among the ruins. A week previously I had brought them a small supply of quinine. As there was no doctor in X, I had left the medicine with the parish priest.

Two men stopped my car as it lumbered over the rough track that led towards the ruins.

"Monsignore! You know the quinine you left with the *parroco*?[1] No sooner had you left than he came round the caves, selling it on the black market."

I registered disbelief.

"It is true!" A woman pushed forward, spitting forth the words venomously. "I bought a tube from him for three thousand lire. It had your mark on it."

"Do you have the tube?"

"I have it somewhere. But everyone knows that it is true."

When I met the parish priest he looked embarrassed.

"I have a confession to make. I have not distributed any of the quinine you gave me."

He brought out the boxes, sealed and numbered as I had left them.

"I am sorry. You see, I know some of these people. They are not bad, but misery plays strange tricks with human nature. If an agitator put the idea into their head—as sure as I am standing here—there would be someone ready to swear that I had sold the quinine on the black market or given it to my relatives."

September came and we knew that the next forty days would be the deadliest ones. Our little team moved on rapidly from one hamlet to another, trying to cover as much ground as possible. We gathered the children in some open place among the ruins and,

[1] The parish priest.

with a rough board on two trestles as an examining table, the doctors investigated each one in turn.

Each night we boiled a couple of eggs over a primus stove and threw ourselves down to rest. We tried not to listen to the drone of the mosquitoes; with our primitive equipment there was no way of protecting ourselves against their bites. I had taken quinine as a preventive for a day or two, but when I found my hearing dulled I had abandoned it, hoping for the best.

Our emergency supply of quinine was running out and I had to return to Rome in a desperate search for even a little more. To no avail.

On the eve of my return to the Pontine marshes I had a chance encounter and a very important one. Mr. Myron Taylor, President Roosevelt's Personal Representative to the Vatican, paid a visit to the headquarters of the Pontifical Refugee Commission. When he came to my office I naturally spoke to him of the anti-malarial work on which we were engaged.

Next day he called to tell me that Admiral Ellery Stone, Chief of the Allied Commission, was sending out an SOS for anti-malarial medicines. Two days later, a large supply of German atebrine—enough for the now sixty thousand malaria victims—had already been located farther north and was being shipped to Rome.[1]

On December 29, 1944, I drove south to Valmontone. For months its name had been on everybody's lips: the strategic centre closing the long valley leading to Cassino. Now it was a derelict village, a pitiful collection of ruins. Some of its inhabitants had returned, to live in the caves on the fringe of the town, without clothing, furniture or money.

We met in a damaged building perched high above the town. The children had been summoned there from the caves, children

[1] Thus began my long association with Mr. Taylor in relief projects, an association that developed into warm friendship. It was at his request that I accepted the responsibility of supervising the distribution of all the medical supplies which would be arriving from American Relief for Italy, Inc., the voluntary relief agency of which Mr. Taylor was Chairman of the Board and Judge Juvenal Marchisio President. Later on, after the departure of Mr. Howard Barr and Colonel John McSweeney, I served as the official representative in Italy of American Relief for Italy.

with old men's eyes, with grey parchment skin pulled tight over their bones. They sat on the hard benches, like miserable little birds huddling together on a branch. Their ragged dresses and thin pants could not shut out the cold and they wept, overcome by the misery for which they knew there was no remedy. Their bare feet were blue with the cold and they tucked them back so that they would not feel the icy agony of the stone floor.

As the names were called, the crying ended. Only one little boy continued to sob. He was clad in brown wrapping paper, held together with wire. One by one the children came up to receive their packages. As their tiny hands felt the warm wool and the strong, smooth leather of the boots, their eyes opened wide in astonishment. Inarticulate sounds of joy issued from their mouths. Clutching their bundles as though afraid that unseen hands might snatch them away, they rushed out of the room and down the hillside to their cave. They were experiencing the first intense, incredible joy of their lives.

I was to be present at hundreds of distributions of food and clothing in the months to come but none of them, heart-warming though they might be, would dim the impression that I received that winter's day. For the first time I had seen the unbelievable miracle that organized charity can perform. "Foreign aid" can sound so bureaucratic, so cold and distant and impersonal. Not when it is people giving and people collecting and people transporting and people distributing and people receiving, each one of them adding something—intangible, perhaps, but very personal —that can transform an organizational process into a manifestation of brotherly love. How many poor mothers whispered a prayer because their children had been given succour and health and a moment's amazing joy and had learned that there could be kindness in the world, because men and women hundreds or thousands of miles away had known how to stretch out a hand to help them.

I have seen at close hand the activities of American, Swiss and British voluntary aid and of the Marshall Plan. Mistakes were made but they were surprisingly few. Relief supplies often found their way to the black market because their recipients sold them, but who could blame them for disposing of what were luxuries in order to buy larger quantities of basic foods? The great good that those agencies did, and the goodwill that animated most of the men connected with them, the noble spirit that had inspired the aid in the first instance: these were some aspects of the most beautiful act of human solidarity ever to emerge from the devastation of war.

I lay on my iron cot in Pontecorvo the night of the distribution in Valmontone. It was raining outside and the water from the ceiling was dripping noisily into the tin cans placed strategically round the floor. Towards midnight the rain turned to snow and the wind blew the flakes under the canvas that masked the glassless window. I was fully clothed and I had a blanket on my bed and yet the cold was unbearable. There was nothing that I could do, except lie there and wait for the long agony of the night to end.

Then I thought of the thousands of people living in the ruins and I felt ashamed. They had no blankets and no mattress to lie on and no roof over their heads. They huddled together in the unbelievable torture of the flooded grottoes. They longed for the dawn not only of tomorrow but of that unpredictable day when the sun would shine again. Then the crops would grow and their children would have a bed and clothing and food. They would learn how to play and to laugh and would go to school. Only when that day came—if it ever did—would they, at long last, be able to rejoin the society of men.

CHAPTER SEVENTEEN

No Love at Christmas

Two DAYS before Christmas I drove along the Appian Way to Naples. The bridges between the hill towns had been destroyed and the road swept down the slopes in improvised loops to circumvent the ruins. The plain—until recently a German battiefield —stretched desolately towards the sea.

In what had been the town of Cisterna a few women were digging forlornly among the rubble. A nun in a soiled habit stood at the door of a hut made of gasoline containers and salvaged wood. Morning classes were over and the ragged children were running home to their caves. Three sisters lived in the ruin next to the improvised schoolroom. When it rained during the night they had to huddle on chairs in the corner of the room while the water poured unimpeded on their army cots. They were lucky; it was the only room left standing in the town.

After Cisterna, the road swept on in an inexorable line for forty miles, an isolated causeway between the watery wastes of a once fertile countryside, where only the half-submerged farmhouses broke the monotony of the swamps. Another ruined town and then—a startling vision of beauty—the Bay of Terracina. I gazed across the blue waters to the violet-grey mountains clear-cut against the December sky. For a moment I had the illusion that the clock had been turned back and that we were in the tranquil, radiant Italy of pre-war days.

At Fondi we halted by the side of the road. It was pleasantly warm in the sun and the air was heavy with the scent of oranges. As we ate our sandwiches a group of boys passing by stopped to beg for food. We had seen other bands of ragged youngsters, varying in age from seven to fifteen, making their way on foot in the direction of Rome.

They were different from the boys we usually saw hanging round the railway station in Rome. They, too, might be fatherless and homeless, but they had not yet had the long schooling in the sordid underworld of the streets that these young vagabonds from Naples and Calabria and Sicily had had.

They greedily devoured the food that we gave them, but there was insolence in the way they accepted it. Their hard gaze and their tight-lipped smiles defied us: "If you don't give us any, we don't care. We know how to get what we want."

There was a subtle obscenity in their young faces, still physically beautiful as the faces of the children of the south are: oval-shaped, with soft, lazy eyes, long eyelashes and full, pouting lips. Dark curls fell low over their broad foreheads and over the unwashed nape of their necks. They eyed me doubtfully but they were perfectly at ease with the American officers who ate with me. American slang and army profanity mingled grotesquely with their southern dialect. One sensed the hardness in them and the cynicism, and there was speculation lurking in their eyes. In spite of their extreme youth, there was nothing even remotely childlike about them, except in a repulsive, equivocal way.

After they had eaten, the boys moved on, pushing each other and laughing loudly, obviously aware that adult eyes were following them up the road.

The few townsfolk, standing nearby in silence, also watched the retreating figures, but there was no pity in their look.

"Thank God, they have gone. They are passing through every day now, these gangs of kids from Naples."

"They are only small. What harm can they do?"

"What harm! Yesterday they entered the *carabinieri*[1] barracks down the road and stole their guns. They are young bandits. They are not afraid of anything."

Next day was Christmas Eve. After lunch I attended a meeting at the Allied Commission Headquarters down by the port. A liberty ship had arrived from New York with clothing, blankets, flour and powdered milk. The supplies had been stored temporarily in three damaged churches, but we were anxious to have them transported to the distribution centres in the hills before the

[1] Italian state police.

first snows came. It was late when our meeting ended and night had fallen by the time I made my way home. I was staying with two army officers in the Palazzo Gaetani in Via Egiziaca a Pizzofalcone.

I hurried past the San Carlo Opera House, heading towards the open space of the Piazzo del Plebiscito. Instinctively I glanced up at the ornate façade of the Royal Palace. Its windows had been alive with smiling faces on October 2, 1943, the day after the Liberation of Naples. The royal statues in the niches had been festooned with agile *scugnizzi*,[1] hanging on to the baroque monarchs with one hand and waving to the liberators with the other.

The day before, the Allies had entered the city almost unobserved. It was raining and there had been a German bombardment. But it was not the rain, nor the bombardment, nor indifference, that shrouded the city in silence. That day, Naples was burying its dead. The last Germans had been swept from the city and the splendid, tragic "four days" of popular uprising had ended. There was exhaustion, hunger, famine, disease. "I felt that I was riding through ghostly streets in a city of ghosts," wrote General Mark Clark.

Next day, the evacuees came down from the Vomero; they emerged from the alleys, the caves and the cellars—old men and young, women and children—and flocked to the port. It was a riotous welcome, an explosion of joy mixed with relief. The experiences of the past months had been drastically brutal; the hundred and ten major aerial bombardments of the Allies—thousands of homes crumbling into ruins and the sidewalks cluttered with the piled-up bodies of the dead—had been followed by the savage destruction of the port areas by the Germans, leaving another one hundred thousand people homeless. There had been fighting in the streets, public executions, famine and drought.

The Neapolitans had expected the Liberation to bring them, not only the blessed freedom they yearned for, but also an end to privations. At first it had seemed as though their dream had come true; there had been free cigarettes, candy and canned goods for everyone. Allied soldiers in their thousands had strolled through the streets: English, Americans, French, Indians, Algerians and

[1] Neapolitan street urchins.

Moroccans, well-fed, cordial, only too eager to spend their money. The Americans, with their clean-cut boyish faces, their friendly smiles and their lavish generosity, had won the hearts of the populace. They had been like young gods descended from the fabulous Olympus of America, where every Neapolitan had an uncle, a cousin or a son.

The idyll had lasted only a few days. Then the hard realities of life had returned. The armies had moved on; the battles of the Garigliano, Minturno, Cassino and Anzio had still to be fought. In Naples the scanty bread ration—for those who had the money to buy it—continued to be the only staple item of food.

The misery was appalling. There was cold and hunger in the midst of devastation. As far back as 1942 the Prefect of Naples had warned the people not to persist in getting themselves arrested "to find something to eat in prison". In 1944 the hunger had increased and now there was a lack of water. No light. No heat. No food. Hundreds of thousands of people without homes massed together in horrible promiscuity. As many as three large families —twenty-five or thirty people—living and sleeping in a single room. A pall of squalor had settled over the city.

If starvation had to be warded off, if money had to be made, then it must be done by trafficking, by pilfering, by begging or prostitution. Vice was the only desirable commodity, easily available, eagerly sought. A moral pestilence swept through the fetid alley-ways; the children were caught up in it and carried along like flotsam on the crest of a wave.

As I started up the hill I heard the patter of bare feet behind me. Three youngsters rushed by. Close behind them, wild-eyed and panting convulsively, came a fourth. There was a cut across his cheek and blood running down his face. It was a fleeting vision of terror. Then he, too, was swallowed up in the obscurity of the alley-ways and the patter of feet faded into silence.

In the narrow Via Egiziaca it was night. Even in the darkness, however, I could still perceive the deeper shadows close to the houses. I stepped into the centre of the street to avoid tripping over the bodies of the children sleeping on the bare cobble-stones. They were piled together, arms and legs intermingling, instinctively seeking warmth, now that the tepidity of the sunny day had receded and the bitter cold of a winter's night had advanced.

After supper the officers and I sat round the fire in the living room. The flames crackled merrily, gradually extending the rays of their warmth into the chill of the vast chamber. We were contentedly silent, feeling the heat penetrating into our bones. With idle curiosity we watched the colonel opening his Christmas package from home: a box of candy, a bottle of whisky, a woollen sweater, a scarf, a letter. He read the letter gravely, turning back once or twice to scan some paragraph anew. In silence he held it towards me so that I could see the kisses and the childish signatures added at the end.

"My kids," he said.

He folded the letter and put the gifts back into the box.

"Just to think," he mused; "those might be my kids lying out on the street, if God had disposed things differently."

We spoke at length of the thousands of homeless children that had gravitated to Naples from the south. They were a menace to the war-effort with their pilfering and their connivance with gangs of adult thieves. They were like termites, seemingly insignificant, but actually capable of undermining the stability of society.

The police captain told us of the latest discovery, of the youngsters who had been riding down the sewers on gasoline drums to get into the port. The docks represented an earthly paradise for every street boy in Naples. Each morning, clusters of them could be seen at every gate, their thin faces pressed against the iron railings, their sharp eyes following from afar the unloading of the ships. They knew that the thousands of cases contained not only ammunition but also shoes and clothing and army rations. Their great objective was to evade the guards and get inside the port.

Some of the street boys of Naples were old hands at the game, authentic *scugnizzi* from the lurid back-alleys of the city, brought up in the midst of misery, aggravated by the terrible experience of the war years. Others were new arrivals, fresh recruits to the thieving and prostitution of an occupied city. They were the more adventurous of the child victims of the bombardments of Sicily and Calabria, who had followed the advance of the Allied army northwards to Salerno and had flocked into Naples after its liberation. They had once had homes of their own, with a father and mother and brothers and sisters. Now their only possessions were their own instinctive will to live and the companionship of other homeless children. In the cruel school of survival they had soon learned that there is one supreme rule, that the weak go under and only the hard and the cunning live to tell their story.

Some of the boys had attached themselves to adult gangs and were their go-betweens with the Allied soldiers, whom they enticed into their schemes with money and women and liquor. Some boys worked alone, each one pathetically inventing his own small plan to outwit his elders and scrape together enough money for food.

Gennaro was one diminutive ten-year-old who could be found each morning with his baby sister on the steps of the Allied Commission building in Piazza Duca D'Aosta. No Allied officer could resist the baby hand held out in mute appeal and the pitiful little figures shivering in the cold. Both of them were without parents but little Rita was not Gennaro's baby sister. He rented her by the day from a friend who preferred to traffic in black-market cigarettes. Later in the morning he would take her down to the port. They would stand close to the gate, their blue noses pressed between the iron bars. Their soft, luminous eyes, startlingly beautiful in the hunger-ravaged baby faces, would fix the guard reproachfully. He would pretend not to see them but eventually he would relent and let them into the port area. "What harm can those tiny kids do?"

Salvatore had a different technique. He was a comical figure in his British army jacket and his men's trousers, roughly cut down to size. His broad smile was unquenchable and his air of friendliness proof against any rebuff. At first, a facile tongue and an air of candour had sufficed to get him past the gate.

"Sergeant Murphy wants to see me about a matter."

When police regulations became more severe he had to sharpen his wits. He borrowed two unclaimed army shirts from Mario's sister, who took in laundry. He packaged them neatly and carried them down to the dock.

"I have to take these shirts to Sergeant Brown." He always invented the name of a sergeant. It seemed to have more effect on the guard than the name of an officer.

"Who is Sergeant Brown?"

"He is on the ship over there. He is the big sergeant with a red face."

"Let me look at the package." Sure enough, they were army shirts.

"My sister washed them for the sergeant." He gave a knowing wink at the sentry.

"All right. Go ahead, but be quick about it."

One morning there was a disaster: he lost the shirts. The soldier at the gate had not been amenable to persuasion. Despite Salvatore's protestations, he had taken the shirts and put them into his sentry-box.

"I will see that the sergeant gets them."

He could not tell the severe soldier that there was no such person as Sergeant Brown, or Smith, or Jones.

The following morning Salvatore turned up at another gate. He balanced a succulent pizza pie on a cardboard tray.

"I have to take this pizza to Sergeant Smith."

The guard refused to allow him to enter.

"The sergeant won't like it if his pizza gets any colder."

The soldier was obviously weighing the pros and cons.

"O.K.! But make it snappy."

Make it snappy? Salvatore would sell the pizza to the first buyer but he would not leave the port until evening, when he would slip out among the crowd of dock-workers heading for home.

There were street boys everywhere, shining shoes, surreptitiously holding out their packs of American cigarettes, leading drunken soldiers by the hand up ill-famed alleys, tendering the photos of the girls who were up for sale. Ragged, dirty, emaciated, brutalized children, whose own indomitable spirit was the only force to keep them alive.

What was to become of them?

The colonel and the captain and I talked until midnight, when a solitary little Christmas bell began to ring.

Christmas! Two thousand years ago a Child was born, to bring peace on earth to men of goodwill. He had invited men to follow Him: "By this shall all men know that you are my disciples, if you have love for one another." And, tonight, on the birthday of that Child, men were planning to kill each other and the victims of their hatred were sleeping on the pavements of the cities, hiding in caves and rotting in the concentration camps.

Perhaps it was because it was Christmas, the feast that we instinctively associate with all that is beautiful and magical and wondrous in our own childhood, that the hurt of those children of the streets penetrated more deeply into our soul.

The colonel was speaking, roughly and humorously as was his custom. It was the final word before we went to bed. It was addressed to me, but it was a reproof and a condemnation and an invitation for all of us.

"What I want to know is this: what is an Irishman doing in Italy, if he can't attend to a little job like this?"

We laughed and we went to our rooms to sleep. I lay awake and I looked up at the ceiling, the vast painted canvas that had once adhered to the plaster and now sagged loose. The courtly scenes depicted there swelled as the wind blew through the rafters, and the noise was like the billowing of sails on a schooner riding the high seas. Rats scampered in the attic, and the woodwork creaked. I was comfortable and warm. I had the certainty of sleep, and tomorrow I would awaken again to the certainty of food. Outside, children were huddled together in the cold, with no certainty except the one big central tragedy of their lives: they were alone and no-one loved them and no-one cared for them. Tomorrow they would die, perhaps, of starvation or disease or exposure to the cold, and somehow they would be put under ground or thrown into the sea and their miserable, purposeless little lives would have ended. Or they would continue to survive, to go on suffering, to corrupt inside more rapidly even than their bodies could show the signs of physical decay. They would go on stealing and begging and prostituting themselves, and tomorrow they would be the tools of others who would use their innocence to make of it their own instrument of power.

The words of the colonel returned to taunt me: "What are you doing? What are you doing?" What were any of us doing in the world if we could remain inactive when faced with the tragedies which were the criminal consequences of adult guilt?

CHAPTER EIGHTEEN

No Alibi for Failure

"HOLY FATHER, my little boy is in the Santo Spirito Hospital. The doctor says that if he could only have that new American medicine he might be saved."

The little woman with the black shawl was oblivious of the hundreds of other people pressing forward to speak to the Pope. She had kissed his ring and in her anxiety she still held on tightly to his hand. Pius XII had to bend to catch the softly-spoken words, his whole attention momentarily concentrated on this one human problem, the ascetic lines of his face softened by the deep compassion in his eyes. Now she was fumbling in her worn purse for the doctor's prescription. After the audience the Secretariate of State would probably send it to my office for attention.

The matter might not end there. At some future audience the Holy Father might suddenly ask me, as he had done before, whether the child in the hospital had received the American medicine. He would be gently surprised if I could not remember that particular case immediately.

The Pope had moved on; it was an old man now who was speaking to him, leaning heavily upon the shoulder of his grand-child for support. A clean white rag, neatly knotted, could not disguise the fact that he wore neither collar nor tie. Was he telling the Holy Father how the child's parents had died? Three times his free hand gestured eloquently in her direction. Her innocent eyes studied the face of Pius XII with the instinctive trust that children always showed in his presence.

To rest my eyes from the sea of faces I studied the frescoes on the walls: the Battle of Lepanto; Gregory VII granting absolution to the Emperor; the seizure of Tunis by Charles V; Alexander III and Frederick Barbarossa. Did the great Sangallo, who designed the Royal Hall for the reception of ambassadors, ever imagine that one day it would be used as an audience-chamber for the miseries of humanity? Was there a painter today, like Vasari, to illustrate the new history of Europe: millions of people being massacred and others dying of hunger?

Later that morning I had an opportunity to speak to the Pope alone. I described what I had seen of the vagabond children round the docks in Naples; there were thousands of other homeless boys in Rome. From the immediacy of his reply it was obvious that he had meditated on this subject at painful length. He told me that reports reaching him showed that children in many parts of the world were suffering atrociously; in China alone they spoke of millions of little ones having been orphaned. How many more would have been made destitute before the war ended? If I wished to try to help some of them he would gladly give his consent. From that moment until the time of his death fourteen years later I never made any request of Pius XII on behalf of the children that was refused.

In January, 1945, it did not seem that Pope Pius would be long for this world. His mortified life and the anxieties of the war years had seriously weakened his bodily fibre.[1] When he raised his hands in blessing, the tapering fingers were as transparent as alabaster.

If the Holy Father expressed no surprise at my wanting to start another activity, some of my friends reacted differently:

"What, another organization! There are a hundred thousand children on the road; what do you think you can do about it?"

It was only after I had given them some hesitant reply that I realized how unfair their question was; it was not a matter of how much I hoped to do as that I hoped to do something.

In normal times it might have been different. There would have been social agencies equipped to deal with some of the children's problems. In the chaos of 1944 the Allies were the only ones who could have done anything to help and they were still fighting a war. Presumptuous though it might seem, it could only be by each

---

[1] Pius XII was six feet tall but when the war ended he weighed only 125 pounds. He had cut his diet to a bare minimum; he would allow no heating in his apartment; he had pushed his working day to two o'clock in the morning.

private citizen contributing what little he could that those home-less ones might possibly be saved. Useless to try to measure our resources and weigh our experience. Only one asset was worth putting on the scales to counterbalance the difficulties of the task: our faith in the Providence of God.

So much for our good intentions. But what could my friends and I actually do for the children? It would take time before we could find food and arrange for its distribution; impossible to find shelter for them at a moment's notice. Medical aid? Even at first sight it seemed like mockery to give a hungry child medicines for its ailments and then let it go back to the starvation of the streets. Yet this was the only help that we were equipped to give them at once. It would at least be a sign of our good intentions, a token to them that somebody cared enough to want to help.

The first month of our street-boy programme was wrought with frustration. Each day ended with a deep sense of humiliation. Very few boys came to the new medical dispensaries. Those that did were obviously not the ones who needed help the most. We wanted to run and we were compelled to crawl. We wanted to feel the satisfaction of giving and we had to recognize our own futility. We were not even able to see that there was one positive feature in this limited activity, namely that our volunteer helpers had time to study not only the ailments but also the personality of the boys that came for treatment.

What did one still need to find out about the street boys? Very little, it would seem. They talked freely about their experiences and appeared to have little reticence in revealing their innermost thoughts.

Nothing could have been farther from the truth. Their spon-taneity was highly deceptive. It was one of the defences they had unconsciously erected, not only against the world, but against the hurt of their own memories, defences so complicated that their real face—their authentic "I"—was often concealed even from themselves.

The nurse-receptionist at one of our dispensaries confessed that she had felt like boxing the ears of the first young ruffian who had swaggered in arrogantly, slamming the door and sprawling in the waiting-room chairs. Then she noticed that, even while they sniggered among themselves, their eyes were wandering anxiously from the surgical instruments in the glass cabinet to the white-robed doctors glimpsed through the swinging doors. It suddenly dawned on her that under their aggressive exterior they were frightened children.

By the time they met the doctor they were no longer in the mood to delve into the phantasy life in which they normally sought refuge. There was painful truth in their accounts of hungry nights spent under the viaducts, of promiscuous mingling in cellars, of prostitution, bestiality and savagery.

More than once at the end of an evening, removing his white smock and washing his hands, a doctor would remark meditatively: "I feel ashamed to go home tonight, knowing that these poor kids have no place to go."

Michele was one of the first boys to come to a dispensary. There was nothing physically wrong with him. As he confessed later, his only reason for coming had been to try to get something for nothing. After his fruitless call the nurse did not expect to see him again. When he did turn up, some weeks later, he was on the verge of tears. Sandro, his companion, had been run over by a jeep. The nurse phoned to me and I drove to the dispensary to pick up Michele and take him to the hospital. We could not see Sandro that evening; he was in the operating theatre and they were amputating his right leg. We went again next day and, from then on, Michele spent most of his free time at Sandro's bedside. Sometimes he was so tired in the evening that his head would fall on to the quilt and the nurses would find him sleeping soundly when it was time for him to leave.

In the ensuing weeks I came to know both boys well. On the street they had been anonymous urchins similar to all the rest. Now, because of the tragedy, their true personality had begun to re-emerge.

Sandro, in his hospital bed, had lost the wild look of the streets. Except for his excessive pallor, it was not difficult to see in him the ingenuous country boy he had been only two years earlier. At five he had been old enough to take the two goats to pasture on the mountain slope behind the stone cottage in the Abruzzi. After his father went to war he had become the man of the house. He was only eight when his mother was killed. When they took her from under the ruins, he could not recognize her—her face was so disfigured.

He stayed in his devastated native village until the Allied advance turned the whole area into a battlefield. He attached himself temporarily to a neighbour's family and moved with them from one refuge to another. He had lived mostly in caves. He had eaten wild roots and the strange, tough bread that the women had baked in the ashes of the fire. When the fighting ended he had not gone back to Orsogno. What was the use? The village had been destroyed and the only relative still there was a cousin of his father and he was an old man.

For the past six months he had been in Rome, sleeping in the tunnel of the unfinished subway. Hundreds of people slept down there at night: boys like himself, broken-down old men, and women of a sort. One night it had been Michele who had lain next to him and had stolen his cigarettes. They had fought and afterwards they had become friends.

Michele was from Naples. He had always had to rough it, even before the war. There were eleven of them in his family, if one counted his grandfather and an aunt. They lived in one room, in a decayed tenement off the Via dei Tribunali. Neither light nor air could filter down the alley-way where the multicoloured rags of clothing hung in limp festoons from morning until night. The only piece of furniture in the room was a monumental iron bed. Nine of them slept on the bed, four one way and five the other. He and his brother slept on the floor. He was not aware of the acrid odour of unwashed bodies. It was no worse than the stench from the drain in the courtyard or the rancid smell of cheap oil that lingered on after the fish had been fried and the petroleum cooking-stove taken in for the night.

The day his mother died she had been the only one of the family to go to the air-raid shelter. She was buried with hundreds of others when the mouth of the grotto collapsed. Two days later, the rescue squads had laid out the bodies on the sidewalks. Some of the people had taken home their dead. His father had wanted to bring her home but his aunt said no. They could not have afforded a casket, even one made with rough boards. If she was to be taken away on the sanitation cart it was better that it happen at once than under the pitying but critical eyes of the neighbours. And where would they have laid her with ten of them already in the room and her already dead two days? Such were the problems of the poor in Naples. They were not new to Michele and they did not cause him any particular surprise, only a vague discomfort, an awakening intuition which might explode one day, that these things should not be, that the alternative offered to the poor should not be so inexorably cruel.

His father had never been good for anything. After the death of his wife he had lapsed into a state of hopeless apathy. When the Americans arrived, Michele had stopped going home even at night. He had trafficked in the Galleria Umberto I; he had shined shoes, begged and stolen like many another *scugnizzo*. He was one of the first Neapolitan boys to go north with the troops after the liberation of Rome. He had joined up with one companion after another until he met Sandro.

It was he, Michele, who had provided the idea and the capital for the shoeshine stand near the Grand Hotel. It was a good stand —perhaps the best in Rome—and everything had been going well until Sandro was knocked down by the jeep.

I was not in Rome when Sandro left the hospital. When I returned, the nurse told me that Michele and another boy had come to fetch him. They had brought him some clothes and a wooden crutch. She did not know where they had gone.

I found them next day outside the Grand Hotel. Michele was shining shoes and Sandro was sitting beside him, propped up against the wall. The crippled boy saluted me with forced gaiety and explained the new basis for their partnership. Michele would do the work and he would provide the pathetic note—he waved his crutch at me to make his point—which they expected would double the day's takings.

The two boys were probably better off than hundreds of their companions. Yet the thought of abandoning them now, without doing something to put their feet on the first rung of the ladder back to happiness, was intolerable to me.

I wondered whether a Boys' Home might be willing to accept them. Before making inquiries, I broached the subject to the boys themselves, cautiously, as I had no illusion about my proposal being well received. I must confess that I had not foreseen the violence of their reaction.

"I am not going to any orphanage," Michele stated flatly.

I started to say that it would not be an orphanage, but I realized that the name was a mere technicality.

"What about Sandro? He needs special care. He should have an orthopaedic limb, if he is to walk normally again."

For a moment it seemed as though Michele might weaken. "Sandro can go, if he wants. I am staying as I am."

"I am staying with Michele," Sandro butted in defiantly.

Both boys were looking at me with open hostility. I had betrayed them. I was threatening to rob them of the one worthwhile thing they possessed: their companionship.

"All right! Have it your own way."

In the weeks that followed, whenever I passed the Grand Hotel I stopped as usual to talk to them. One day their stand was vacant; after a day or two it was occupied by two other shoeshine boys. Michele and Sandro had vanished.

I never forgot Michele and Sandro. Even when several years had gone by and other children of their age had grown up round me, my thoughts would sometimes return to those first two vagrant boys I had known. I wondered whether I would ever see them again, just to be told that they were living a happier life, that they had a family of their own and had learned to forget the horrors of the war. Or perhaps I had been mistaken, after all, in thinking that those two children must survive. Perhaps they had just been two homeless street boys like the rest: born with a name and yet nameless; having lived and yet without a past; continuing to exist but deprived of a future; with a face, but indistinguishable one from the other. Just two anonymous little urchins in the vast multitude of the lost children of the world. They had only seemed to emerge for a moment. Then they had been swallowed up again in the vast blackness of night where the forgotten children wander, the little ones whose names are known only to God.

CHAPTER NINETEEN

Hunger

IT WAS a morning in early January. The Neapolitan sun was rising lazily into the sky: no longer the cruel dominator of July, flattening the houses into one harsh reverberation of light, but the delicate artist of winter, weaving the lingering haze, the deep azure majesty of the sea and the ancient ochre of the city into one stupendous tapestry.

The sea-front at Mergellina was deserted. Only one person walked ahead of me. His bare feet padded softly on the sidewalk and his ragged trousers flapped grotesquely against his slender brown legs. He turned for a moment to see who was behind him. He wore no shirt under the torn jacket and his ribs stood out against the skin. I was sure that the one glance from the vigilant eyes had told him all that he might need to know.

"He will not turn around again," I told myself. "Yet he is conscious of all that is happening behind him."

I was wrong. As he drew abreast of a wooden stall on which black market cigarettes were exposed for sale, he did turn again, with a decisive swing of his body, as though he were responding to my call. His action was so brusque that the old woman sitting by the stand instinctively followed his gaze. It was a golden opportunity: a flick of the hand sent a packet of cigarettes flying into the strange cloth bag hanging over his arm.

Instinctively my pace quickened. I overtook the boy as he turned the corner.

"I saw you steal those cigarettes."

He made no attempt to escape. His face was sullen but not alarmed.

"You know that it is wrong to steal."

He looked at me bitterly. From close at hand I could see that he was not even twelve years old. He spat out the words: "What do you want me to do? Die of hunger?"

Hunger!

"Hunger persuades to evil," wrote Virgil two thousand years ago. During his Neapolitan sojourn did he see the *scugnizzi* of the day scraping among the offal like starving dogs searching for food?

'A hungry people," said Seneca, "listens not to reason, nor cares for justice, nor is bent by any prayers."

The ancients knew hunger; not the polite hunger that adds zest to eating, but the hunger that "breeds madness".

"Death in all its shapes is hateful to man, but the worst is death from hunger." Did Homer see Greek children too weak to cry, too weak to care, while famine sapped the substance of their bones? Centuries later, a nurse would visit the children in his war-torn land: "They have only skin stretched over their bones, and their faces are like those of old men."

Probably few of us have experienced hunger. It is only by feeble analogy that we can form even a pallid idea of its horrors.

I went without food for two days one spring, confined by a blizzard to an Alpine refuge. The gnawing pangs of appetite were difficult to bear. On the evening of the third day my fellow-climber discovered an ancient half-loaf of bread lying in the filth between the firewood chest and the wall. At any other time the mildewed smell of it would have nauseated us. We dried it on the stove. Never before had there been food so delicious. We had been hungry, ravenously hungry, but we had not known hunger, *the* hunger.

Hunger! Wherever I went there was hunger. In the foundling hospitals the infants lay exhausted, opening their mouths to cry as little kittens do, with no sound emerging. Their baby bodies were devitalized; their stomachs, so long unaccustomed to food, were no longer able to hold it. Tiny children stopped me in the street, gazing not at me but beyond me, with the terribly vacant look of the starving. *"Ho fame."*[1] *Fame!* It is an awful word—like *hunger*—two syllables, so easy to say: *fame*.

"What do you want me to do? Die of hunger?"

The *scugnizzi* stole to ward off hunger. The mother, the sister,

[1] "I am hungry."

could not bear the sight of the starving children at home and gave themselves, out of hunger. Up to that moment they had been brave, resisting threats and enticements. Now they ceded, to hunger.

Hunger knew no frontiers.

In 1946 I was in Hamburg. Five o'clock: a middle-aged man—briefcase in one hand and umbrella in the other—a respectable clerk, halted in front of me to uncover the garbage can on the sidewalk. Incredible? No! He was looking for food, any food. He was hungry.

Italy, Greece, Germany, Yugoslavia, Poland: children begging for food, committing crimes for food, prostituting themselves for food.

"What do you want me to do? Die of hunger?"

There was no joy, only heartache, in watching the children eat in the difficult days after our first soup kitchens were opened. Their hunger was too great; their need too obvious.

When the iron cauldrons were carried from the kitchen and the sisters began to serve, even the fragrance of the soup was like a long-drawn-out torture, pinching their nostrils and twisting their bowels agonizingly. Their eyes did not detach themselves from the huge pot until the ladle had filled their own plate to overflowing. Their bodies were tense in expectation. They were devouring the food with every organ, with every nerve and fibre of their being, even before they put it into their mouth.

They gulped the first few spoonfuls but almost immediately their pace slackened. They dawdled over each mouthful, but not because they were satiated. Looking at the pasta and beans rapidly disappearing, they were conscious that the joy of eating would soon end.

The dieticians agreed that the two daily rations were sufficient for the minimum human requirement. The children, however, could have continued to eat until they had gorged themselves, contenting not only their bodies but also the unsatiated hunger of the soul. Food had become a symbol of many of the precious things that they had lost: a mother's love, the warmth of a home.

They could have gone on eating, but the supply of food had to be stretched out to feed as many hungry mouths as possible. The quantities of flour, of spaghetti, oil, dried vegetables, tomato paste and salt needed for one ration of bread and soup seemed infinitesimal, when measured in grams. Multiplied by the tens of thousands of children who would soon have to be fed, they added up to tons.

It was not easy to find the food. American Relief for Italy supplied the flour and the milk, Ireland the meat and the butter; the rest had to be bought.[1] It was even more difficult to organize the preparing of it. It would not have been possible at all if the good sisters in each town had not assumed the task of cooking the food and serving it to the hordes of wild youngsters who invaded the quiet of their convents.

From afar, all the street children had looked the same. Seen at close range in the feeding centres, the differences in their personalities stood out strikingly: timid or aggressive, bitter or optimistic, calculating or generous. The younger ones—only two or three years old when the war began—had never known anything else than the grey misery of privation. Others—now fifteen or sixteen —could still remember the different world in which they had lived. The disruption of their lives had started as far back as 1940. Their fathers and elder brothers had been called up to fight, their mothers had had to go out to work and family life had disintegrated. The schools had been closed because of the bombardments, and the boys had been left to their own devices on the street. They had tried to find in the Fascist war the glamour that could fire their imagination. They had not succeeded. It had not only been the terrors of the bombardments, the nights spent in the air-raid shelters, the food rationing and the black-out. It had been the dull squalor of life, the defeat that followed defeat. It had been the confusion and discouragement that they discerned in the attitudes and conversations of their elders. When Fascism fell, the last dream had faded and tar had blotted out the grandiose slogans painted on the walls. No more *Figli della Lupa*,[2] no more *Avanguardisti*,[3] with tiny rifles slung over their shoulders and

[1] When UNRRA came to Italy, I approached Mr. Keeney, the Director, and he agreed that all the street-boy centres should benefit from their distribution of food.

[2] Sons of the Wolf: the Fascist organization for elementary-school children.

[3] Pioneers: the Fascist organization for young teenagers.

Sunday afternoon parades and summer camps! Life had become a
struggle for survival, a black market operation. Petty com-
promises with truth and honesty had come to be accepted as an
everyday necessity of living.

The Resistance Movement had given some of the youngsters a
sense of purpose. They had carried messages after the curfew; they
had stolen German supplies; they had participated in the fighting
during the "four days of Naples" and the defence of Rome.
Grown accustomed to violence, it had not been easy for them to
readjust after the Liberation, just because the Allies had arrived.
It had been a praiseworthy thing to steal from the Germans; why
should it be so wicked to steal from the Allies? The obvious
affluence of the Americans—well clothed, well fed and wasteful—
made misery even more painful to bear.

Most of the boys who came to the soup kitchens had lost their
homes; they had had no alternative but to take to the road. When
their family died they had experienced all the terrible anguish of
bereavement. Then, apathy had settled upon them, a numbness
deadening the pain of loss. In self-defence they had instinctively
shut out all the memories that could hurt, all the gentler influences
that could hinder them in their cruel fight for survival.

Other boys—and there were many of them—still had relatives
with whom they could possibly have lived. They had generally
been involved in the mass executions and had known the degrading life of the refugee camp. When they had returned to their
desolate villages they had been restless and bewildered, intolerant
of restraint, exasperated by the miserable hopelessness of life.
They had decided to follow the soldiers and seek the excitement
of a vagabond existence.

On the road the clever ones had discovered their unsuspected
gifts for survival. They had become masters of guile. There was
no vice unknown to them, no human weakness that they could not
discern or were incapable of exploiting. Their knowledge of the
depths to which human nature can sink blinded them to the possibility of disinterested kindness.

They sometimes allowed themselves to be used by older people,
when it was to their own advantage to do so. They sold their

stolen goods to adult receivers and bought black market items that they themselves could sell. They worked with older gangs and often served as bait to entice a victim into a trap. They smoked and drank without restraint and prided themselves on their toughness. The first time that the police had arrested them they had been scared, but when they had been released the police did not know what to do with them—"We can't detain all the kids. Where would we put them?"—they had awakened to a cynical realization of their own impunity.

Respectable citizens quickened their steps at the sight of a group of young vagrants. In their excessive prudence they did not learn to distinguish between one homeless boy and another, between the psychopaths, the hardened young criminals and the great mass of pitiful waifs, still unconsciously longing for security and affection.

All of those boys in the street had stolen, perhaps, at some time or another, or had broken into a cellar to get out of the rain, but not all of them were *bad*.

When they told me later—in happier moments—of their experiences on the streets, I saw again the things that I had witnessed but with different eyes. They spoke of the men and women whom they had met on the sidewalk, of the glance of pity hastily repressed, the hurried drawing away as from contaminated beings. They recalled their own bitterness, their own hardening, their despair. They looked back with a strangely detached wonder to those far-off unhappy things. They had been hurt by the world of grown-ups and, instead of helping them, the grown-ups had hastened on their way.

I was amazed and moved by their fortitude. They had experienced every heartbreak; they could not possibly look to the future without a feeling of terror and yet they could still find the courage to smile. They pushed forward along the roads, bare-footed and half-naked, undernourished and sickly, exposed to every physical and moral danger. I was amazed, not by the temptations to which they had succumbed, but by the virtues which they had preserved. Behind the older boys trailed the smaller children, not bound to them by any bond of blood but only by the brotherhood of the road, protected by them, fed by them and—why not?— loved by them in their own rough and often profane way.

"Suffer the little children to come unto me and forbid them not; for of such is the kingdom of God."

An American truck appeared at a refuse heap not far from the Basilica of St. Paul and dumped its load of condemned cans of food. Even before the truck had disappeared, a swarm of emaciated children were crawling over the refuse like scavenger beetles. They fought for the valuable cans—the stomach-satisfying foods like corned beef and Spam—and left the vegetables as consolation prizes for the losers. Next day the number of hungry children at the dump had increased. It did not matter: there was food enough for all.

The third morning, after the soldiers had unloaded the cans as usual, they sprayed them with gasoline. There was a wail of dismay. The smaller children burst into tears. As soon as the truck left, they rushed to the burning refuse, poking frantically with sticks, trying desperately to snatch the blackened cans out of the flames. What did they know of ptomaine-poisoning? They only knew hunger. Contaminated or not, the cans contained food.

« Then, some evening, as I had sat in the protected
peace of one of our little communities and seen
the contentment shining from the children's eyes... ».

« You know the old aunt who is taking
care of my little sister? She is very poor.
I send her my savings each month ».

CHAPTER TWENTY

Horror

"MY MOTHER is dead. She was killed by the Germans."
"Where was your home?"
"In Tuscany, near Lucca."

His tone was matter of fact, his face expressionless. Was it hurt
I glimpsed through the studied indifference of his eyes? It was
difficult to say. From Tuscany! Strange! It had been in the
cathedral at Pisa, close to Lucca, that, only a few months before,
I had received a first inkling of the dreadful reality that can lie
behind the dead eyes of a child.

I recalled the two children who had survived the massacre, and
the words that the grandmother had uttered to reassure me:
"Don't worry. They don't understand anything any more." Before
I had fallen asleep that night in Pisa, I had found myself wondering. Did those children not understand? Had a merciful door
really been shut on their suffering or were they themselves holding
a barricade tightly closed against the world?

In April, 1945, I again found myself in Tuscany, driving north
from Pistoia to Bologna. At long last the Allies had broken
through the Gothic Line. Americans, Brazilians, British, Indians,
Italians, New Zealanders, Poles and South Africans swarmed into
the plain of Romagna and headed triumphantly towards the key
cities of the north.

The Porretta pass took me through the mountains. From the
summit the road followed the winding course of the River Reno
down into the valley. There were the usual scenes of devastation;
even the remotest cottages had been destroyed. With still fifteen
miles to Bologna, I reached the little town of Marzabotto. I had
been there before the war to see the famous Etruscan necropolis.
It had been a hot day and I had sat in the cool shade of the cedars

of Lebanon. Now I sat on a stone, looking at the ruins of the houses and the mutilated stumps of trees, and listened to the story of its martyrdom.

All through the summer of 1944 there had been killings up and down the valley. For every German shot by the partisans there had been brutal reprisals against the civilian population. On September 28, with the arrival of two regiments of the Adolph Hitler SS Division, the general massacre had begun.

At Spericomo, a bare mile away, only one poor soul had survived, a blind woman whose hysterical screams had been heard across the valley for three long days. At Casaglia, the villagers—fifty of them children—had been herded into the graveyard and slaughtered. Only after the SS had departed had a little boy crawled from under the dead. He had clung to the closed gate and screamed to an empty village: "If there is anyone alive, please run." Hearing his voice, two little girls had taken courage and crept out from the death pile.

In Caprara, of a hundred and seven who died twenty-four had been children. They had been thrown into a room, slaughtered with handgrenades and finished off with flame-throwers. The SS had amused themselves by spying at their torments through a hole in the door.

Altogether, in Marzabotto, 1836 people had been killed.

The tragic story came to an end. In silence we watched a little boy climbing laboriously up the hill. His right arm had been amputated above the elbow. The old man sitting on the tree-trunk answered my unspoken question.

"All his family was slaughtered."

There was room on the stone and I motioned to the boy to sit beside me. His silence was gentle. I put my arm around his thin shoulders. Instinctively he moved closed. I touched his cheek softly. His head rested slowly against me as though he were tired, very tired.

What goes on in the minds of these children of the road? What dark thoughts brood there during the day and what obsessive dreams frighten them during the night? Do they wake up screaming and is the awakening worse than the dream? From now on there can be no comfort, only torture, in remembering.

Tortured minds, mutilated bodies!

There were more than fifteen thousand mutilated children in Italy as a result of the war.

After every major bombardment there had been tragic scenes in the hospitals; surgeons had often been obliged to amputate the limbs even of tiny children to save their lives. After each German retreat abandoned shells and land mines had exacted an even heavier toll. Long stretches of the public highway were bordered with ominous signposts, but actually there was no knowing where a mine might be found.

A boy peered into my car as I waited at the level-crossing near Furbara. Was it a cynical expression in his eyes? Or was it bitterness? A few more steps, a blinding flash, and another victim, with all his riddles, had been added to the interminable death list of the war. A group of children were playing on a bare plot of ground as I drove through the outskirts of Rome.[1] The mysterious object they had just dug up exploded, and I carried the four living but mutilated bodies to the Santo Spirito Hospital.

For countless children close to the battle areas experiences such as mine were calmly accepted as a part of daily living.

"One morning I was with my brother Ivo", wrote one young Tuscan, "when we heard a terrific explosion in the direction of La Casetta. Two little girls had been playing near a pile of stones. The foot of the older girl had struck a mine and she was blown to pieces. The smaller one lost her sight. The mother came running up, crazy with grief. At first we were frozen and could not move. Finally Ivo went to a nearby house and asked for a cloth. I held it while he picked up the remains."

In 1945, the Order of Malta opened a home for mutilated children in the grounds of the Quirinal Palace. Practically every afternoon thereafter I went to visit them.

Franco and Lino were usually the first to recognize my step. They were brothers and they held each other by the hand. Then came Giuseppe, placing the stump of one of his handless arms trustfully in my grasp. I shuddered internally, but I had schooled myself not to reveal the horror that I felt. When I spoke, his dark eyes turned so spontaneously it was difficult to realize that they

---

[1] Piazza Irnerio.

were sightless. The childish beauty of his oval face was in dreadful contrast to the desecration of his poor body.

"*Monsignó!*" It was Vittorio, the tiniest of them all, who generally arrived with little Giovanna leading him by the hand. His brain had suffered and he lived in a dim twilight of understanding. To speak to him, however, was to look into heaven, to discover a spiritual radiance that transcended reason.

"*Monsignó!* I have prayed to Jesus for you."

"Thank you, Vittorio."

The tiny lips were parted in the most delicate of smiles and the sightless eyes were straining upwards, as though the force of his effort could pierce the veil of not-seeing.

On several occasions during the summer I took them into the country. Once it was to the Pope's private garden underneath his window at Castel Gandolfo. They sat on the circular rim of the fountain and trailed their fingers happily in the water.

"*Monsignó*, let us run."

Holding them by the hand, I ran across the smooth grass, where no stone could trip their unsuspecting feet. The breeze blew into their face and they quivered with joy at the unseen, wonderful world that they sensed around them.

"*Monsignó*, is it beautiful? Is everything beautiful?"

"*Si, caro.* Everything is beautiful, very beautiful."

With those mutilated children, cared for by loving people—so unlike the unwashed, bitter children of the streets, sleeping in the tunnels, trafficking, prostituting and stealing—it was not difficult to remember that they had their angels beside them, guiding their steps. There was a joyfulness and a spiritual radiance that only God's grace could explain.

Why did God permit them to suffer? The tragedy of the child victims of the war was once again the great mystery of evil and sorrow and pain. In God's divine plan for the world men are not automata, controlled by inexorable command. They have the power to love their brother freely and to bind up his wounds. But able also, because they are free, to hate him and stab him to death. Able, too, to involve even innocent children in their fratricidal strife.

What was to happen to those tiny victims of man's cruelty to man? Were they to be excluded, because of their youth, from the communion of suffering? Were they not to be allowed to see their acceptance of it elevated by God to the heights of the Cross, for their own purification in love and for the redemption of the world?

Surely those victims of the war were destined to become the new messengers of peace and goodwill among men! No-one would ever again even speak of war without the tragic vision of children with sightless eyes and truncated limbs rising up to make him desist. No-one would ever again indulge in the luxurious follies that had marred the pre-war world, now that the message of homeless little ones was there to shame him out of his selfishness. No longer would little sisters from orphanages have to go wearily from office to office each day to beg. No longer would men say: "Why should I pay to keep other people's brats?" No longer would newspapers tell of fabulous sums spent on one night of folly. No longer would men's consciences allow them to waste while children starved. The victims of the war would be there, the mutilated and the orphaned, to awaken compassion and to reveal to men the goodness of God, who allows them to use the riches of their purse and the kind urgings of their heart to make the world a better place to live in, a place of peace and of love.

No longer . . . ?

CHAPTER TWENTY-ONE

Prodigal Sons

"SHE IS the mother of three young children." A tear rolled down the wrinkled cheek of the old man and fell on my desk. It was not difficult to read his thought: on the yes or no of this man depends the life of my daughter.

"You have a kind heart. You are a priest. *Sia buono!*"[1]

Was it selfishness that made each person see his own sorrow as *the* great calamity, fight for its alleviation as though it were the only tragedy in the world? No. Millions of other people might have worse misfortunes, but that did not lessen by one iota the immensity of each human sorrow. Who could blame this old man if he steadfastly closed his ears to reason? She was his only daughter and she was bound to die,[2] unless she received the penicillin that she needed.

"Tomorrow I will present your request to our Medical Commission."

"I know what their answer will be, the same as at the hospital. They will not give ten million units for one person."

The hospital was not wrong. The total quantity of penicillin available in Italy was insufficient for the needs of even one small city. Ten million units of it might save the life of several people. Yet was it right to base decisions exclusively on mathematical calculations? Each request covered a human dilemma, a problem of living creatures, of mothers, of families, of sole surviving children.

In Greece a children's clinic had only sufficient milk to keep five hundred babies alive until the next supply would arrive. What should the doctors do? Be quantitatively just and give a little milk

---

[1] "Be kind!"

[2] She was suffering from a chronic myocarditis.

to each one of the twenty-five hundred babies and have them all die in the end, or should they select five hundred babies—and which babies?—to be saved?[1]

Two thousand mothers must have cursed the doctors for their favouritism, weeping as this old man was weeping. *"Sia buono!"*

I stood for a moment at the front door as the old man shuffled into the darkness. The *carabinieri* on perpetual guard outside bade me goodnight. I put the bolts and chains in place and climbed wearily upstairs. My helpers had long since gone home, frozen after a long day in the unheated rooms, eyes strained by the glare of the acetylene lamps.

The giant crucifix at the top of the staircase was impressive in the semi-darkness. My fingers touched the feet of the dead Christ. How many times had the mutilated soldiers hobbling downstairs stopped to touch those nail-pierced feet reverently with their lips! Until recently the house had been a military hospital. Memories still lingered in every nook and cranny. At the head of the next ramp of stairs was the room where Ahmed, the Moslem soldier from Somaliland, had died. He had suffered patiently in his solitude, isolated by the barrier of language. His hand had searched for mine that night as I stood at his bedside. He had found it and placed it gently over his breast to gather the last beat of his heart. How great is the brotherhood of man! Feeble as we all are, and pathetic in our loneliness, how easy to have compassion for each other, and love! As little children do.

The memories of old sorrows lingered on and the shadows of new tragedies joined them in these vaulted halls, day by day.

It was ten o'clock. Supper would be awaiting me. Raniero, the caretaker, refusing to go to bed before I had eaten, would be there to serve it. I would spread the newspaper next to my plate, try to shake off the worries of the day and enjoy the luxury of being alone.

Entering the dining room, I stopped short. I was startled to find a tiny figure already seated at the far side of the supper table. I had forgotten all about Peppino.

"I am sorry, Peppino. It is late. You must be hungry."

"I gave him some supper two hours ago, but he wanted to stay

[1] *Hellas*, London, May 14, 1943.

up and now he is hungry again." Raniero had already incorporated the care of Peppino into his daily routine of duties.

"I never go to bed before midnight," Peppino said tonelessly.

I had met him that afternoon in the courtyard of San Damaso, inside the Vatican. He had been talking to my driver when I came out of the elevator.

"I wanted news of an aunt and they told me to come to the Information Centre in the Vatican, but no one here knows her."

"Where does your aunt live?"

"In Rome."

"And where is your home?"

"I don't have a home. I don't have anyone. They are all dead."

Peppino had been born in Italian East Africa. His father and mother had been peasants from the Veneto, who had emigrated to the new land immediately after their marriage. Everything had gone well for a time. Then the father had been called up to fight, the mother had died, and Peppino had been left alone.

In 1942, he had been repatriated to Italy and placed in a refugee camp. After September 8, 1943, the Germans had rounded up the men to work on the defences of the Brenner pass and, although Peppino was only twelve years old, he had been taken with them. Somehow he had survived the hardships of forced labour and the winter cold of the mountains.

With the arrival of the Allies it had seemed that his sufferings were to end at last. An officer had put him on a truck and sent him south to look for the aunt whom he confidently expected to find in Rome. Disappointment awaited him, and he was alone in the inhospitable streets of a hungry city.

Peppino stayed with me for several days. Most of that time he spent in my study, silently disappearing as each visitor entered, and returning again as soon as they had left. He stood with his nose glued to the window, looking at the people hurrying to and fro in the street, but refusing to go for a walk. I gave him books and toys, but he did not know how to read and still less how to play.

"I want to sit here."

I became so used to the bullet-shaped head resting on the folded arms sprawling over my desk that I was no longer conscious of the two eyes attentively following my every action, seeking a hidden significance in each stroke of my pen. From time to time, unblinking, they returned to scrutinize my face. When I smiled there was no answering ripple, and no embarrassment when suddenly our gaze met. I found that I, too, was pausing to scrutinize the sad, childish features. If the eyes are really the mirror of the soul, then there was greyness within, a monotony of not-caring which was terrifying in its emptiness.

I had to find a home for Peppino, a place where he could go to school and learn a trade. He had already lost too many useful years. Two of the institutions that I visited were willing to make room for him. Yet I hesitated. I wondered whether he would be happy there, whether the problems of his confused little personality would be understood, whether he would receive the care and the love that he needed to banish the frozen look from his eyes.

Was Peppino different, then, from every other boy I had met? The difference was not in Peppino. It was in myself. My closeness to his sorrow had given me a closer insight into the immensity and complexity of his need—of every lonely child's need—than I had ever had in the past.

Unfortunately, in those unhappy war-torn days, there were tens of thousands of children who were homeless. It would be a miracle if all of them could receive even the bare minimum of custodial care.

It was obviously not only the boys who had lost their homes during the course of the war. For many reasons, however, the girls had not taken to the road as their brothers had done. They had not been moved by the same spirit of adventure; surviving relatives had been more willing to take girls into their families; the numerous local convents of sisters had given a home to those who were quite alone.

The work of the street-boy organization was therefore principally, if not exclusively, directed to the care of boys. Four months after its foundation, more than one hundred thousand children were being fed; tens of thousands had been clothed.[1] Yet what

[1] Hundreds of communities of sisters prepared and served the food. Others—notably the Calasanctian Sisters and the Sisters of Charity—organized sewing groups to unravel the tens of thousands of old woollen garments we had collected and knit them into new sweaters, to wash and cut up old army uniforms and make them into boys' trousers. Many indi-

satisfaction could there be in giving a child a bowl of soup and then watching him disappear alone into the darkness? In seeing a momentary flash of joy give way at once to the empty gaze of the unloved?

"What good are we doing keeping them alive when all they have to live for is to rot on the streets?"

"We must do what we can; after that . . ."

Nevertheless my friend was right; it was humanly impossible to go on feeding them, clothing them and giving them medical care and not try at least to tackle the seemingly hopeless task of providing them with a home.

Hopeless, indeed, to think of finding empty buildings in the cities or of erecting new ones! What about the existing institutions? The larger religious congregations were already doing everything they could. The smaller institutions? Those that had escaped destruction were in a state of extreme poverty. Perhaps for that very reason they might not be filled to capacity.

In the spring of 1945 we sent a questionnaire to several hundred orphanages. The answers far exceeded our expectations. While they were arriving, telling us that they would be able to house more children, if only they had additional cots, blankets, tables and chairs, we were already filling our warehouses with discarded hospital beds, firemen's bunks and other equipment. "American Relief for Italy" supplied the bed-linen. The "Don Suisse" came to the rescue with railway-cars full of crockery and cutlery collected in the Swiss homes.[1]

It was not merely a question of the initial equipment; the orphanages needed a continuing supply of food, and money for day-to-day expenses. "Take the children. We will find you the

---

viduals gave all or most of their time to helping the street boys. Princess Gabriella Pacelli, the niece of Pope Pius XII, dedicated a half of every day to supervising our clothing programmes; Count Mauro Faina came straight from his bank every afternoon to work with us until nine or ten o'clock; an Air Force colonel, a captain in the Navy, an engineer, an accountant and others gave their whole day to the heavy organizational work.

[1] Altogether, 230,000 sheets, blankets and towels, 28,000 beds and other pieces of furniture, 270,000 plates, cups, knives and other utensils were collected and distributed.

money." It was a hazardous thing to promise so much to so many. On the other hand, even to carry on the work we were already doing, we had no resources, except those that Divine Providence sent us. If it should become impossible at any time to continue our help, no one but ourselves would have been damaged by our having made the effort.

In the end our imprudence was justified. At a distance of less than six years from the end of the war, with the aid of thousands of little donors, it had been possible to provide a home for more than twenty thousand children.

On May 4 the German troops in Italy surrendered. Five days later, the war in Europe ended.

I was in San Giovanni Valdarno, on my way to Florence, when the church bells started to ring. The men were already in the streets, discussing the news they had heard over the radio. The women were hanging their coloured bedspreads from the windows as they did on religious feast-days. Improvised flags—most of them red—had made their appearance as if by magic. In the main square a Communist orator was haranguing the crowd.

My tiny car was greeted with a menacing salute as it tried to edge its way through the crush and a hostile face glowered in at me. Only the children in the crowd seemed to be smiling. They pressed their noses excitedly against the glass and made friendly little signs with their hands as I continued on my way.

Leaving Florence behind me, I pushed on over the Futa pass to Bologna and devoured the last two hundred miles that separated me from Milan. I was anxious to find out as quickly as possible what new problems we might have to face in the north.

It was already night when I reached the outskirts of the city. The streets were deserted; the silence was broken by sporadic bursts of rifle fre. The crackle of a machine-gun sounded uncomfortably close. It seemed imprudent to venture farther in the dark. I parked my car in the courtyard of an apartment building and slept as best I could, stretched out on the back seat.

Next morning, as I drove through Corso Magenta towards the Cathedral square, two bodies were being removed from the side-walk. During the day there would be hysterical denunciations, followed by summary executions in the street. Mussolini's ravaged body would hang in Piazza Loreto. The war might have ended but the killings were starting all over again, this time in revenge.

A solitary church bell was ringing. A few women were hurrying to Mass. As I passed close to the cathedral several ragged children were poking among the ruins of a house.

PART THREE

Child Victims in the Aftermath of War, 1945-63

CHAPTER TWENTY-TWO

Prepared to Serve

"I AM sorry. I can't take any of these older boys. The twelve-year-olds you sent me are bad enough."

Practically all the children for whom we had succeeded in finding a home up to the late spring of 1945 had been the younger ones. It was not only that the directors of the orphanages had hesitated to mix hardened adolescents with the other children. The boys themselves had often refused to become inmates of an institution. A year or two before, they had been ingenuous children, only too eager to accept a substitute for the love they had lost. As the months had gone by, however, and their illicit activities had solved their immediate need for food, drink and cigarettes, they had grown accustomed to the hardships of a vagabond life. Their contacts with the adult world had only served to make them harder and more cynical, while promiscuous sexual experiences had destroyed what traces of innocence remained.

If we could not find institutions willing to accept them, why should we not attempt to open homes for these tough boys ourselves, better adapted to their particular needs? I knew hundreds of them by name. I had met them time and time again, in Palermo, Bari, Naples, Rome and Leghorn. Most of them had come to the feeding centres for a meal or had been given a change of clothing. There had been hesitancy at first. The priest's garb had been an obstacle for a time, but not for long. Once I had been accepted, it became my most valid passport. When I drove into any large town and left my car in one of the main streets, two or three old acquaintances were often waiting for me when I returned. They would grin sheepishly, offer me a cigarette and give me news of other companions on the road. Sometimes, in one of the bursts of warm-heartedness that were not untypical of them, they brought me younger boys who needed care. I was amused and yet touched by their good-natured advice. In Naples, where I had come to know most of the *scugnizzi* who trafficked round the port and the Allied offices, one hardy young fifteen-year-old had offered me protection.

"*Se qualcuno Le da fastidio, ce lo dice.*"[1]

It was in Naples, too, that I ran into Totonno.

"You don't remember me?"

I hesitated. There was something very familiar about him.

"I used to carry the medicines for you when you came to Velletri. I lived in the Fosso with my Aunt Maria and Uncle Gaetano."

I looked in amazement at the bold-eyed youth with the bitter mouth, forming a mental picture of the fresh-faced little boy who had run alongside me, bare-footed, down the country lanes. How proud he had been when we entered the caves to show that he carried the rucksack with the food and medicines!

"My uncle used to beat me. I put up with it until my aunt died. Then I ran away and came back to Naples."

Useless asking him where he lived now.

"How are you getting along?"

"I manage somehow," he answered, with a mirthless laugh and a significant glance. 'You know."

From then on, on my weekly visits to Naples, Totonno was my inseparable companion. There was no need to let him know when I would be arriving. After two or three stops—at the port, at the Allied Commission and the Prefecture—he invariably caught up with me. News travelled like lightning in the underworld of the street boys.

After making my round of the feeding centres and the places where most of the *scugnizzi* congregated, I began my search for the relatives of the Neapolitan boys I had met on my travels. Here Totonno's help was invaluable. He led me unerringly through the narrow streets, interrogated the old women sitting outside their basement homes,[2] ran ahead of me up the malodorous stone stairways and banged without ceremony on the decrepit doors.

---

[1] "If anyone bothers you, just let us know."

[2] The typical Neapolitan *vasci*, with the doors opening directly on to the street.

Pope Paul VI presides over the Assembly in the Boys' Town of Rome.

The Court in the Boys' Town of Rome.

It was generally the womenfolk—the sisters and the aunts—who were at home, and the mere mention of the wandering youth automatically let loose a flood of tears. Exclamations of pity and pious ejaculations mingled with threats of chastisement if they ever set eyes on him again. There was seldom any doubt about the existence of a deep family tie, but this did not hide the hard fact that the re-appearance of the absent one would only create an added problem. The pinched features of the children and the prematurely aged faces of the women showed that they had their own problems of misery to bear.

I never gave Totonno any money, nor did he ask me for it. My ready acceptance of his services restored his self esteem. Sitting on the sea-wall at Santa Lucia while he shared my lunch, he talked freely about himself and his companions on the road.

"Don't let them kid you. They are scared stiff. We are all afraid."

"Afraid of what?"

"Oh, I don't know. Afraid of getting sick, like Raffaele—did you see him the other day? He can hardly drag himself along. He use to be stronger than any of us—afraid of lots of things."

"Afraid, too, of the future?"

He shrugged his shoulders and gave the little laugh which served as a non-committal answer.

He would not admit it but it was true. The one chink in the armour of the seemingly impervious street urchins was their fear of the future. The lives they were leading might satisfy the material needs of the moment but they had no logical outcome, except crime, prison and dereliction. They were illiterate and unskilled in any trade. If they ever spoke of the future, they ended up, as Totonno did, with an expressive shrug of the shoulders and a resigned "What can I do about it? *Che sarà, sarà.*"[1]

The only way in which this vicious circle could be broken seemed to be to place them in an institution where they could go to school, learn a trade and start life anew. From the adult viewpoint the logic was perfect, but it did not take into account the obstacles created by the boys themselves. Their fear of another change, their defeatism and tragic fatalism deprived them of the power to alter their mode of existence.

[1] "What will be, will be."

Some of the boys had actually spent a short time in a Boys' Home. They had ended by running away or they had been dismissed as incorrigible. They had bitter things to say about their experiences, but there was obviously another side to the picture. It could not have been easy for a director, after years of more or less routine handling of docile children, to be unexpectedly asked to cope with hardened young ruffians.

Nevertheless, I had to smile when Gennaro recited from memory the farewell speech that the director of one orphanage made to him when he was expelled.

"He kept wagging his finger at me and patting his tummy with the other. '*I cannot understand you,*' he said. '*We have given you everything: food, clothing, a good bed, the chance to learn a trade and go to school. All that we asked of you, and it seems to me—umph, umph—to be a reasonable request, was that you be respectful and obedient.*'"

"Wasn't he right? Wouldn't it have been better for you to put up with the difficulties in order to learn a trade?"

"I know. But I just couldn't take it. Don't ask me why! I just couldn't take it."

Caught in the treacherous bog of the evil habits they had formed, what they needed were not reprimands but a realistic understanding of their difficulties and the day-to-day encouragement that could sustain their efforts. The impersonality of institutional life had profoundly disillusioned them. In retrospect their resentment at the lectures they had received increased rather than diminished. They, too, had their "logic" and it could burst into words like a torrent destroying a dam.

"I never asked anyone to drop a bomb on my home and kill my mother. I never asked anyone to shoot my father. I didn't choose to go hungry and not have a home and have to beg to survive. Maybe I am dirty and maybe I am not nice and I don't know how to read or write and I am a bad example for their measly little kids in pinafores. Or maybe all this is my fault and I should be shot. Then I wouldn't bother anyone any more.

"Let them that run the institutions go their way and let me go mine, but don't talk to me any more about orphanages." Thus the discussions would end.

"I am too old to go to school." It was a younger boy speaking.

He knew nothing about institutions, except by hearsay and by observing the subdued inmates walking in crocodile, with their prefects bringing up the rear.

"You could learn a trade."

"I would be no good. I am no good at anything."

"You could try. I am sure that you would succeed. Then you would be able to get a job and make your own way in life."

"I am not going to an institution. The bell ringing all day long and everyone marching from one place to another in a long line. *Yes, sir! No, sir! Thank you, sir!* Not me. No, thank you. I'm better off as I am. Nobody orders me around."

What could be done for those boys?

"There is nothing that anyone can do for them now. They are young criminals, too corrupt and too vicious to change. It is a pity. Some day they will fall foul of the police and they will end up in jail. You had better face the facts."

There was truth in what my friends said. There were probably only heartaches in store for anyone trying to help them. There was one uncomfortable fact, however, that could not be overlooked. Whatever those boys had become, it was our doing. We were all responsible to some degree, by deed, or omission, for not having made the world a place where children would not be robbed of their families and left to rot on the streets.

One thing was certain: if the purpose of the new centres that we intended to open was to *serve* the children and to serve *those* children, they would have to be organized to meet their needs, not as we thought they should be, but as they actually were. Adjustments would have to be made, not only in the institutional routine, but in our own mental approach to their problems. Instead of preparing an alibi for failure—"it will be the fault of the boys, if they do not take advantage of the opportunities we are offering them"—we should make success a possibility by deepening our own capacity for sympathy and understanding. We should protect ourselves against the ever-present dangers of wounded pride and easy discouragement by allowing greater unselfishness and warmer charity to deepen the roots of our faith.

CHAPTER TWENTY-THREE

Shoeshine Hotel

IT WAS ten minutes to five and no-one had put in an appearance. I sat at the rough wooden table in the cellar and idly turned over the pages of a book. Five o'clock! A timid step was heard descending the stone staircase, and a tousled head—a mop of black hair and two dark eyes in an unwashed face—peered round the freshly painted door. At the sight of the empty corridor, it disappeared again.

"*Avanti!* Don't be afraid. The others will be here soon."

Where were the others? When the news had been spread among the boys at the station that the "Shoeshine Hotel" would open that evening, there had been an enthusiastic response. Perhaps, when the crucial moment arrived, they had been put off by our insistence that they be in by five. At seven there would be supper. There would be clean cots. Next morning there would be hot milk and bread before they left for their day's activities.

It had been a young Salesian priest who had told me of the existence of the unoccupied cellar under a war-damaged school in Via Varese.

I had been discussing with him the need for a night-refuge for the boys who spent their day trafficking at the railway station.

He himself lived close to the station, at the Salesian House in Via Marsala, and his tall angular figure could be seen several times a day, crossing the road from the terminal to the church. He strode so energetically that his thin black cassock flapped against his legs, and the ragged youngsters who trotted alongside had difficulty in keeping up with him. His noisy followers filled the courtyard of the school, to the dismay of an older confrère who saw that the high-school boys, with their nice woollen sweaters and zouave trousers, were being frightened away by the barbarian invasion.

The great disadvantage with most of the new centres we had opened that spring was that they were far removed from the usual haunts of the street boys. Necessarily so; there were no buildings available anywhere near the big cities. If receiving centres could be opened in the vicinity of such places as the railway terminus the youngsters might be attracted to them more easily.

Permission was obtained to occupy the cellar. A week went by in installing showers and giving the place a thorough cleaning. With chintz curtains to hide the bars on the narrow windows close to the ceiling, the cellar was given a more home-like appearance.

There were thirty clients the first evening, all old acquaintances from the railway station. I was glad to note a few sixteen-year-olds among them. When they went back to their friends next morning they would be bombarded with questions. "How was it?" "What did they give you to eat?" If everything went well, they would be our best public relations men.

The second evening, at five o'clock, a small group was already waiting at the rusty iron door. Yesterday they had found it strange to walk openly into a house, without the fear of being chased away; now, after only a few hours, they had acquired a feeling of proprietorship. This was *their* hotel, *their* home.

For the next half-hour other newcomers drifted in. They came diffidently—the very sound of their footsteps on the stone staircase betraying their hesitation—like kittens cautiously putting their paws on an unfamiliar board. At table they affected an air of confident ease, but their eyes were watchful and their bodies still tense with suspicion. "What is he getting out of this?" "Where is the snag?"

The days went by and each night there were new recruits, until we had a hundred guests jamming the cellar to capacity. I had to cut short my work at the office to be home before five. It was awesomely silent when I entered, unless the two Salesian students who had received permission from their superior to pass the night there had arrived before me. A few minutes later the mob would begin to surge in, the lights would go on and the place would hum with activity. The feet no longer crept cautiously down the stairs.

They clattered rhythmically against the stone and there was gay expectancy in the sound. Some of them were whistling and their salutations flew clamorously right and left. They had a hundred stories to tell of the day's doings, of policemen and black marketeers and of the fights between the prostitutes and their protectors. They repeated word for word what the fat lady had said to the detective and what they themselves had answered the "cop", when he asked them: "Don't you have a home?" In their eagerness to be heard they pushed each other aside, afraid that their story would be lost if it waited until later. What they wanted most of all, before settling down for the evening, was a playful punch in the chest, a pat on the shoulder, a contact that would tell them that they were noticed and that they, too, belonged.

It took some time to sort them out for their various duties. The oldest boys, Michele and Spartaco, went to the boiler-room kitchen to prepare the supper. Their system of marshalling their helpers was rough but effective. Giovanni and Mario would peel the potatoes; Franco and Massimo would cut the bread and chop the vegetables for the soup; Giorgio and Tommaso would take the dried cod out of the tank where it had been steeping since the previous evening.

This basic element of our meal never changed. I do not remember where it came from, the unpalatable-looking mountain of dried cod which lay in permanence on our kitchen table, draped in muslin. I developed such a deep-rooted aversion to it that many years went by before I could be persuaded to try it again.

The rest of the menu was always a surprise. It depended on what the policemen brought us after their raids on the black market. This unexpected alliance with the "cops" created a notable conflict of interest in our family circle. Up to then the shoeshine boys had unhesitatingly sided with the black marketeers in their conflict with the law. Now, an evening raid on the illegal sellers of cheese, salami and ham offered us the prospect of a delicious supper.

We had our black moments. The night that the police came to visit us, looking for a boy who had got into trouble, we also discovered that there was an outbreak of scabies. Useless our attempts to isolate the contaminated. The boys had to stay indoors and be plastered with sulphur ointment for three consecutive days.

With almost a hundred vigorous youngsters so closely confined, the breakage rate of everything that could be disintegrated shot to the skies. Sheets, blankets, towels, clothing had to be boiled and hung in the little courtyard to dry. The mattresses went to the disinfestation centre and everyone was obliged to sleep as best he could on the bare cross-wires of the bed.

Except for such moments of crisis, life in the cellar was becoming more pleasant. The ear-splitting clamour of the first few days had diminished. Unconsciously the boys were becoming accustomed to living in a house. They were no longer uncontrolled young savages, following their primitive instincts. They still ignored the nicety of verbal thanks, but they manifested their appreciation of every little kindness in innumerable delicate ways. Their defences had been lowered and they were no longer afraid of showing their desire for affection. It was pathetic to see how they sought an assurance of interest from every glance, from every word of praise, even from every scolding that they received.

Life was better organized. Most of the younger boys had agreed to attend classes during the day and arrangements had been made for them to have their lunch at school. The rest were still shining shoes and carrying valises at the station. The basic rule remained : by five o'clock everyone must be home.

After supper, when the dishes had been washed and the living room made tidy, came the time for games and home-made music. Little Pierre, the son of a French circus clown killed in a bombardment, was our favourite entertainer. Mounted on a table, his body swaying rhythmically to the music in his head, he sang to us the songs he had learned under the big top. He was the youngest member of our family and this increased the enthusiasm of the rest when he ended by throwing out his arms in a Gallic invitation of applause. As a grand finale he reached the floor with a handspring and executed cartwheels up and down the room.

Nine o'clock came and we went to our little chapel to end the day. God seemed very close to us in the cellar. It was the poorest of places, a bare, low-ceilinged room, with a home-made altar, rickety benches to sit on and a floor that was cold to the knees. The children were distracted sometimes during the prayers and their attention wandered during my brief talks. But when we prayed for their dead parents there was a deep stillness, and when

I told them of the birth of Christ in the cave at Bethlehem, of the Child fleeing with Mary and Joseph into a distant country, there was understanding and appreciation in their attentive eyes. They, too, had known hunger and misery; they had lived in caves and they, too, had fled as refugees from their own land. Never had the words of the New Testament been so poignantly real.

No sooner had their heads touched the pillow than they were asleep. The only sound was that of footsteps on the sidewalk filtering through the air-vents. The pedestrians hurrying by were unaware of the hundred children sleeping soundly underground.

Before I retired for the night I paced the corridor, reading the last pages of my breviary. This was the peaceful moment of the day. The deep breathing of the children was as soothing as the gentle murmur of the sea, interrupted only now and then by a strangled cry.

A hundred children at peace! They would awaken tomorrow to a world still filled with shadows, but there would no longer be the bitter stab of dawning consciousness. They were no longer alone, no longer unwanted, no longer unloved.

The walls of my little room were damp. Under the cold light of the electric light bulb hanging desolately from the ceiling, I could see the moisture glistening. I had the only private room in the cellar—it even had a window looking out on to a sunken yard—but it was also the only unhealthy place in our Shoeshine Hotel.

I was not feeling well when I drove to Berne, with an Inspector-General of the Department of Public Health and the head of the Italian Relief Distribution Agency, to confer again with the directors of the *Don Suisse*. When the talks ended, I was well pleased with the results: twenty-five prefabricated houses had been placed at my disposal for the street boys.

On our return journey there was snow in Milan. All night long a racking cough kept me awake. On my arrival in Rome the doctor had no difficulty in making a diagnosis: double pneumonia.

The separation from my family in the cellar was a painful one. It was strange to reflect that there could be a hundred poor boys whose lives collectively and singly had become such an integral part of my own and, now, by what might have seemed like a blind turn of fate, this close relationship was to be dissolved. I was not worried about their essential welfare. They had grown accustomed to their home, and the Salesian students would take good care of them. To some extent, however, and through no fault of mine, I had failed them. I knew the individual history, the personal tragedy and the character of each one of them. I understood their moods, their tendencies and their daily difficulties. Now, suddenly, they were to lose a prop on which they had come to lean.

Instinctively I knew that when I recovered things could not be the same. During my weeks in bed I saw more clearly the reason why. For five years I had been caught up in an unending whirl of activity: the war-wounded, the people in the battle zones, the evacuations, the medical dispensaries, the anti-malarial campaign, American Relief for Italy, the street-boy organization. Each of these varied fields of activity, overlapping and intertwining, had absorbed every moment of my day. Now I could look at the ceiling and ponder on the mysterious workings of Divine Providence. A decision had to be made. Either I was to confine my activity to the temporary one of relief, or personal service to unhappy children was to become the central purpose of my life—subject, of course, to the approval of my superiors.

I could not have forgotten the shoeshine boys during my illness, even if I had been so inclined. Every day, one or more of them walked the three miles from the railway station to leave a message at my door. Only two succeeded in circumventing the doctor's orders and reaching my bedside. To have them standing there, grinning a little ruefully, unbelievably comic and yet pathetic in their oversize battle-jackets and baggy trousers, was a better tonic than any medicine. The obvious sincerity of their concern was a proof that our work had not been in vain. We had succeeded, in some measure at least, in reaching their more intimate needs.

My experience of the past months had confirmed my belief: a boy may have become hardened and embittered through abandonment, evil habits may have been formed, but things are not hopeless. There are hidden resources that can still be tapped, well-springs of hope that can be liberated, miracles of love that can be performed. Above all, there are the divine remedies of grace that only await the goodwill of men to perform their own great miracle of redemption.

To restore the integrity of youth is not an easy task. The distortion of a personality cannot be eliminated by organizational ability, by bureaucratic process or simple humanitarianism. Only personal dedication can hope to break down the barriers of bitterness and disillusionment; only patient self-sacrifice can possibly bring to an unhappy child the living knowledge of love, whether it be human or divine.

It was during my illness that I dreamed of a future Boys' Town, of a community where an ancient adage, *Maxima debetur puero reverentia*,[1] would be meditated and applied. A community where the innate rights and duties and the God-given mission of each child in society would be respected and fostered. A fraternal community where suspicious youngsters would learn the difficult art of living together in liberty, in mutual tolerance, in peace and brotherly love. A joyous place where the anti-social boy would find understanding for his difficulties, encouragement in his efforts to advance, confidence and trust as a bulwark against the temptation to despair. A place where the bitter child would learn through the patient dedication of his elders that there is warmth in the world and goodness and self-sacrifice. A place where each day could be a period of growth, encouraging the children to develop the gifts with which nature had endowed them. A place which would have as its ultimate goal to help each boy find his true place in society as a responsible, God-fearing citizen.

I could see now how providential it had been for me to have lived in direct contact with so many of the tragedies of the wartime world, to have been with the children in the terror of the bombardments, in the agony of the operating theatre, in the squalor of the caves, to have seen them in the concentration camps and in the desolation of the malaria swamps, to have followed from close at hand the tragic Odyssey of their demoralizing existence in the streets.

The ghostly faces of children peered at me beseechingly from out of the darkness: Pasqualino, cut down by the machine-gun, moving his head painfully to smile; Michelino, whose hunger-consumed body I had carried through the woods; Gennaro and Vincenzino huddling together for warmth in the drainpipe at Santa Lucia. The victims of the war advanced in spectral procession, their luminous children's eyes filled with pain. Not for themselves

[1] "The greatest respect is owed to a child" (Juvenal, *Satires*, xiv, 47).

—they were beyond further suffering—but for those other children adrift on the vast, cruel sea of sorrow in the world.

The faces of children, animal-like in their wild abandon: could these be the future citizens of a happy community of boys?

Then I remembered their generosity, devoid of the external delicacies of form, primitive, often obscene, but none the less sincere. I thought of their solidarity, especially towards children younger than themselves. I recalled their heroism under fire, their endurance on the road, their enterprising spirit, their will to survive. These could be the qualities that might enable fierce children to become responsible citizens tomorrow.

I thought of their pathetic need of affection, a raging hunger which they tried to deny. In the city of boys there must be a key capable of opening up the sanctuaries of the heart, where all the tender memories of yesterday had been hidden away, the memories of things that reached so deeply into the fibre of their being that even to recall them was to suffer hurt. These precious memories must be set at liberty again by the magic key that is love, so that they might not hurt any more but re-acquire their old potency to console and to inspire.

Trust and love: the two great forces which could built a city, not merely a group of edifices built with stone, but a community of free, responsible young citizens living together as brothers under the sovereign Fatherhood of God.

CHAPTER TWENTY-FOUR

The Children's Village

I TOOK advantage of my period of convalescence to stay at the Tor Marangone, a locality on the sea-coast forty-five miles north of Rome. This was one of the places where, a few months before, one of our street-boy centres had been opened.

It was an enchanting spot. The hills that rolled gently down to the coast, the rock promontory that jutted into the sea, the violet-grey islands of Monte Cristo and the Giglio in the distance, formed a picture of exceptional loveliness.

There was space at the Tor Marangone and the site was splendid. Would it be possible to have this temporary shelter grow into a "Town" such as I had dreamed of—a real town, with streets and houses, workshops and schools—a place where homeless, anti-social youngsters might receive a chance to become useful citizens?

The possibility of such a development seemed very slight. There was nothing substantial with which to start. The two rustic buildings, made attractive on the outside by the purple bougainvillaea, were practically worthless.

When another priest, Don Rivolta, and I had driven out to inspect it in June our hearts had sunk. Even the garden, littered with refuse, was a desolate sight. It had only been the natural beauty of the countryside, looking its best on a summer's day, that had overcome our doubts.[1]

"I had imagined that the Village was a big thing," wrote one of the group of boys who arrived there on October 28. "Instead, there it all was right in front of me. There was the front of the

[1] As Don Rivolta and I could not reside there ourselves at that time, a dedicated married couple, an ex-journalist and his wife, looked after the children.

house as it is today, but all broken. The only room was the dormitory. The beds had straw mattresses. There were enough blankets but, when it rained, water dripped from the ceiling. Dirt fell down on us from the broken roof boards. As there was some space left, two big tables had been put in there and we ate at them."

The one bleak hall, with the plaster crumbling from the walls and the rough brick floor broken and worn, had to serve every purpose: as dormitory, living room and study. The paneless windows, filled in with cardboard, could not keep out the cold, and the two electric light bulbs dangling from the lofty ceiling seemed only to accentuate the gloom. The situation during the colder months would have become intolerable if one of the wooden chalets that I had obtained from the Swiss Relief Agency had not arrived.

Winter had been a cold and cheerless season, fraught with discouragement. It was amazing what a miracle the coming of spring had wrought. The place was beautiful again; the trees were green and the bougainvillaea had started to bloom. Even the crumbling stucco of the walls seemed picturesque in the soft, golden light of the sun. Each morning I put a rickety table in the garden and worked peacefully on the mail that reached me from my office in Rome.

Medicines were running short in our dispensaries in Naples; a new supply of powdered milk was needed in the feeding centres; the organization of a night refuge was urgently requested for the vagrant boys at Tombolo. It was disconcerting to note how remote these problems seemed in that tranquil garden by the sea.

There was quiet in the morning but, when the noon bell rang and the bare-footed boys came running over the little stone bridge and down the dusty path that led from the rural school, the air was filled again with clamour. Each day I wondered idly whether the young teacher would come to complain about their pranks. Perhaps I should tell her that one of the reasons why the boys got into mischief was that she laughed at their mistakes in front of the neighbouring farm children. Yes, here she came!

"Roberto behaved intolerably this morning. I insist that you punish him severely."

"What did Roberto do today?"

"I had to send him out of the class for talking. After five

minutes he came back without permission, stood on a bench and made a speech."

"What did he say?"

"He came out with a lot of nonsense; 'Is this justice, Miss Teacher? I ask you: is this the way to treat a poor father of a family?' He is impudent and he must be talked to very severely."

After morning classes the boys were free. They ran to the beach or played incessantly with a cloth ball in the dusty clearing behind the ruined pigsty. With no space in the house, no instructors and no equipment, it was difficult to fill in the rest of their day.

It had been a wonderful thing last autumn to have given them a clean cot to sleep in, a table to eat at and a warm-hearted couple to look after them. Now that the months were rapidly passing by, one had to look at the situation with a different eye. Some of the youngsters were already fifteen; there was no time to lose, if they were to receive the minimum training they would need for a job. Unlike the other centres that we had founded, there was no trade school nearby that the boys could attend.

Some buildings at least must be erected and a large sum of money would be needed, but that was not all. If Don Rivolta and I were convinced that this experiment in getting the boys to accept community responsibilities was sufficiently important, then we must devote our personal attention to running it, not from a distance, but by living there ourselves.

"When are you coming back to live with us?"

I lacked the courage, at first, to tell the boys at the Shoeshine Hotel that my home was now established elsewhere. They would soon know it; two of their old companions at the railway station had already gone to the Tor Marangone on foot. Others would be following them. Better that I should tell them myself.

"You remember Cecco and Alfredo at the station? I had to find a home for them. And there are many boys like them who have no family. There is no more room here at Via Varese, so I must look elsewhere. That is why I can't be with you all the time as I used to be."

Each time that I went to Rome, my first visit was to Via Varese. The boys were well cared for and I was delighted to see the progress they had made.

Emotionally they were more stable. A few months previously it would have been difficult for me to change my abode without giving them a feeling of rejection. Now I was happy to see that there was a growing realization of the fraternity to which they and the boys in our other centres belonged. Any feeling that they were less thought of soon vanished.

I had a continuing responsibility, however, for this former family of mine. Some of the boys might come to the Children's Village, but the group as a whole needed a new home. Even before I was taken ill I had initiated my futile search. So hopeless a task had it become that His Majesty King Umberto, who was deeply interested in my work, had offered to allow me to use the rear wing of the Royal Palace as a temporary refuge.

At last a glimmer of hope came. I discovered the presence of some dilapidated military sheds at Forte Prenestino on the outskirts of Rome. After months of negotiations with the Ministry of Defence the concession was made.

My joy was short-lived. Up to that point the important objective had been to obtain possession of the site. Now it suddenly became clear that the real difficulty lay ahead. Where would I find the tens of millions of lire needed to make the sheds habitable and how could I obtain the still larger sum necessary to erect the other buildings? Our resources were already grievously overtaxed by the continual drain of the soup kitchens and by the day-by-day demands of our child-placement programme. The bills for the construction work at the Children's Village were coming in with inexorable regularity and it was taking a superhuman effort to pay off the debts on that programme alone.

I had become accustomed to waking up with a start in the middle of the night in my little room at the Tor Marangone, where the floor shook perilously at every step and the rats scampered boldly over the rafters. Once awake, it was difficult to fall asleep again. A thousand thoughts would flash through my mind, piling one upon another like a waking nightmare. Finally I would turn on the light and sit at the little table near the window, scribbling figures and making hopeful estimates that turned out afterwards to have very little basis in fact. When morning came and I awoke again to the cheerful light of the sun, the heavy worries of the night slipped back into proportion. The hardy young citizens would be merrily making their beds and sweeping the paths with their long-headed brooms, and in the serenity of their smile I would see the answer to my dilemma. During the night I might say: we must reduce expenses! During the day, seeing the seemingly unending lines of hungry little waifs waiting their turn in our soup kitchens, how could one think of limiting their number? When the actual moment of decision came, I did not have the courage to risk turning anyone away.

CHAPTER TWENTY-FIVE

Freedom and Responsibility

"WE'RE FREE, aren't we? Well, I will do as I like."

Tommaso eyed the popular assembly defiantly and sat down with such force that little Pasqualino at the other end of the bench was almost catapulted into the air. The boys sitting in orderly rows in the garden turned to look at him. Tommaso was a relative newcomer. Two months before, he had had an ugly colouring to his skin, the sign of unhealthy living. Now he was as brown as a berry, with not a spare ounce of fat on his hard little body. He was tough in his attitudes, as well, ready to take offence at a moment's notice.

The incident at the evening meeting had grown out of a complaint of one of the citizens.

"Every evening, as soon as I fall asleep, someone comes in and makes a lot of noise and wakes me up."

Tommaso jumped to his feet.

"Are you talking about me? Then say so. I will make a noise if I want to. We are free to do what we like."

The younger citizens were obviously perplexed. The older ones were waving their hands to attract the attention of the mayor.

"Enzo, you can speak."

"I think that Tommaso is right. If we are free, then he can make a noise if he likes."

Other hands were raised, but the mayor ignored them to take the floor himself.

"Tommaso may be free to make a noise, but what about Mario? Doesn't he have a right not to be awakened? Why doesn't Tommaso go and make a noise somewhere else?"

The clash between Tommaso and Mario led to the citizens passing a new law: silence after lights out. Normally this is a rule that youngsters love to break. In the village, if anyone was tempted to do so, he knew that his action would no longer have the prestige of a rebellion against adult authority; it would meet with the weighty disapproval of public opinion. The citizens themselves had made the law because they had clearly seen the need for it.

Only nine months had gone by since the founding of the village and already the boys were reasoning differently. It had not been easy for them to understand that loyalty and not guile, trust and not suspicion should inspire their dealings with their fellows. As one of them wrote afterwards:

"At the beginning the citizens talked a lot about loyalty, sincerity and justice, but they understood very little about it. Brotherhood was the only thing they really understood, because when they had been on the road and had gone stealing together they had all been friends."

Lino was one newcomer who was amazed at the new set of values he found in the village. A few days after his arrival, he was seen to approach some city folk having a picnic on the beach. They handed him a piece of cake. In the assembly that evening he was asked for an explanation of his conduct.

"I bet you told them that we don't get enough to eat."

"What if I did? What does it matter to you?"

"Don't you realize that you have damaged the good name of the village?"

"What do I care?" was the cynical reply. "I wanted the cake and I got it."

The mayor rang his bell to still the clamour that broke loose. Once again there was a self-appointed devil's advocate ready to defend the rebel.

"We are free, aren't we? Then he had a right to say what he did to those people, if he wanted to."

The mayor gave the legal quibbler a black look.

"You would butt in. You think the same as we do, but you have to argue just to be different."

He turned to the culprit, who was patently enjoying the commotion that he had caused.

"We can speak badly of our country to other people. We can do it, but we shouldn't, because it isn't right. It is the same here.

We can speak badly of our village to outsiders but we shouldn't, because it isn't right and it isn't just."

Carried away by the vehemence of his conviction, the young mayor burst into tears.

The culprit was dumbfounded. He would have liked to laugh off his embarrassment, but he found that he could not. It was not merely because the citizens were eyeing him with open resentment. The sincere emotion of the mayor had made him realize that there were important things that he must learn, if he wanted to be a respected member of his community.

It was to give the boys an idea of law and order that, from the moment of their arrival in the village, they had been encouraged to elect a mayor and have their own law-making assembly. Perhaps their anti-social attitudes might be overcome by having them accept definite responsibilities in the running of their community. Certain elements in their character seemed to favour the success of such an experiment. They had a spirit of solidarity, an instinctive respect for a leader, and a rudimentary but powerful sense of justice. They were deeply attached to their freedom, to the faculty to be able to do *what I want, when I want*, to stay in a place or move on at a moment's notice, to sleep when the impulse took them, to eat and drink, smoke and gamble whenever the circumstances might permit.

There was freedom in the very air of the Children's Village. Freedom in the limitless expanse of the sea, in the rolling hills, wild and uncultivated, stretching aimlessly into the distance. There was freedom in their relationship with the adults, untrammelled by institutional protocol. There was freedom in the daily measure of their life, more, in fact, than we had actually planned, imposed on us by the poverty and primitive structure of the house, but providential in those first difficult months of adjustment. I can see now how fortunate it was that their way of life bordered so closely on the very extreme of poverty, that they slept on empty sacks filled with straw and shivered in the winter's cold, that the food served out of a big pot twice a day by "Zia Maria" was less palatable— though more wholesome, perhaps—than the food they could have bought with their own illicit earnings on the black market in Rome.

"Magniammo mejo a Roma,"[1] they grumbled, but they did not abandon the village. They boasted of their war-time exploits, making them sound like a pleasurable Odyssey, but their attachment to their broken-down abode and what it stood for increased from day to day. The village was like the Shoeshine Hotel: an extremely poor place, but their own. Not so well organized that they would inevitably feel a sense of obligation; on the contrary, so primitive as to make their help seem essential to its very existence.

Many of them ran away, either as an immediate reaction in a clash of personalities—a childlike protest against authority—or just because the old wanderlust had returned. All of them came back sooner or later; some returned so quickly that no-one had even noticed their absence. One youngster seemed to have left for good; the call of the road must have been too strong to resist. A month had gone without any further news when I saw him from afar, coming up the road. He stood his dilapidated bicycle against a tree. It was noon and the boys were at table. He took his place among them as naturally as though he had never been away. He had come home for good.

One democratic process leads to another. If the village had its own legislative body and an executive branch of government, it was inevitable that there would soon be a judge and a court.

Naturally, just as some of the boys had found it difficult to understand why they should set up rules that would restrict their freedom, they balked at setting penalties that they themselves might have to incur.

"We made the law because we wanted to, didn't we? Nobody forced us to, did they?"

"No, but——"

"Then we must see that everyone obeys the law. Otherwise there was no sense in making it."

"Yes, but I'm against having one of us be judge. Why should anyone boss me——?"

"Who do you want to boss us? Mario?"[2]

"No, but why should one of us have all the say?"

---

[1] "We ate better in Rome."
[2] The adult counsellor.

"Because we pick him. He represents us. If he doesn't do right, then we can do what Zio Pietro says and have a court of appeal."

The powers of the judge were clearly defined. For minor offences he could impose the penalties set by the penal code. For more serious misdeeds a citizen must be tried by the court; convicted, he must have the right to appeal.

Some of the original penalties invented by the citizens contained a direct symbolism that appealed to their primitive sense of justice. If two citizens fought, the right wrist or ankle of one must be tied to the left wrist or ankle of the other. If a boy begged for food outside the village, he must carry a piece of bread round his neck from the four o'clock snack until supper-time. Even though the culprits accepted them without protest, I was relieved to see that, as the boys matured, these crude punishments began to disappear.

Other early elements of their town system, introduced by aping adult institutions rather than to fill a real need of the community, were also gradually eliminated. Other essential ones, such as the monetary system, were introduced.

When classes started in the rural school on the far side of the railway tracks, a few of the citizens became regular truants. To start learning the alphabet at their age was a humiliating task. How could they be persuaded to go? To try to force them would be a mistake; they would take to the road at once. Let the assembly deal with them? Their truancy was not harming the other citizens; would they feel inclined to infringe on the personal liberty of their companions?

It was the truants who made the first big mistake; they flaunted the joys of their wrong-doing in front of the other citizens. "You have been in that stuffy school all morning. We spent the whole time down by the beach."

The matter was discussed in the assembly.

"It is not right! We work all morning while they enjoy themselves and then, when noon comes, they have dinner just like the rest of us."

It was decided that henceforth *"chi non lavora, non mangia"*[1] should become the basic rule of the community. In order to receive

---

[1] "He who does not work, does not eat."

his meals a citizen must pay for them with *merits*, which he himself would have to earn in school and at his daily chores.

What was a citizen to do with his surplus currency? If there was to be a monetary incentive for him to work with greater diligence he must obviously have the possibility of spending it. On what? The only commercial article available at first was powdered milk, a delicacy that the boys liked to eat by the spoonful. I gathered together as many copy-books, candy bars and tablets of soap as I could, and made up my mind that, close to the old toolshed that had been turned into a dignified city-hall, I must erect a tiny building for the bank and the store. For the responsible position of storekeeper, Armando, the smallest boy in the village, was the citizens' first choice.

Only a few months after he came to the village, he had taken the Italian lire he had accumulated by growing potatoes and selling them to the cook, tied them into his handkerchief and climbed the hill behind the village farm. The old shepherd who lived up there was already familiar with the diminutive figure that came scrambling up the slope.

"How much do you want for the little lamb?" asked Armando.

The old shepherd chewed reflectively for several moments before naming a price.

Armando whistled increduously and made his own offer. Little by little the shepherd's price sank and more slowly still Armando's rose. At last they reached an agreement.

"The lamb still needs milk," said Armando. "You should throw in milk to feed it for the next two weeks. I will come for it every morning."

The old man reluctantly agreed.

"It is still too small to drink from a basin. I will have to buy a feeding bottle. Let's knock the cost of the bottle off the price of the lamb."

By this time the shepherd was anxious to see Armando leave. Satisfied at last, the boy untied his handkerchief, counted out the money and ran back down the hill with the baby lamb in his arms.

As I looked at the young citizens sitting in orderly fashion on the benches of their assembly I wondered: would these once unhappy youngsters of the war—"Bull-dog," "The Neapolitan," "The Old Woman"—ever have submitted willingly to a barrack-like routine of discipline? Even if they had, how effective would it have been in making them good citizens?

The village, in a short time, had proved its worth. The time had now come for the makeshift and temporary period of its existence to give way to a more permanent structure. It must keep pace with the needs of the boys and the rapidly changing conditions of the times. Secondary schools would soon be needed; well-staffed vocational schools must take the place of the little artisan shops. The boys must be given a reasonable hope of being able to contend favourably with an economically hostile world. Otherwise, youthful ambitions would suffocate, stagnation would set in and the good that we were trying to do would be seriously compromised.

How could all this be accomplished? That was the question.

CHAPTER TWENTY-SIX

To be a Man

BY THE spring of 1947 the youngsters in the Children's Village at Tor Marangone were such an exuberant group, healthy and bright-eyed, that a casual observer might have judged them to be without a care in the world.

Their days were tranquil and filled with a sense of purpose. After school they ran light-footed through the fields and chased each other merrily over the hills that rolled softly upwards from the sea. In the water their slim, golden bodies, as graceful as long-finned fishes, cut smoothly into the depths where sea hedgehogs awaited them, to be picked for later eating. They tugged at Roman vases embedded in the floor of the sea, among the ruins of ancient streets and houses where other boys had played and run, laughed and wrestled as they did, two thousand years ago.

When the day ended and they sat in a circle in the soft darkness of the garden, only the crickets and the far-off barking of a shepherd's dog interrupted the heavy silence of the night. Old tales were told and newer experiences of yesterday, and the listeners hung breathlessly upon the words of the story-teller. The cracked bell clanged unmusically for prayers; a tiny lamp was burning in the whitewashed chapel; a genuflection, a good-night hug and peace descended upon the community.

Sometimes my eyes wandered unobserved over the shadowy faces in the evening circle. I knew their stories: a brother massacred by the Nazis; a father in prison for murder; a mother killed in a bombardment; months of starvation, vice and vagabondage behind them. Were they insensible to the lash of memory or were they not, perhaps, less carefree than they seemed?

Moments came when there was no further doubt. Their secret sorrows welled up out of the depths and surged over them like the turbulent waves of the sea. An anniversary, a chance remark would touch a chord, and the boy, no longer a self-reliant adolescent, would quietly disappear to some secret spot to cry alone. The affection with which they were surrounded, the companionship that they enjoyed and the variety of interests that filled their day could not wipe out completely the pain of their memories. Nor could they erase the deep, instinctive hunger that every child has to be possessed and loved by parents of his own. Only the passing of years and their own maturity would succeed in weakening the force of this.

Deep within them, colouring their thoughts and dulling their aspirations, was a fundamental sense of insecurity. It was not only that their vagabond life had robbed them of a sense of belonging. They were painfully conscious of their own inadequacy. Most of them could neither read nor write. Even to complete five years of elementary school seemed like an unreachable goal.

Culturally they were starved. Cut off as they had been from all the normal sources of a child's spiritual growth, they were incapable of even the most infantile appreciation of beauty. The glories of the spring, the flowers ablaze in the garden or a splendid sunset over the sea left them unmoved.

A benefactor sent a radio-gramophone, an object of astonishing luxury on the broken brick floor. Its arrival was hailed with wild excitement and the eager expectancy of the boys was almost painful in its intensity. Dead silence fell when the first note emerged. As one tuneful record followed the other the interest died. The boys shuffled their feet in embarrassment. One by one they drifted into the garden, amazed and vaguely disturbed that anyone could enjoy listening to mere sounds.

I sat on the terrace of the Boys' Town at Pozzuoli, with twelve-year-old Antonio perched on the arm of my chair. His interest in the rough sketches I was making was so marked that I offered him my pad and pencil.

He shied away in alarm. "I am no good."

"How do you know if you have never tried?"

The very same day I came across him on the rear steps of the house, hunched over a piece of white wrapping paper. The figure he had drawn—stove-pipe hat, stiff legs, spreadeagled hands—was a small child's image of a man.

"It doesn't look like anything," he said, in self-depreciation, but the way he threw back his head to look at his creation gave the lie to his words.

To get them to try: that was the difficult task. Their pessimism, so easily mistaken for laziness or indifference, could not be cured by a scolding. Good-humoured encouragement was its only remedy.

Their basic lack of security revealed itself in many ways. As a student of criminology I had often seen that the aggressiveness which was characteristic of many juvenile delinquents, came not from over-confidence, as one might have surmised, but from a lack of it.

It did not surprise me, therefore, to see aggressiveness erupting every now and then among our own young citizens. Their apparent self-assurance was merely a mask for a deep-rooted pessimism. Abusive words or a blow were often the only way they knew to assert themselves, a throw-back to the violent impetuosity that had characterized their former life. Only by patient counselling would their emotional excesses slowly diminish and eventually disappear.

In their relationship with the adults in the community, dark clouds often loomed on the horizon. Perhaps it was a frightened child striking out blindly in order to hurt, reacting instinctively to his own emotional disturbance; sometimes it was the clash of a budding personality, a teenager testing his wings and beating them frantically against the restraining hand; sometimes it was a crisis almost deliberately provoked, created by a youngster's deep need to test the solidity of the affection of the people for whom he, too, wanted to care. Whatever the cause was, however ridiculous some of these little upheavals might seem, they could not be laughed at or ignored. Each one of them provided either a possibility of inflicting further hurt or an opportunity of adding one more delicate touch to the building of a future man.

Carlo was a judicious boy, normally on good terms with everyone; he was also self-opinionated and even obstinate on occasions. One day I came on the scene just as he had given a resounding smack on the head to a newcomer. Afterwards I learned that the blow was more than well deserved. At the time, however, I accepted the occurrence at its face value.

"Carlo, I am surprised at you, hitting someone smaller than yourself."

That evening Carlo slipped off to bed without saying good-night.

Next morning he avoided me again. He was probably waiting for me to comment on his sulking, which would give him an opportunity to tell me how I had misjudged him. By now he was thoroughly miserable, yet too proud to give in without justifying himself. He, too, had to learn his lesson, that while the self-pitier mopes, the rest of the world goes unconcernedly on its way.

That night, after the boys had gone to bed, I was in my study finishing the recital of my breviary. Half an hour had gone by when I thought I heard a light step outside. Perhaps I had been mistaken. No, there was someone in the garden! I went to the door. In the shadows was Carlo. He was distressed and obviously hunting for words.

"Good night, Carlo," I said warmly, and rapidly enough to save him the embarrassment of speaking.

He took two rapid steps forward and threw his arms around me while I patted him on the back.

"Good night, Carlo. Sleep well!" I punched him lightly on the chest and caught the glimpse of his tearful smile before he turned to run lightly back to bed.

How many heart-aches, how many stumbles and falls before a boy grows up to be a man! How difficult for a child born in tragedy to acquire the certainty of himself and to believe in the possibility of love!

This is not only true of human love. It is true of divine love as well.

It is difficult for a child to awaken to a knowledge of God, unless his father and his mother have opened his tiny mind to the possi-bility of love! Psychologists tell us that the "personal" aspect of God that first deeply moves children is the *love* of their heavenly Father; God loves me! How can they reach this concept easily if they do not see around them the manifestations that are the interpretation of love?

What happens when a child does not have a home where the first delicate foundations of his spiritual life are laid? What happens to a child who is robbed of a mother's love and of the delicate religious guidance of her mind and of her heart?

Père Duval tells us how, as a child, he used to look at his father kneeling on the kitchen floor:

> "And I thought: My father, who is so strong, who is head of our house, who can drive the oxen, who doesn't kow-tow to the Mayor, or to the rich people or to any ruffian . . . my father, when he is in the presence of God, is just like a child."

He looked at his mother.

> "And I thought: God must be a very homely person if one talks to Him with a child in one's arms or with an apron on. And He must be a very important person if, when mother speaks to Him, she does not pay any attention either to the cat or to the storm. . . .
>
> "The hands of my father and the lips of my mother taught me more about God than my catechism. God is *a person,* very close to us, to whom it is very pleasant to speak when one's work is done."

The children of the street came to us and inside there was a void. God was a word, demanding respect because of an instinctive attitude that had percolated down to them through the grime of war, but meaning nothing personal, nothing that was theirs to hold on to, to live with, to console and inspire them.

Perhaps in a few of them there were memories of a father kneeling on the kitchen floor and a mother sitting in her long, black peasant's dress, with the youngest child in her arms. But for most there were no such happy recollections; better if there had been no memories at all to torment them and to deform the images of their mind.

"My father came home angry. When he saw that supper was not ready he began to shout. He picked up the big pot off the fire and threw the water over Mummy. She screeched and ran out into the street. They took her to the hospital. When she died, men came and took daddy away." I was in the garden outside the little Home we had opened on the hill above Leghorn. The tiny child looked vacantly into my eyes and the words, told and retold, fell mechanically from his lips.

Another boy, an eleven-year-old, stood sadly by my desk at the Tor Marangone. He was silent and his face was tied into hard knots of pain. Perhaps it was Christmas that had brought him nostalgia and sadness. He had no father. His mother had no fixed home, and kind neighbours had looked after him, until they sent him to Boys' Town.

"Mother has not written to me even for Christmas."

I told him gently how many cares grown-ups have and how weary they can become and how, involuntarily, they postpone and even hurt, not because they mean to, not because they have really forgotten, not because they do not love, not——

"Yes, I know," he said gently. "But she is my mother."

CHAPTER TWENTY-SEVEN

One World

IN THE late spring of 1947 I flew to New York to report to American Relief for Italy on the needs of the Italian people.

There had been some improvements during the preceding twelve months but there was little reason for rejoicing. The value of the lira had fallen and unemployment had increased. No-one dared to predict what would happen to Italy's economy now that UNRRA aid was coming to an end.

Politically, 1946 had been a turbulent year. Italy had become a Republic but only by a slight margin. In the local elections the Christian Democrat majority had declined heavily, to the advantage both of the Communists and of the extreme right-wing party. There had been widespread strikes, riots in Trieste, the threat of a partisan rising in the north, a separatist movement in Sicily.

The news from the peace conference in Paris had been disastrous. Italy would lose most of the Venezia Giulia. She would lose her fleet, her colonies, her claims against Germany. She herself would have to pay three hundred and sixty-five million dollars in reparations.

Even nature had been unkind. There had been floods, a grasshopper plague in Sardinia, snow and ice all over the peninsula. The death toll from the cold had reached unprecedented figures.

When the year drew to a close, if it had not been for the growing understanding shown to Italy and the determination shown by the people of Italy itself, the situation might well have been called desperate.

"Do you really believe that Italy will recover from the war?"

It was the question the newsmen asked me time and time again during my stay in the United States. In San Francisco, in particular, where I held a two-hour press conference in the study of

A. P. Giannini, they were surprised and more than a little sceptical about the optimism of some of my replies.

The Italian Americans I met were obviously trying to relate my descriptions of misery to the little town where they or their fathers had been born. When I spoke of the children, the older women did not disguise their tears. *"Poveri piccirilli!*[1] May the Mother of God protect them!"

As I left a hall on the lower East Side of New York, a little woman, shabbily dressed, was waiting to speak to me.

"Father, I want to help the children but I must wait until I draw my pay at the end of the month. I am only a cleaner."

"Are you Italian?"

"No, Irish."

After a brief talk in a clothing factory in Boston, standing on a cutting table during the lunch hour, two negro women approached me to ask whether there were any coloured children in Italy as a result of the occupation. There were a few, I told them.

"Poor little things! They must feel out of place. We are willing to adopt two each, or even three, if that would help."

The older men held back, outwardly impassive. As I passed their tables, however, each one stopped me with some inquiry that showed how deep their feelings were.

"Have you been to Avellino? I was born there." "How are things in Sicily? *Io sono di Marsala.*"[2] "I was born in Russia. I am a Jew. I know what suffering is."

In every part of the country I met men who had served in Italy during the war. Some of them, old acquaintances from Naples and Leghorn, travelled great distances to see me. They had formed little committees among their friends to raise money to help me in my work for the shoeshine boys. I could tell them truthfully that the boys, even though they were on the threshold of manhood, still remembered their soldier friends, not so much for the food they had given them, as for the way they had treated them, warmly and understandingly, like the neighbour's kids back home.

I marvelled at the enthusiasm with which men whose names were Burke and Cohen and Kominski could listen to my plans for the future. My admiration for an extraordinary people grew by leaps and bounds. Their faults might be evident, as defects always

[1] "Poor little things."　　　　[2] "I am from Marsala."

are, but what an encouragement to find men so spontaneous in their enthusiasm, so direct in their generosity, so self-assured and yet amazingly humble in offering their service?

My best encounter was yet to come.

I had only five minutes to catch a train and I was running down the steps of Grand Central Station. Turning the corner, I almost collided with a middle-aged businessman hurrying in the opposite direction. We both started to apologize.

"Colonel!"

"Monsignor Carroll!"

It was my colonel from Naples, the colonel of that famous Christmas Eve! We forgot about our trains and we sat in a noisy coffee shop and talked. He was no longer in the army; the war and Italy were things of the past. But as we talked there was nostalgia in his eyes and he chuckled as one episode after another came to his mind. I reminded him how the lights had gone out every night in his apartment in Naples.

"Do you give the repair men anything when they leave?" I had asked him.

"Not a thing," he had replied.

"Are you sure?"

"Absolutely! I only give them a bite to eat when they finish their job."

He had laughed when I told him that, if he wanted them to put in a wire that would carry the current, he had better stop giving them supper.

"Poor lads. Salvatore has four children and Mario has three," was all he had said.

I returned to Italy fired by fresh enthusiasm. Even the shock of rediscovering its misery was not able to quench it. In the Neapolitan grottoes and in the ruined warehouses down by the port, hungry people still stagnated in hopelessness. In the windowless hovels of the Calata in Palermo many of the tiny tots had had their fingers nibbled away by rats. Wherever I looked there were homeless children, desperately in need of assistance. How much there was that needed to be done! Useless, however, to rush off blindly in many directions. Our scant resources must be utilized with the maximum care. Our plans must be carried out a step at a time.

The village for the boys at Via Varese must be completed; the schools, workshops and cottages at the Boys' Republic[1] must be erected; the other shelters must be enlarged and consolidated. In the meantime, in one way or another, other towns must be erected for the urchins of Naples and Palermo; new centres must be opened throughout the south; emotionally disturbed children must have the special care they needed. Why put limits to the Providence of God or to the charity of man?

[1] The new name of the Children's Village.

CHAPTER TWENTY-EIGHT

An Iron Curtain

WHEN I went down to Rome that morning I found a telegram waiting on my desk: TODAY MY SON'S BIRTHDAY WILL SEND YOU TWO HUNDRED FIFTY DOLLARS TO TAKE POOR BOY OFF STREET.

Only vaguely did I remember having met the sender of the telegram at a luncheon in New York. I had a much clearer recollection of another Italian American who had been seated to my left. He had regaled me with a description of his beautiful home in New York and his villa in Florida and casually spoken of the de-luxe sports car he had just bought for his teenage son.

The little man to my right had said very little. Two months later, however, his telegram was on my desk.

I would have no difficulty in finding a new candidate for Boys' Town. There were still young vagrants aplenty round the railway terminal. Walking down Via Veneto in the direction of the Piazza Esedra, I was impressed by its new air of animation. The café tables under the trees were crowded with well-dressed tourists. There were no more derelicts huddled on the steps of the Capuchin Church—the derelicts still existed, but the police had banned them from the centre—and the old man with the beard, who sat in the nearby doorway, had disappeared. Perhaps he no longer had a market for the tobacco from the cigarette-butts the street boys used to sell him.

A boy in a ragged jacket was standing in front of the Bernini Hotel. The thought of the telegram made me look a little closer. I noticed that he had been crying and stopped to speak to him.

I wondered afterwards what would have happened to Pino if the businessman on getting up that morning had not had his generous thought and so started the chain reaction that ended in his becoming a citizen of a Boys' Town. It was awesome to reflect that the welfare of children could so depend on the generous or selfish decisions of others. It made one realize, too, what a responsibility it was to have their happiness depending on one's ability to plead for them, to move men to help them!

By the beginning of 1950 the Sea Village and the Agricultural Village had been added to the Industrial Village at Tor Marangone to form the Boys' Republic. The Boys' Town at Forte Prenestino had been completed. The Citadel of Youth had been opened on Monte Mario for emotionally disturbed children. Boys' Villages had been built at Pozzuoli and Palermo. Much had been accomplished, but more remained to be done and the daily difficulties of our task had not diminished.

As general living conditions gradually improved and the memory of the war-years mercifully faded into the distance, there was the temptation for all of us, under the pressure of our daily business, to forget the lessons that distress had taught us. During the war there had been a brotherhood of suffering and a sharing of each other's burdens. Now, in a more orderly society, poverty and misery had once again been forced into hiding. They had retreated into the hovels on the fringes of the city, to the villages in the hills, to the bare attics where the solitary poor grow old and starve. It was so easy to forget, in the satisfaction of achievement, that the decent aspect of thousands of working families was a thin cloak concealing their daily struggle for survival. The fear of sickness or unemployment hovered over them like a spectre, threatening to rob them of what little they had and plunge them into destitution. The iron curtain of our modern way of living had once again created a barrier between each man and his neighbour.

Was the war so far distant? Sometimes it seemed so. At other times I wondered.

Peppino crept into my little cottage one day. He was only ten, but even for a ten-year-old he was tiny. A tuft of unruly hair fell over one eye, leaving the other one—black, intelligent, mischievous—even more prominent in the wizened little face.

He had come to us in the fall of 1948. He was the first of a new generation of children who had not belonged to the homeless vagrants of the streets, but who still bore in their undernourished bodies and their old men's ways the imprint of the war.

Peppino sat on the edge of an armchair and pretended to read his comic. Even without looking up, I was conscious that he was glancing at me from time to time. Soon he would come over to my desk and play with my pencils. If he only wanted an excuse for a chat he would ask me how the pencil-sharpener worked. If he had some request to make he would edge round the desk and sit on the arm of my chair. That afternoon he came and sat on the arm of the chair.

"How is everything, Peppino?"

"Fine."

Then, like an avalanche: "May I borrow your mousetrap?"

"Do I have a mousetrap?"

"Yes, Signor Spaccia put one under your book-case. He saw a mouse in here last week."

"What do you need a mousetrap for?"

"To catch birds."

"You can't catch birds with a mousetrap," I told him.

"With this kind you can," he answered confidently.

"Why do you want to kill little birds?" I was leading up to a talk on how cruel it was to catch God's little creatures that had done us no harm and were so happy singing in the trees. His answer caught me off guard.

"What for? To eat, of course!" He was looking at me as though I were crazy. "I used to catch them all the time at home."

"You lived with your grandmother before she went to the hospital?"

"Yes. My father was shot by the Germans and my mother died of pleurisy. I don't remember her."

"How old is your grandmother?"

"Eighty-five. It isn't true, is it, that old people die when they reach a hundred? The other day I read of someone who lived to be a hundred and ten. I wish she would live another twenty-five years."

He told me of his life with his old grandmother in the attic near the Colosseo. The neighbours, poor like themselves, had tried to help them. When he was four he had gone every day to the Franciscan Monastery on Via Merulana and they had given him soup to carry home. Some mornings he would get up early and set traps for birds in the park where a Roman Emperor had once had his palace. He would take them home triumphantly to his grand-mother. Little birds . . . to eat!

In the older boys, too, memories lingered.

Salvatore was in my study one afternoon, reading a book by the window. As he read, he hummed and the haunting tune was always the same.

"Ti piace quella musica?"

"Me la porterei sempre appresso se potessi."[1] Only a Neapoli-tan could voice a sentiment so poetically but, even for bright, impudent, warm-hearted Salvatore, the expression seemed exag-gerated, unless it held a deeper significance.

"What does it remind you of? What did you feel—inside you—when you first heard it?"

"I thought of my mother's death."

"It . . . made you sad?"

"No. I thought how beautiful she was, and how good."

I hesitated.

"I didn't know that you remembered your mother. It is many years since she died."

"Yes, I remember her." There was a pause. "But, if anyone ever asks me whether I do, I always say no. I remember her as though she were still here. She was young and I remember that when she died the neighbours on our floor said: 'bad people never die and she . . .' "

It had been a rich young American who had been responsible for Salvatore coming to Boys' Town. He had met the little *scugnizzo* with the sunny smile outside his hotel on the waterfront in Naples. He was a young man on his honeymoon, and the hand-some little boy, with his few words of English but a quick grasp of meanings, had been an ideal guide. The young couple had bought him two suits and when they went to Capri and Ravello they had taken him with them and he had stayed with them in the de-luxe hotels. They had grown fond of him.

"Would you like to come to America with us?"

His eyes sparkled and he had nearly jumped out of his skin.

"We will find some place for you to stay until we can arrange for your papers." There could be no problems for a young couple

[1] "Do you like that music?" "I would carry it with me always if I could."

in love, especially when the man was the son of one of America's richest millionaires.

The American Consulate had given them my telephone number and they had called me. Salvatore had come to Boys' Town. Before he left Naples he had gone to say good-bye to an old friend.

"So you are going to America. . . ." The old boatman had fallen silent. "Listen here, Salvatore; don't set your heart on it. The United States is a long way off."

"But they promised me and the lady kissed me and she was crying. . . ."

"They mean well. But a lot of people . . . when they come to Naples . . . they see the blue sea and the sun and when they leave they are sorry and they would like to take a little bit of Naples home with them. . . . But, when they are back in America . . . they soon forget."

Salvatore had been angry with the old boatman. He told me the whole story one day.

"Tommaso was right. They did forget."

I knew it too. I had received a check for a hundred dollars when Salvatore came to us and—after that—silence. I had written every year to give the young man news of the boy's progress. One day, picking up my morning paper, I read of his death. He had become a millionaire in his own right since his father died. Salvatore mentioned it to me the next time he came to visit me.

"Poor man. I shall always be grateful to him. He did mean well and it was through him that I came to Boys' Town."

Gaetano was another little Neapolitan boy who was with us in 1948. His brother, Mario, was already in Boys' Town and it was he who told me one fine day that he had a younger brother.

"A brother! Where is he?"

"In Naples somewhere. He stayed there with his friends when I came to Rome."

The next time I went to Naples I took the youngster with me. It was afternoon when we arrived.

"Where shall we go to look for your brother?"

"Oh, it is too early. The best time to find him is about eleven o'clock. That is when people have been drinking and they give more easily."

It was almost eleven, after we had driven through many streets and Mario had gone to peer into one bar and restaurant after another, that we saw a diminutive figure emerge from a fashionable café.

"Gaetano!"

The brothers greeted each other with casual affection, as though they had only been separated for a few hours. Mario took Gaetano to the nearest fountain to superintend his ablutions before he would let him into the car.

A few days after he entered Boys' Town Gaetano had to go to the hospital. I visited him each day and took a bag of fruit with me. On the third day Gaetano asked me to give it to another boy in the ward.

"No-one ever comes to see him and he is very sick. He loves fruit. Sometimes the nurse buys him some out of her own money."

I took the bag across the ward. I was shocked to see the pale boy, propped up with pillows. He was too weak to smile, but his eyes showed his pleasure and his surprise. After that I brought two bags of fruit with me on my daily visit.

One morning he was not in his bed. Perhaps he had been taken downstairs for an X-ray.

No, Gaetano told me, the boy had died during the night.

"But," he added, "he knew that someone cared for him, before he died."

I went out into the bustle of the city. A hundred people whom I passed on the sidewalk would willingly have opened their purse to give a sick youngster a bag of fruit. How tragic that in our watertight compartment world men are no longer in contact with sorrows outside their own small circle of daily life!

I had stood at a window in Philadelphia a few months before, looking at the people hurrying by, and a similar thought had crossed my mind. I was visiting a friend at the local office of one of the unions. As we talked, an old man waited patiently by the door.

"He is in no great hurry. He has been on a pension now for some years."

I moved over to the window, conscious of the fact that the old man, after much fumbling, was placing a handful of coins on the desk.

"I wanted to send $15 for the children in Italy. Then I heard that the Father would be here himself today. I have only $13.50. If you can add the $1.50," he said in a confidential whisper, "I will bring it to you next week."

I looked at the bustling sidewalk below. "When this old Russian Jew in the baggy suit walks down the street, no-one will even bother to look at him. Yet most of us, well-dressed, well-schooled, busy with so many important matters—or so we think—are not worthy to shake his hand. This toil-worn workman's hand, stretched out in brotherly love, has become the hand of God Himself."

CHAPTER TWENTY-NINE

Requiem

IN 1951 my mother died.

The previous September she had undergone a serious operation. Six months later the evil had returned and this time she knew there was no hope. The faith that had sustained her through all the sorrows of her life reached out yearningly towards its logical goal. I had returned to Ireland to be with her.

"God doesn't seem to want me." It was a lament as light as a feather and the first one that I had ever heard pass her lips.

A special blessing arrived from Pius XII and her mind went back to the last time that she had seen him. It had been at Castel Gandolfo and he had come out of his study to greet her with outstretched arms.

"How can I thank you for giving your son to me!" Words inspired only by charity, but calculated to cancel out twenty years of loneliness for an Irish mother and console her for time to come.

Each morning, coming back from church, groups of boys and girls passed me on their way to school. The boys tipped their caps respectfully and saluted me with their piping voices. One tiny colleen, with eyes as clear as a summer morn, stopped to whisper to me: "This morning I remembered your mudder in my prayers."

One evening my mother insisted that I go to visit an old friend at Merrion. It was a family anniversary and I was invited to supper. At eight o'clock came the children's bedtime and our host and his wife, with a simple word of excuse to their guests, accompanied the youngsters upstairs for the family rosary. What a strange experience, to find oneself back in a world where beautiful customs such as this evoked no surprise! Thank God, these children had not lost their homes! What would they have become if they had had to walk the streets alone? What would I have become without such a mother?

She was laid to rest in the quiet graveyard among the fields and woods that she had loved so dearly and I returned to Rome.

I had expected sympathy from the boys; I knew the delicacy of their feelings under a rough exterior. I was not prepared for the depth of their sadness. They were frozen in grief, mute, but looking at me with big, sorrowful eyes. One little fellow reached up to pat my cheek with his grubby fingers. Before going to bed I knelt to thank God for one blessing above all, for having created children with such a great capacity for love.

CHAPTER THIRTY

The Children of the South

OUR LITTLE waiter put the two cups of coffee on the table, took our money and gave a professional dab with his napkin where a glass of water had overflowed. His intelligent black eyes never left our face. There was friendly interest in these two human beings descended from another planet.

"Sugar, please," said my friend.

"It's sugared already."

"Well, a spoon, if you don't mind."

"Already stirred."

I broke into this exchange to head off an explosion. My friend, an elderly engineer from Turin, was not long in patience.

"How old are you?"

"Eleven."

"Don't you go to school?"

"I used to."

He broke off to call his mother from the kitchen. A road-mender had come in to buy a pint of wine.

We left the cottage store and drove on to Locri. Difficult to imagine that this small town had been one of the opulent cities that had given that stretch of the Ionian coast the name *Magna Graecia*. The Great Greece! Today, only the ancient names and a few ruins remained to remind the traveller of its former glory.

It was already the third time in the course of that year, 1953, that I was covering Southern Italy, by-passing the large towns and penetrating into the remotest recesses of the hills to reach the tiny villages. They were for the most part mere clusters of roughly-hewn stone, isolated hamlets where the arrival of an automobile was a memorable event. The children were eager to look at their distorted image in the shining enamel of the hood, but too shy at first to come forward. They stood in little groups, as wooden-faced as the adults, silently observing from a distance what the mysterious visitors would do next. They were ragged and bare-footed, their sturdy brown legs marred by scabs and sores.

I had thought a great deal about these children of the south. Most of the boys that I had met on the road after the fighting, the majority of the citizens now in my Boys' Towns and Villages, had come from the southern regions. They were lively Neapolitans, acute observers, convinced of their cleverness; brown Messinesi, clear-brained, diffident, impulsively generous; tall, blond boys from Brindisi, of obvious Norman extraction; mountain boys from the Abruzzi, tenacious and dependable. In the background of each one of them, the beautiful, poverty-stricken lands where tens of thousands of other youngsters were growing up without a reasonable hope for a better life tomorrow.

It was late that afternoon in November when I took the winding road that led from Locri to Gerace. The car climbed rapidly from sea-level to the chain of mountains that dominated the narrow coastal plain. I found it difficult to shift my gaze from the ancient citadel ahead of me, an unassailable fortress perched high on a promontory of rock.

In the dusk the bare mountains were even more forbidding than in the daytime, when one's eyes were easily distracted by the cobalt splendour of the sea and the white-gold glitter of the sand. The village was as gloomily aloof as the Scottish castles in the early editions of Walter Scott.

Dark had fallen as I drove under the crumbling stone arch into the cobbled streets. Silence everywhere. Not a person to be seen. Not a glimmer of light in any of the houses. How was I to find the bishop's residence? Strange though it might seem, Gerace, with only two thousand six hundred inhabitants, was still the seat of a bishopric. The majestic Norman cathedral, the largest in the whole of Calabria, alone could testify to what had been its ancient splendour.[1]

With the aid of a torch I discerned a coat of arms above a dilapidated doorway. I pulled a cord and a bell tinkled emptily in the distance. Just as I was wondering whether the house was

---

[1] "Dives opum Geratis," the Normans had said of it.

really deserted, there was the grinding of bolts and the creaking of the huge door on its rusty hinges. The cheerful face of the Franciscan lay-brother, who was the bishop's secretary, chauffeur and servant, peered out at me.

"It is only five-thirty, yet there isn't a soul in the streets or a light in the houses!"

"As soon as it is light the men will be out on the hillside again, even though it is winter. Now it is dark and, when the stomach is empty, the best place to be is in bed."

The bishop smiled at me with his wise old eyes and pulled his heavy woollen cloak around him for warmth. The electric bulb hanging forlornly from the rafters cast little light on the miserable room.

Before his appointment as Bishop of Gerace, Father Perantoni had been the Father-General of the Franciscan Friars Minor. His brethren in America had given him a small car to enable him to visit his diocese. At least in this respect he was better off than his aged predecessor who had had to take the rickety bus down to Locri each morning to teach in the public schools and so earn enough for his own keep.

My first stop on that November trip had been at Sant' Agata dei Goti, a little town not far from Naples. As its name implied, it had once been a colony of the Goths. Even before that—three hundred years before Christ—there had been mention of it as a participant in the Samnite Wars. In the ninth century it had been seized by the Lombards; it had sided with the Greeks and had been besieged by the Emperor. Once coveted for its wealth, for centuries now it had been sinking into the stagnant poverty of a thousand similar communities throughout the south.

The morning that I visited it there was excitement in one of the narrow streets leading to the town square. Two little girls and their baby brother, home from school, had not found their customary lunch of hard bread and raw onions awaiting them. Their father was out, but someone who refused to answer was locked in the back room of their cottage. The neighbours had called the police.

When the *Maresciallo*[1] had pushed his way to the front of the crowd and invited the intruder to come forth in the name of the

[1] Marshal.

law, the door had swung open immediately. To everybody's surprise it was the children's father who emerged. Only the twitching
of a nerve at the angle of his jaw betrayed the strong emotion
under which he was labouring.

"How could I look them in the face?" His dark eyes rested
sombrely on the three little ones clinging to his legs. "Since my
wife died I have had to be both father and mother to them. Today
I didn't even have a piece of dry bread to put on the table. The day
before yesterday, yesterday, this morning . . . not a person able
to give me an hour's work . . . to dig a ditch, to unload a truck
. . . anything."

He held out his powerful arms, not for dramatic effect, but with
the stupefied hurt of a man wounded in his most essential pride.

There was misery in all the communities that I visited, in the
coastal hamlets, in the environs of the larger towns and particularly in the tiny villages lost in the hills.

Eighty-six per cent of Southern Italy is mountainous, a bare
desert of stone that has been stripped of its trees. With every year
that goes by, more of the little remaining earth is washed away by
the floods that follow the winter rains. In summer it is the shortage
of water that arrests the vegetation and leaves the countryside
scorched and desolate under the blinding heat of the sun.

There are few houses on the plains. The need for mutual defence
against the pirates, and the ever-present scourge of the malaria,
long ago drove the inhabitants to group their homes together on
higher ground. Often they were an hour's donkey-ride away from
the fields they had to cultivate. It had not been difficult for the
land to be taken over by absentee landlords. The new owners
spent no money on improvements; they used the soil only for
what easy profit it could give.

A numbing fatalism settled upon these wild and beautiful lands.
The inevitable was too strong to be fought, the course of things
too foreseeable to allow hope to survive. A young man might
deceive himself for a while, in the vigorous optimism of his youth,
but, deep within himself, he knew the future pattern of his life. He
would marry and bring his bride home to the two miserable un-
paved rooms where his father and mother, his brothers and sisters
and his grandparents already lived. Soon he would see his young

wife ageing prematurely and his children being born and, ahead of them, the same cycle of misery and hopelessness that no-one could escape. He might start a life of banditry, choosing the only feasible way of breaking his bonds. He would be protected by the silence of his neighbours, but his rebellion would only end in tragedy.

Hundreds of thousands of men, women and children left their native land in desperation to seek a new life overseas. As the immigrant ships slipped out of port the primitive cries of the women, the weeping of the children, mingled with the lament that arose from the dockside. Tear-dimmed eyes watched the land until even Vesuvius and Mount Pellegrino had disappeared below the horizon. Then they went below to the fetid air of the steerage, in which they would spend the long-drawn-out weeks of misery at sea. For better or for worse there could be no return.

The New World!

"Darkness and dampness and dirt. Dirt and discomfort and disease. Diphtheria and death."[1] These were the conditions of the immigrant neighbourhoods where the Italians would live in close proximity to the Irish and the Polish Jews.

Insults, jibes, prejudice! The "dirty Micks", the "Wops", the "Kikes" gritted their teeth and laboured, twelve hours a day, six days a week, a dollar a day in the factory, slave conditions in the sweat-shops. Why had they come? Why did they stay? The thought of the bracing air over the coasts of Mayo, the soft caress of the Sicilian dawn: the mere thought of it weakened a man, set his bowels ayearning. Only hope gave them the strength to carry on; the hope that democracy, freedom, brotherhood, would cease to be mere words, would become symbols of life for their children and their children's children after them.

Forty years had passed. From the labourers on the road had come the skilled workers, the machinists, the small tradesmen, the restaurant owners and the builders. Their success had proved that the peasants of the south had only needed a chance to make good.

When the Committees of Boys' Towns of Italy launched their appeal for the creation of children's centres in Southern Italy, it was from the immigrants of thirty and forty years ago that I

[1] The New York City Housing Survey, 1905.

looked for a special response. They would understand the problems that we faced; they would know that no matter how much
the new Italian democracy might try to do, the Government alone
could not solve them.

The first results of the appeal were not encouraging. Individu-
alism and parochialism, the perennial stumbling blocks of Italy,
were to blame. Mr. X would not join a benefit committee because
of the personality of the chairman—"Why should I build him
up?" Mr. Y would only give a contribution if the children's centre
was to be built in his particular village of origin. The attitude of
some was tinged with resentment: "Why don't those people do
something to help themselves?"

Have you forgotten the hopelessness of those barren lands?
Have you forgotten the misery that compelled your father and
mother to leave their native soil, taking their family with them?
Have you forgotten the little boy that you were, minding the few
goats on the mountainside, the little girl gathering the chestnuts
to be ground up for flour? Can you not visualize the baby left
under the tree while the mother worked in the heat of the sun?
Can you not recall how you, too, padded many miles each day
along the dusty roads for an hour's teaching in the tumbledown
school? The cuts on your bare feet have healed, your hands are
protected now against the painful chilblains of winter. Is it possible that scar-tissue has formed on your soul, robbing it of its
ability to feel and to suffer and to understand?

As usual it was often those who had the least to give who gave
the most. Engaged in their own daily struggle to make ends meet,
they did not need to be told the value to us of even a single dollar.
For our part, we knew the sacrifice that even a single dollar had
probably entailed; it became a sacred thing, to be used in the
most careful way.

I relied a great deal on the help of the local populations. They
might be extremely poor, but I knew what their collaboration
could mean.

Living in the battle areas during the occupation, I had called
upon the men to assist by disinfecting the caves. After the Liberation we had distributed food and clothing to hundreds of poor
mothers, but they, in return, had given many hours of their time
to sew the garments we needed for the street boys. The doctors

had been aided in equipping their clinics, but they had more than repaid their debt by donating their services to the people whom we sent for treatment.

In building the children's centres down south, if the local people could not afford money they might give materials; if not materials, labour. In one little village the men cut the stone blocks in the quarry and the women carried them on their heads up the hill. In every place I asked them to pledge themselves to maintain the centres once they had been built, become partners in charity, not recipients of aid.

The Festa was drawing to a close. The representatives of the Sicilian Government had already left for Palermo. The family groups from the nearby villages were wending their way home, some on horse carts, most of them on foot. The band was playing half-heartedly. The bustle and the excitement were over, and only a few townspeople still lingered in the square.

I made a last tour of the nursery with the mayor. The bright classrooms, the immaculate kitchen and dining room, the medical dispensary: it was the most beautiful Children's Day Centre I had seen in many a day. Outside, an old woman, black shawl over her head, had stopped to take a last look at the building. Her wrinkled hands, lifted in admiration, spoke as plainly as words. With a polite bob to the visitors, she was on her way.

Giovanni was waiting to drive me the fifty miles back to Palermo. It was sixteen years since I had first met him, outside the railway terminal in Rome, with shoeshine box over his shoulder. He had taken the day off from his job to drive me to the ceremony.

"We have come a long way since the cellar in Via Varese."

"I was just thinking the same thing. What is the date of your wedding?"

"I wasn't speaking about myself. I meant the Boys' Towns and the Nurseries."

I was silent. This had been the fortieth institution built since the war. On each occasion I had said: this is the last. Then, some evening, as I had sat in the protected peace of one of our little communities and seen the contentment shining from the children's eyes. the vision of other eyes, bitter and unimaginably sad, had shaken me out of my complacency. As long as there are hungry children and unhappy children in the world one has no right to rest. Their need and the charity of men must meet once again to accomplish another miracle of love.

CHAPTER THIRTY-ONE

The Boys' Town of Rome

IN 1951 I had been fortunate in obtaining a large expanse of land six miles from Rome, between the city and the sea.

It was bare land. Wells had to be sunk; the soil had to be irrigated; trees had to be planted. It was two years before I had sufficient money even to start to build. Not until 1954 was the first nucleus of the Boys' Town of Rome completed—a little community with a big name—the Medico-Psycho-Pedagogical Observation and Therapy Centre.

It had sometimes seemed so easy to look after the vagrant children of the war—tough and unprepossessing though they might appear—if only one had the vocation and, of course, the money. Then—out of the blue—to destroy one's self-complacency, would come a boy like Nato who, when the impulse took him, would bang his head violently against the wall. Or Lino, who would retreat under a table and bark for an hour like a dog. Or Gino and Piero and Antonio, who wet the bed every single night and were twisted up inside. Or Mario, who would stop in the middle of a sentence and stand with his hand half-raised, a million miles away from everything round him.

Were they crazy?

"No," said the doctors; "only disturbed."

In my daily contacts with the children it had been impossible not to be aware of the emotional problems that afflicted them. In the Boys' Towns we had tried to ensure that each one would receive the individual care that he needed. The more difficult cases, however, seemed impervious to all our efforts. They had convinced me that we needed to know far more about the background of each boy than we actually did. We must have competent professional consultants, a staff trained to observe the day-by-day manifestations of each complex personality, and the possibility of applying the proper individual treatment.

As early as 1949 I had started our first residential Observation and Therapy Centre in the ancient fortress on Monte Mario.[1] Its success, even in such an unsuitable setting, had encouraged me to seek a permanent site elsewhere. This time I planned to make it a village, and not only in appearance. The Boys' Town system of giving each youngster definite responsibilities suited to his age and capabilities might help these boys to adjust, give them greater confidence in themselves and assist them in establishing satisfactory relationships with the people round them.

What would happen to them when their period of basic readjustment ended? I could continue to send them to one of the other Boys' Towns to complete their schooling and start their vocational training as I had been doing with the boys from Monte Mario. I had observed, however, that to uproot them from surroundings that had become familiar and from adults with whom they had begun to feel safe often caused a fresh emotional shock. This might be avoided by creating a new Boys' Town, with schools and workshops and playing fields, on the same ample estate as the Therapy Centre. The two communities, distinct from each other and yet co-ordinated, would create one big family: the Boys' Town of Rome.

As our boat approached the island of Procida, the fortress-like building crowning the southern cliffs loomed dark and menacing. To divert the attention of the boy who was with me I pointed out the nearby island of Ischia and, farther off, the pyramid of rock on the horizon that was Capri.

The tiny harbour with the quaint cottages strung along the waterfront was a picturesque sight. Primitive horse-carriages were waiting patiently by the landing stage to take travellers into the interior of the island.

---

[1] As on earlier similar occasions, Monsignor Giovanni Battista Montini, Under-Secretary of State to Pius XII, attended the inaugural ceremony. The future Pope Paul VI never failed to show his deep interest in the welfare of the vagrant children of the war. On occasions too numerous to count I had gone to him for help and never in vain.

"We had better take a carriage. The prison is quite a distance from here."

"Was that the prison we saw on top of the cliff?" The boy had not missed the significance of the dismal edifice that dominated the island.

Mario had been in the Garden City, as the Observation Centre came to be known, for almost a year. He had come to us from an orphanage where nine of his ten years of life had been spent. He had been only an infant when his father was sentenced for life. Once, when he had asked the sisters about his father, they had told him that he would do well to forget him.

Easier said than done! How can a small boy eliminate from his mind the fact that he does have a father? "I wonder what he is like?" "I wonder whether I resemble him?" "I wonder whether I will turn out like him?"

"He is a very disturbed boy," the sisters had told me, but there were few clues as to what lay at the root of his trouble. Only after several months did little things—fragments from out of the past— begin to emerge. I mentioned his father once or twice, but he feigned indifference, which made me wonder all the more.

I wrote to the chaplain to find out what kind of a man the father was and entered into correspondence with him. It was at my suggestion that he wrote to his boy for Christmas. Up to that moment he had accepted being shut out from his son's life as part of the penalty that society required him to pay. The day before Christmas the letter and a package arrived.

When I stopped at Garden City on my way back to the Boys' Republic they told me about the parcel. Mario had blanched with excitement and run off to open it alone. Its contents were pathetic —a few oranges, a candy bar and a biscuit or two—but it was the first postal package of his life and . . . from his father. When I arrived, the boy came to me at once, with pride in his eyes, to offer me a biscuit.

Both Mario and his father had written frequently after that. Now, several months later, we were in Procida for their first encounter. They met, not in the visiting room with the iron grille, but in a little whitewashed room off the outer courtyard.

I met the father first and I was surprised at his youth. He was more nervous than the boy and pathetically unsure of himself.

"Why don't I bring him in at once?"

They had stood for a moment, eyeing each other uncertainly, each one unable to make the first approach. Then it had been a single rapid movement. They had clung to each other, without a word. I had left them and sat on the low wall of the courtyard, looking out over the azure sea. I finished the reading of my breviary and said my rosary and watched an old convict mumbling childishly to himself. I wondered how long he had been there. Had he, too, been a young man, twenty-two years old? What could the father and son be finding to talk about for so long? Three hours had passed. How would the visit affect the boy?

I need not have worried. When Mario did emerge he was smiling and serene. He slipped his hand childishly into mine and chattered gaily all the way back to the boat. From that day on he was a happier boy; the terrifying figure of the unknown convict father had disappeared for good.

Giovanni was another young citizen of Garden City who had his father in prison. He had been six years old when his father was arrested. He wrote regularly and Giovanni had even gone to see him while his mother was still alive. He had a small child's memory of a wonderful man, strong and clever. As time went by it became more obvious that, even from inside his prison cell, the father was exercising a maleficent influence on his son. It was not so much what he wrote—the usual recommendations to study and to look after his health—as the continual projection upon his son of his own unsatisfied dreams of grandeur. If Giovanni told him that he was a full-back in the soccer team, his father answered that he must insist on being a forward. If Giovanni wrote that he wanted to be a mechanic, the father discouraged him. "There is no future in it. You must become a highly specialized electronics engineer. They make good money."

To forbid the boy to receive letters from his father was unthinkable. The only way to counteract their disturbing effect was to encourage the boy himself to examine each phase of his own life with a realistic eye.

Two boys without a mother, two fathers in prison, but two entirely different cases and the need for two different approaches to the deep human problems involved.

CHAPTER THIRTY-TWO

The Door to Greater Good

ON DECEMBER 31, 1954, I drove to Florence. At the top of the Radicofani pass, Memmo stopped the car for a moment to look back into the valley. Ten years ago we had had to trail behind the Allied tanks labouring up that precipitous slope. We had not dared to stray even a yard or two off the road, the land on both sides was so heavily mined.

We dined at a wine-shop on the outskirts of Buonconvento. The inn-keeper's wife placed a brazier of live charcoal under the table to keep us warm. A dish of home-made macaroni, roast chicken and Chianti wine put us in a festive mood. It was only ten o'clock but groups of villagers were already bringing in the New Year with song.

"Do you realize that it is exactly ten years since you began working for the children?" Memmo broke in reflectively. He was a senior Vatican chauffeur, assigned to me during the war, and who had remained with me afterwards.

"Ten years? You're right. It seems like yesterday. One thing is certain. I wasn't eating chicken and drinking Chianti on New Year's Eve in 1944."

"I was only eight then." It was Ezio, a citizen of Boys' Town, speaking. "I imagine that I spent New Year's Eve, like every other night, in the railway yards or in the tunnel by the Colosseum. One night was the same as the next, colder perhaps or hungrier but always terrible."

"Next month you will be leaving us. In a few short years it will be you who will be getting married."

We left Florence early next morning to drive north into the mountains. Snow was falling as we reached the Futa pass. It had been the heart of the famous Gothic Line that the Germans had defended so successfully in the winter of 1944. Two young brothers, Carlo and Graziano, had been living there. Tragedy had struck the family and their home had been destroyed. When the fighting ended, starvation had driven them south and brought them to the Children's Village. Today, Carlo—a successful ceramic artist—was going back to be married in the little hamlet where he had been born.

The news of the coming event had caused great excitement among the citizens of the Boys' Republic. Incredible that some-one who had been one of themselves only three years before was about to be married. The youngsters, who had gathered in my cottage that evening, had discussed it animatedly. Only one boy had not joined in: Giovanni, a stolid thirteen-year-old from the Abruzzi. Lolling back in my most comfortable chair, with his eyes fixed on the ceiling, he had looked supremely bored by the conversation. At last he had been able to stand it no longer.

"So what? Carlo is getting married. Soon he will have children and then . . . then Monsignor will be a granddad."

On the surface the years from 1948 to 1955 might seem carefree ones in the history of our Boys' Towns. They had been years of accomplishment. Boys' Villages, Children's Homes and Nurseries had sprung up in more than forty localities. The Boys' Village at Tor Marangone, now the Boys' Republic of Civitavecchia, had taken on its final form. From the high land behind the railway down to the tiny fishing port by the sea, cottages, schools and workshops had grown into an imposing pattern of streets and public squares.

In June, 1955, ten years had gone by since I first drove up the narrow road leading to the war-damaged villa. The villa was still there, incorporated into a network of imposing new buildings. The second-floor room was there, too, where I had lain awake at night. So was the mountain chalet, which had been the boys' first real dormitory and had later become my cottage. Three genera-tions of young citizens had come in and out of that little wooden house every evening when the day's work was done, laughing over the comical happenings of the day, listening to the radio, revelling in the happy confusion and the noise.

The sound of a musical instrument was wafted to me across the garden; a young citizen was practising "Cavalleria Rusticana". I remembered the first time the band had played in public. It had been in June, 1949, the evening I returned from my second trip to the United States. It had been eleven o'clock before I reached the Boys' Republic. The boys were still waiting by the roadside, some of them fast asleep on the grassy banks. They had scampered up the drive to warn the band. The musicians had lined up hurriedly in two straggling rows and embarked on the one piece they had learned during my absence. It was a war-time melody: "Good-bye, My Love, Good-bye!"

At the foot of the medieval watch-tower on the coast lay the Sea Village. It had been on Christmas Day, 1946, that the idea had come to me of creating a second village at the Tor Marangone, this time on the promontory of land stretching out towards the sea. It had been another hard struggle to make that dream come true. The adults in the community had perhaps taken it for granted that the construction materials should arrive regularly and the labourers' wages always manage to be paid, but the children had not been deceived. No matter how I had tried to smile, their own intuitive sensitiveness had told them when the hidden problems were sometimes heavier than usual and their sympathy had manifested itself silently in an added warmth of affection.

Strange, as one looked back, to see how the very loneliness of the daily burden had transformed it into a consolation. The truth had clarified itself: personal dedication—no matter how generous—was not enough. It must be by sacrifice—by the acceptance of whatever worry God might permit—that one would win back for the children the happiness they had lost.

The spring and early summer of 1955 had been filled with activity. Three new Children's Day-Centres had been inaugurated in Southern Italy; Boys' Town, Chieti, was nearing completion; Girls' Town had just been founded.

In September a change came to my own daily life: I moved my habitual residence to the Boys' Town of Rome.

It had been evident for some time that my living in so remote a spot as the Tor Marangone was becoming an obstacle to the greater expansion of our work. In spite of this I had not had the

courage to make the logical move. The Boys' Republic was particularly dear to me. It was the first-born. It had been my home
for ten years. Every stone in the buildings, every machine in the
workshops was bound up with some memory of the boys and of
the friends that had made them possible. I had hesitated, but
God's Providence had mercifully stepped in to help me.

When the organization I had founded started to erect the first
Boys' Homes after the war it had been suggested that it keep
permanent title to all the property. This was not my thought nor
that of the other members of the Board. We had no intention of
creating a rich agency, top-heavy with administrative responsibilities. We would keep title to those institutions which we ourselves intended to direct, but there were countless other children
who urgently needed assistance. To help them we were soliciting
the co-operation of every group that was qualified and willing to
help. If we could provide them with the tools to do the job, that
was all that we desired.[1]

With the Village at the Tor Marangone it had been different.
From the moment that Don Rivolta and I had decided to make it
our home I had never foreseen that the property would be owned
by any other group. The owner of the land, a friend of Don
Rivolta, was willing to sell it at a very low price and there seemed
to be no obstacles in the way. In the purchase of the land title
passed to the Institute to which Don Rivolta belonged. He had
thought that this would be the best way to ensure the continuity
of our work after our death. This was true, but I foresaw that it
might lead to complications in the future. What mattered more
than anything else, however, was the welfare of the children. In
spite of this changed situation, the Board and I decided to go
ahead with the construction of the town and, in fact, brought it to
completion within the next four years.

As was inevitable, the complicated relationship between the
Boys' Towns Organization and the Company of St. Paul with
regard to the Boys' Republic became increasingly cumbersome.
When his superiors decided, in the summer of 1955, that they
needed Don Rivolta in Rome, the time seemed to have come for
me, too, to leave the personal direction of the Republic and

[1] The Boys' Village at Palermo was given to the Don Orione Fathers
and the Village at the Forte Prenestino to the Salesians.

transfer all the direct responsibility to the Company of St. Paul.[1]

The uprooting was painful; the distress of the boys made it all the more difficult. Once again, however, I was to learn that it is through the acceptance of such sacrifices as God allows us to make that the door to greater good is opened.

The sun was setting as I approached the Boys' Town of Rome. It had been the golden magic of the sunset that had first won me to this rolling countryside. How squalid it had seemed in the colder light of the morning, with hardly a tree to relieve the parched desolation of the land!

Now, after four years, the countryside was transformed. Wells had been sunk, an irrigation system had been installed. Golden vineyards clothed the gentle slopes into the valleys and thousands of young fruit trees, in orderly design, stretched as far as the eye could see.

The buildings that made up the Medico-Psychological Observation Centre—the residence, the clinic, the school-houses and the chapel—were set attractively among the trees round a diminutive square.

The boys were coming out of the town meeting as I entered. It was my usual hour for visiting them. We would have supper together, I would wait until they had gone to bed and then I would drive back to Civitavecchia. Not any more, until God disposed otherwise.

The dining room was bright, with its violet-tiled floor and the chintz curtains at the windows. There was a cheerful buzz of conversation as the boy waiters began to serve. Three boys sat at my table. One of them was Gino. As usual, his eyes were downcast and his face was expressionless.

It was three years since his father had been killed in an accident and his mother taken to the insane asylum. He had been a difficult boy in the orphanage. They had put up with him for two years, but after one disturbing episode they had refused to keep him any longer.

"How did school go today, Gino?"

[1] Three members of the Board of the Boys' Towns Organization, including Monsignor Carroll, remained on the Board of the Boys' Republic. Boys' Towns of Italy is still giving it substantial financial assistance.

Silence. Then, with emphasis, "Badly."

"How is that?"

"I am no good."

Another youngster broke in with a funny story about the kitten that had strayed in through the classroom window.

"Did you play soccer this afternoon, Gino?"

"No!" Then, to head off the next question: "I am no good."

What was the name of the little boy at Pozzuoli, the little boy with the pencil and paper? Antonio! That was it.

"Gino, I knew a boy who was always saying *I am no good*. He really believed it until, one day, he began to discover that there were lots of things that he was able to do. He will probably drop in to see us one of these days. He has his own auto-repair shop in Rome."

Gino's head was still lowered. The other boys chattered on and paid no attention to his silence. They were used to him. That was Gino's way.

After supper most of the boys were in the garden. Some of the youngsters were sitting under the trees, listening to the story that the wife of the director was telling. A group of soldiers was being organized on the nearby meadow to meet an assault of the Red Indians. Rino, tall for his thirteen years, was giving the orders. He was a born leader. His lean, handsome face was sparkling now with excitement. Strange how some human beings are born with such a predisposition to command. I remembered a photo that Rino had shown me of his father: strong virile features, wide-set expressive eyes like his son's. I could imagine the same golden brown flecks in them that came in moments of excitement. Rino's father had been killed in the mountains in a conflict with the police. The boy had been sent to an institution. He had been a turbulent influence, ready to do any mad thing if another boy dared him. He was an exceptional youngster—qualities of courage, of generosity, unswerving truthfulness thrown at one like a challenge. What potentialities for good—or for evil!

Gino was coming across the square. Gino—Rino—now fellow citizens—what a difference between them! Without looking up, he stopped.

"It is true you are going to stay with us . . . always?"

"Yes, Gino."

His eyes flickered upwards for a moment. Was he glad or indifferent? Impossible to tell.

How tiny was this Boys' Town, so pathetic in its youth. Like these children. Lonely, isolated, in need of so much protection and help and love.

CHAPTER THIRTY-THREE

Love

LOVE is a powerful word, so potent, in fact, that many people are afraid of it, even where children are concerned.

When I started the Boys' Town of Rome I was conscious that it must become a place whose law and whose spirit would be love. It was there that the emotionally disturbed, the children with the bitterest problems, must have a home. How could they find a key to their difficulties unless there was patience and understanding and . . . love?

The new community was not being created under the pressure of the post-war emergency. Into its development could go all the fruits of one's experience. It must demonstrate beyond any possibility of doubt the limitless possibilities of young people to grow, when they are given respect, trust, guidance and affection.

The Italians have an alternative expression for *amare*, to love: *voler bene*, to wish well. Is not this the essence of love: to wish well, to desire the supreme good of another at the cost of any personal sacrifice? *Greater love hath no man than this, that a man lay down his life for his friends.*

Love must express itself outwardly. It is in daily dedication, however, that true love lies. A child needs the warmth of his mother's hug, but it is her thousand little sacrifices that will prove irrefutably that its well-being is her main care.

It is not only children without parents who experience the lack of love. There are fathers and mothers whose petty vices, whose selfish passions have robbed them of the power to love.

"I gave him everything," wails the doting mother. Everything: the money and the material things that were the bribe for his affection, the substitute for the daily sacrifices that she herself did not have the generosity to make.

"I never raised a finger to him or said a cross word, and now he treats me like this." The youngster was never taught to restrain his instincts, to grow in self-discipline; right and wrong were never interpreted to him by the sincere distress of his parents. Looking back, the lack of correction is the clearest proof that his parents did not really love him, not enough to care.

Not all of the boys who came to Boys' Town had always been deprived of love.

What was it that little Salvatore had said of his dead mother? "I think how beautiful she was and how good."

How much hurt in memories but what a consolation to possess them, to have the reassuring certainty that one has been loved!

That was the reason why the orphans who came to Boys' Town were often less disturbed than the others. They lacked the warmth of their parents' presence, but they did not have the sense of personal rejection that the unwanted child did. If they had never known their dead parents, their phantasy could build up the ideal image: a wonderful man and the most beautiful of mothers, who would have loved them dearly if they had still been alive. The foundlings could only say: two people made me come into the world but they did not want me.

This sense of rejection might not appear on the surface. Only among themselves, among companions of their own condition, did these eleven and twelve-year-olds talk of the things that hurt. Sometimes, however, their bitterness overflowed. One youngster was found to have lung trouble and must go to the sanatorium. I consoled him as best I could.

"Hadn't they done enough? Had they to put this sickness as well into my blood?" There was unbelievable sadness in his anger.

Impossible to estimate the havoc that these feelings of rejection could wreak in after years. How many men I had found in prison whose records bore the "illegitimate" sign! Even as grown men, any allusion to their parents opened the floodgates of their pent-up feelings.

I was speaking to an inmate of Regina Coeli about the girl with whom he had been living, the child that had been born and abandoned.

"Why should I care? No-one ever cared for me!"

"You don't understand," I told him. "You will never be able to get rid of this child. He is you. He is being rejected by his father as you were rejected by yours. It is you who have been born again."

Among the children to come to us after the war there had been many foundlings, who had been placed with foster families soon after birth.

"My mother—up to that time I had always thought she was my mother—took me to Rome one day. We stood on a street corner and she told me . . . that . . . I was not her child. She had no money left . . . no home . . . she would have to go out to work. She could no longer manage to keep me. She took me back to the Foundling Home."

I had seen this eleven-year-old when I paid a visit to the home. Babies were dying there because of the lack of formula foods, the lack of heating. He was squatting among a group of tiny tots crawling on the floor. When I entered, he had sat up straight so that I should not miss him, and his eyes had cried out to me across the room: "Take me away! Take me away!"

Years later, after he had graduated from Boys' Town, Franco came back to see me. He had heard that another ex-citizen of Boys' Town had found out the name of his mother. Should he try to do the same?

"Another year or two and you will have a family of your own. I would not start to dig into the past." I had Marco in mind when I spoke.

Marco had been one of our first citizens. After he reached sixteen he began to speak to me about his phantasies. When a middle-aged woman passed him in the street, he often thought: "She may be my mother." He was not resentful. "She may be poor. She may need me."

If Marco was less bitter, he was more determined than the rest. He was twenty-three when he finally discovered her identity.

He had rung the door-bell of the beautiful villa on the outskirts of Rome. Two children were playing happily by a fountain. Were they his half-brother and sister?

The manservant had scrutinized him carefully but had obviously been reassured by his gentlemanly appearance. He had led him up the drive and into the villa. He had had to wait several minutes. A woman's voice sounded pleasantly from across the hall. She was talking to a friend over the phone and she was in no hurry. The voice was low and good to listen to and her laughter was musical. The elegant lady who entered the drawing-room fitted the voice. There was pride in her walk and well-bred inquiry in her arched eyebrows. The strange young man was standing with his back to the window. He had searched desperately for an opening word, but before he could utter it she had stopped short, her hand over her mouth and something like terror in her eyes. Resemblance? Intuition?

He confirmed his identity and told her how he had found her.

She burst into tears, begged him to go away and not wreck her life. In her growing agitation words stumbled one over the other. She offered him a large sum at once and more later, if he would only leave.

"I do not want to harm you. I don't need any money. I only wanted to know my mother."

"Now I know who my mother is," he told me. "Now that is over."

Perhaps for you. You will marry soon. You will have children of your own. But the poor woman in the rich villa will never be able to cancel the memory of the handsome boy who only wanted to find his mother so that he could give her his love.

Every Foundling Hospital could tell a hundred stories of the women who come to the reception desk to inquire about a certain child, born on a certain day. "A friend of mine has been thinking of adopting a child born on her birthday, May 8. A child of ten. Can you tell me if a child was brought here who was born on May 8, 1954, in the evening?"

If they succeed in learning a name and a place, they visit the foster home or the orphanage, admitting nothing, just happening to pass by, devouring the child with their eyes. And the child will wonder years later who the lady was who came so often to look and bring a toy and go away again, afraid.

"Why didn't she want me? I may not be as strong as other boys and I know I'm not good-looking, but she is my mother."

Difficult to explain to a child how cowardly a human being can be. Useless to try to assess the blame of the poor mothers, themselves the victims of ignorance and fear.

When Emilio came to the Boys' Town of Rome he was seriously disturbed. He knew his mother. She had not recognized him legally as her child, but she had visited him faithfully every week in the institution to which the public welfare authorities had sent him. She had brought him clothing, candy, toys—some of the other children had been jealous and had said nasty things—but she had never taken him home with her, even for a day. He had become too difficult for the orphanage to handle.

What did they mean by a *difficult* boy? A boy with difficulties, yes. A boy quite capable of throwing the chairs out of the upstairs windows in feeble protest, as he had done. But a willing and generous youngster, too frank to digest the injustices of orphanage life, too sensitive to cope with the strains that his loneliness had imposed on him.

Emilio's mother continued to come to see him every week. I asked her why she did not give the boy her name and take him to live with her.

"How can I? My old aunt lives with me and she has never known about my child. How can I tell her now? And my neighbours?"

"Emilio wonders why he can never go home with you, never write to you, never call you on the phone. He will not accept this unnatural situation much longer. Soon you may lose him for ever."

The next time I saw her she was a different woman.

"I took your advice. Just imagine! My aunt told me that she had known for several years. My absences every Sunday had made her suspicious, and once or twice—something I did not know—Emilio telephoned and put down the phone quickly when she answered. She had often wanted to discuss things with me but she never had the courage."

Emilio went home for Christmas and, the following summer, he went home for good. Often, after that, he would call Boys' Town on the phone.

"This is Emilio. . . . You haven't forgotten me?"

"Of course not. You know that. You know how fond we are of you."

He did know it and it was our aim that every citizen in Boys' Town should have the same great, healing certainty that his happiness and his welfare came first.

It would not always be easy.

It would not be easy to persuade Tommaso, sent away from eleven institutions, that Boys' Town might be different. Why should it? Boys' Town would tire of him, too, and move him on —for his own good: that is what they would tell him.

No use making speeches to him, reassuring him with words and smiles. Only time could bring to him the conviction that it might be true, that there might possibly be a chance that somebody could care.

From the first moment, however, Boys' Town itself must speak to him, delicately, persuasively, in its own inimitable language. The flower beds and the carefully tended garden, the cheerful aspect of the rooms: all telling of the effort the grown-ups had made to render it attractive. For whom? For the children for whom it was home. Not a museum, carefully waxed and always spotless. A lived-in place, where one could move and play and be at one's ease. A place that one could learn to take pride in, and want to give an extra polish to when visitors came, because it was one's home. A place that could smile with the sun and be delicately and beautifully sad with the rain and fit one's mood like a glove. A place that one would want to remember all one's life.

The atmosphere of the place! The freedom and yet the mutual respect. The lively chatter in the dining room, where adults and boys and guests sat at the same little tables, eating the same wholesome food, pleasantly served. The relaxed air of the boys, not afraid to joke, to express their opinions, not afraid that a mistake would bring the world clattering about their ears. How startling, all these things, that put a big question mark in one's mind and set one to wondering . . . not hoping, as yet.

How strange not to be called into an office and interrogated, with that forcedly affectionate tone one knew so well. "Now, Tommaso, let's have a little talk about yourself." The questions, always the same. Why? Why? How strange to have the privacy of one's memories and of one's hidden hurts respected!

How strange to see the ex-citizens of the Boys' Towns return-ing, from the Boys' Republic of Civitavecchia, the Citadel and other places! To see them walk in confidently and smile and joke, as though they belonged. Talk with Monsignor, sit down to lunch like everybody else; interested in everything: "How does the bank function here? Your money is the scudo? Our's was the merit. Who is the mayor? Who is the judge?" How strange! Are they play-acting? Impossible! Perhaps one day I will come back as they do and the boys will gather round me and I will tell them how well our band played . . . not to discourage them but to let them know how close to my heart is the memory of this place.

How tiny the Boys' Town of Rome was in that September of 1955 when it became my home! But how warm and how full of promise! The boys in the Garden City and its Therapy Centre were well housed, but the Boys' Town itself reminded me very vividly of the beginnings of our street-boy centres after the war. It had no buildings of its own. The boys slept on cots, crammed together in an old villa. I camped out there as well, in a diminu-tive room. We took our meals in the recreation room of the Therapy Centre, and our school rooms and artisan shops were temporarily located in the outhouses of the farm. On paper there were streets and squares and cottages, a city hall and a bank. There were workshops and schools and an auditorium. All on paper, as yet.

CHAPTER THIRTY-FOUR

Respect

"CAN I buy you an orangeade?"

The young citizen, making a purchase in the town store, looked up at me expectantly. He would be disappointed if I declined.

The boy store-keeper polished the glasses, and my host pushed his money over the counter with visible satisfaction.

What was so remarkable about this little happening? In a traditional institution it would have been for the adult to buy the boy an orangeade. The final result would have been the same. Or would it?

The thirteen-year-old had always lived in an institution. As a citizen of the Boys' Town of Rome, he really felt like an individual for the first time in his life. He could pay for his own candy; he could even stand treat with money he himself had earned.

There was no self-deception. He knew that, if all this was possible, it was only because the adult world had made it so. For once, however, he had not been made to feel like an orphan, a perpetual recipient of charity. The grown-ups had had the delicacy to consider his feelings, to understand his crying need to believe in his own worth, to regard him, not as one of a crowd, but as an individual to be treated with respect.

Respect . . . for a child! It is the child who must learn to be respectful: respect his elders, respect authority. Love a child, yes . . . but respect him! Yet what was it that Mencius wrote, three centuries before Christ? "To love another and not to respect him is to treat him like a household pet."

When the infant peers up at the man and woman bending over his crib, their mutual warmth awakens the first tiny consciousness of the wonder and the joy of love. The delicate quality of their closeness provides it with the first practical demonstration of respect. It is this love, whose primary ingredient is respect, that should surround every boy or girl throughout the formative period of their childhood. It was this respect that the children of the war had lost when love had been taken from them.

Respect for this unwashed child of the street, with mucus trickling from its nose, for this little girl, scratching her infested head, for this youngster with dirty gesture and cigarette-butt dangling insolently from his lip?

"You dirty little——!"

"I would not use that kind of language to a child."

"Child? What child? They are little beasts."

Could one argue with every exasperated store-keeper in Naples? They had their legitimate grievances. Could they philosophize about every ragged child that hung suspiciously around their door?

Even before I knew them intimately, I had found so many qualities to admire in the lice-ridden adolescents on the streets: their courage, their cheerfulness and their generosity to each other. Whatever I might or might not be able to do for them there was one thing I was firmly resolved they should have: respect. It would not be through me that they would suffer further hurt. I may have known very little of pedagogical theory, but one does not need to be a violinist to suffer as a bow passes stridently over the strings. One need not be a psychologist to discern a false note in the way an adult speaks to a child: the harsh, the condescending, the falsely paternal, the bitter, the sarcastic. At the centre of each, the same common denominator: a lack of respect.

Strange how seemingly unimportant things can remain indelibly printed in one's memory! The voice of my history teacher at school, heavy with sarcasm! How his victims had writhed and how the rest of us had laughed! We had laughed obediently and noted, as children do, the quirk of satisfaction on his lips. Sometimes it was I who was hurt, but I had smiled, to show my indifference and because I knew intuitively that my smile would cut into his defences. I had been punished and, afterwards, when no-one could see me, I had cried.

"Go, call the director and be quick about it!" There was no cruelty in the voice of the instructor in the orphanage I visited in 1944, only a complete disregard of a child's feelings, of his hurt at being ordered around like a dog, of the loneliness that the barrier of tone and attitude could create. Why use that tone to a child? I knew what the instructor would have answered me: "These boys must be taught to obey or else . . . ! If you are soft with them they will just walk over you."

"What do you mean, you don't like eggs? We took you off the street and now you want to pick and choose: I don't like this, I don't like that." The cook in that other orphanage had been red with anger. The boy was standing there in miserable confusion, his budding manhood offended. Tears were ready to fall and this made him angry with himself. Bitter words were waiting to be shouted at her. I prayed that he would keep silent and not make matters worse for himself. It would only end in his returning to the street.

This time, I had reasoned with the good woman.

"What you say may be all right, but *I am not their servant* and I'm not going to be treated like one."

What was so wrong in being the servant of the children, of poor children who had no-one to care for them? What had Christ said to His disciples: "If I, being your Lord and Master, have washed your feet, you also ought to wash one another's feet."

"Suffer the little children to come unto me and forbid them not; for of such is the Kingdom of God." Was it only the well-washed boys and girls that Jesus wanted to gather round His knee, like the golden-haired children in the holy pictures? Would it not have been the homeless boys wandering the streets—the arrogant, dirty teenagers, rude because they were untaught, bitter because they were unloved—that He would have welcomed?

In October, 1945, I had asked Pius XII whether I might bring some of the street boys to see him. Nothing would call their plight to public attention more quickly than their being received by the Pope. Typically, his mind flew immediately to two important details. What about their midday meal? I told him that I planned to take them to our nearest soup kitchens. "They will be hungry long before they get there. I will have luncheon packages prepared for them." How should the audience be referred to? Not as an audience for the street boys or the shoeshine boys . . . nothing that might seem to be a reflection on them. On the spur

of the moment I could not make any concrete suggestion. He
solved the dilemma himself, the night before the audience, by
calling the director of the Vatican newspaper and dictating the
term that must be used: "The Holy Father Receives the *Dearly
Beloved of Christ.*" The audience was a solemn one, not to impress
the boys, but to show the world that these children of the streets
had a God-given right to respect.

Two thousand of them had gathered in St. Peter's Square that
Sunday morning. Those that had shirts had taken them off to
perform their ablutions in Bernini's gigantic fountains. They had
trooped into the basilica for Mass. At the *Orate Frates* I had
turned to face the sea of faces, pathetic in their eagerness. Never
before had I felt so strongly the grandeur of my priesthood. "Let
us pray, my brothers."

They had hurried up the marble staircase—the Royal Stairs of
the Vatican—marvelling at everything, at the gilt of the ceilings
and the size of the columns and the immobility of the Swiss
Guards. They had still not believed it, that they were to see the
Pope. *"Te lo dicono e, poi, non te lo fanno vedé."*[1]

The ten minutes of waiting had been painful in their anxious
expectancy. Then, far away, down at the end of the hall, a slender
white figure had appeared. The hush had been shattered by
strange, inarticulate cries. They had clambered up the marble
columns; they had balanced on the wooden barriers; they had
reached out perilously to touch the out-stretched hand. There was
something in his smile, warm and yet tinged with sadness, something in his voice and in his eyes, that told them of the deep
reverence that was in him and the infinite respect.

My first Boys' Town had been built for these youngsters and
for them I had meant it to be a place of love and respect. How
many reflections had recently gone into the foundation of the
latest Boys' Town, the Boys' Town of Rome. The little store that
had been built—the store where Gino had bought me the orangeade—represented only one of the aspects of its life that were to
give the boys a sense of their human dignity.

Four more years had passed. It was 1959 and Boys' Town,
Rome, was no longer so tiny. The cottages were set on a circular

[1] "They tell you you will and then they don't let you see him."

drive lined with mimosas and cedars of Lebanon. To the east they looked to the Alban hills and to the plain that had been the bloody scene of war. To the west the eye soared over the peach orchards in the direction of the sea.

There was beauty and peace. Beauty for the eye of the child as it rested on the purple bougainvillaea gently scaling the chapel wall. Beauty in the avenues of spruce and cypress that led from the Garden City to the Industrial Town. Beauty in the placid cows grazing under the eucalyptus trees. Beauty on the soccer fields, where contesting teams in white and red or blue or violet surged and ebbed like vibrant waves of youth.

I was not ashamed of our continuous effort to maintain, with paint brush and hammer, with flowers and seedlings, the attractiveness of our town. I was not afraid that someone would comment as they had done years before: "You are getting these youngsters used to a way of living to which they are not accustomed. How will they react when they go back to the slums?"

I had wondered then why it should be taken for granted that the boys would go back to the misery from which they had come. Even if some of them should have to live in a slum, would not their little corner reflect the cleanliness and the attempts at beauty that they had come to know?

The years had gone by and my beliefs had been justified. The ex-citizens brought their wives and children to see me. They invited me to their homes and in all of them, no matter how humble, there were cheerful drapes and flowers and artistic prints on the walls. They were places where human beings could live together in mutual respect.

Roberto brought his youngest child with him one evening.

"Why don't you stay to supper?"

The boy waiter in the restaurant was used to every kind of problem: Americans who wanted hot water to dilute their coffee, visitors from India who could not eat certain foods, small boys who could not reach the table. He brought two telephone books to raise Mariuccio in his chair and fastened the napkin round his neck. The three-year-old, spoon in mouth, stared in fascination at a whole restaurant peopled by boys.

"Take your spoon out of your mouth and eat your soup before it gets cold. What would Mummy say if she were here?"

Was it really twelve years since Roberto came to Boys' Town one evening, cheerfully defiant under the ceremonial politeness he was putting on because of the good lady who was with him? She was a remarkable woman; above all, she was an old-time aristocrat and used to having her own way. She had smuggled Roberto out of the town to save him from a trial in a juvenile court. She had already decided that the street urchin was a good boy at heart and she had driven a hundred and fifty miles to bring him to Boys' Town.

There had been a tug-of-war between Boys' Town and the court. The post-war difficulty of communications had favoured us and Roberto had stayed. Now, here he was back to see us with one of his children.

He leaned closer, so that his son could not hear.

"You know, I worry sometimes. Suppose he turns out like me!"

I laughed. "If he does, I will be satisfied."

I meant it. His father, with the same cheerful challenge in his eyes that I remembered so well, was a man truly worthy of respect.

Girls' Town was holding its first graduation ceremonies. Impossible to recognize in the beautiful young citizens the slovenly creatures who had crossed the doorstep with noticeable diffidence three years previously. A modest house, made beautiful by the tasteful use of colour, from the pastel drapes in the bedrooms to the youthful shades that gave each room a look of spring. It was awesome to contemplate the human transformation that had taken place within its walls.

The young mayor, poised and lovely, waited smilingly by the microphone for the guests to take their seats. In the background the girls of the graduation class in their white dresses, with tiny bouquets of flowers in their hands, looked like a bevy of beautiful young bridesmaids. Strange how the word *beautiful* came so spontaneously to describe them. Analysing their features, perhaps none of them would have met the strict canons of good looks. Yet there was a care in their grooming, a quiet elegance in their movements, a clarity of health in their skin and in their eyes and, above all, a radiance in their glance, that gave the spectator a sense of well-being, an impression of deep beauty.

In English and French and Italian, the fresh young voices blended; in their dancing the lithe young bodies moved in perfect rhythm. A representative of the Department of Education distributed their diplomas in kindergarten teaching. The record of their scholastic achievements was impressive, promising well for their future.

An American actress, Linda Darnell,[1] had set the spark that led to the founding of Girls' Town. For her wedding present she had asked her husband to erect a home in Rome for orphan girls. It had coincided with the request I received from an American nun. After years of teaching the daughters of the rich, Sister Dominic Ramacciotti of Hagerstown, Maryland, wished to dedicate her efforts to giving poor girls the same kind of opportunity that the boys were receiving in the Italian Boys' Towns. In those first graduation exercises, five years after Girls' Town had come into being, we were seeing the results of her inspired guidance.

Most of the first girls had lived for years in an orphanage. They had been astonished when they came to Girls' Town to find that their first lessons had been on the care of the skin and the hair. The slovenly look had begun to disappear; a womanly respect for their person was being acquired. Intellectual neatness would follow—it would not be too great a jump—and a new awakening of the spirit. Respect is not a divisible element; it is rooted in a true set of values, in a reverence for God and his handiwork, in an appreciation of the beauty of a world in which a real life can be lived, if one has the clear-sightedness, the rectitude and the courage to want to live it.

[1] Her tragic death in a fire, in March, 1965, shocked the world.

CHAPTER THIRTY-FIVE

Trust

"I HAVEN'T stolen anything from anybody."

Gianni, the eleven-year-old Commissioner of Labour in the Garden City,[1] was on trial.

He had been an ambitious boy from the moment he arrived. Small for his age, with features too irregular to be good-looking, his sharp tongue had not made him the most popular citizen. There was bitterness inside him. The off-and-on recipient of sporadic acts of kindness from people who took an interest in him and then tired of the effort, he looked at the world with a diffident eye. He was conscious of his own smartness and knew that he could make good if he received a chance. So far, a real chance had never come his way.

In the Garden City he found that all the boys were new arrivals like himself. In this community he could aspire to even the highest office; all that he would need would be the votes of his companions.

His first job was as a street-cleaner. Within a short time his public square was known to be the cleanest in town. Mario, the Commissioner of Sanitation, was only too glad to make Gianni a Controller. He did so well that the incoming mayor actually appointed him Commissioner of Sanitation. After some hesitation, the assembly ratified the nomination; Gianni might be a little too pushing but he was efficient.

At the next election he found three citizens to sponsor him and presented his candidature for mayor. He was soundly defeated. The new mayor was generous and offered him the important post

[1] One of the self-governing communities in the Boys' Town of Rome, where the new boys live. At the end of their first year they become citizens of the nearby "Industrial City".

of Commissioner of Labour. Here disaster overtook him. Among his new responsibilities was that of assigning extra jobs to citizens who had fallen into debt. The mayor gave him their names and he could use his own judgement in setting the special rate of pay.

In the next two months Flavio, the Town Auditor, noticed that the budget of the Department of Labour had soared rapidly. He mentioned the matter to the mayor.

"Why should there be such an increase in overtime? Are Gianni's accounts in order?"

"Oh, yes! He has receipts for all his expenditures."

The mayor consulted with the banker; Gianni's personal account was unusually prosperous. An official investigation was opened and the findings were turned over to the court. Poor Gianni was on trial.

"I haven't stolen anything."

The citizens eyed each other. Perhaps he was right. After all, all that the Commissioner had done had been to ask for a ten-cer-cent commission from the citizens to whom he assigned extra jobs. Was that stealing?

"Whom did the money come from?"

"From the citizens who did the jobs. They wanted to give it to me. I didn't force them."

"But whose funds were you using to pay them?"

"They were city funds. They didn't belong to anybody. They were mine as much as anybody else's."

"City funds are mine, too, but I don't seem to have done as well out of it as you."

All this was very confusing to the citizens. The public prosecutor had an inspiration.

"It is true, isn't it, that our taxes went up two weeks ago?"

"Yes."

"Maybe if you hadn't been so free with the city funds we wouldn't have to pay higher taxes. It was our money he took. Mine, and yours, and yours." His triumphant gesture embraced everyone in the court-room.

The atmosphere had changed. Gianni was the first to sense it.

"How much have I to pay?" He put his hand to his hip-pocket.

"Not so fast," said the presiding judge. "If the attorney for the defence has nothing more to say, the court will recess for ten minutes."

Make restitution; pay a heavy fine; hold no public office for four months. Good-bye to his ambition to be mayor! Before Gianni's period of probation would be over he would be going to the Industrial Town. There he would be with boys older than himself and he would have to wait at least two years before he could aspire to a similar office.

The trial had taught Gianni his lesson. It had given the other young citizens a lesson, too, in public honesty. Public office is not a privilege, an opportunity for personal gain; it is a responsibility, a trust for which one must give an accounting to the public and to one's own conscience.

This is one of the many instances in which self-government went wrong. Went wrong, that is, in the opinion of the people who believe that it is a dreadful thing for a youngster to be given the freedom that may end in his making a mistake or committing a "crime" as Gianni did.

"Youngsters of that age are not sufficiently mature. Suppose they make some stupid law? Obviously, an adult must step in and veto it."

Experience has taught me the contrary. When there is a healthy atmosphere in the community and good individual counselling, the Boys' Assembly is an extraordinarily well-balanced body. Looking back, I see that the mistakes that have been made both individually and collectively in the process of self-government have provided the richest formative experiences for the boys during these past twenty years.

Today no-one denies that youngsters must be trained in responsibility. Some people, however, still want this to be achieved without their being given concrete responsibilities, without their having the freedom to plan, to make decisions, to experience the risk of making choices. In the end it adds up to whether the adult himself is not afraid to accept his own responsibility as an educator and the risk that this implies, whether he does not prefer to seek refuge in the rigidity of external rules than allow the experiment of trial and error by which alone a training in responsibility can be achieved.

Does one really believe that young people are worthy of trust? That is the important question.

Perhaps it is foolish to trust boys and girls. If it is, it is divine folly. God endowed men with free will, not because human nature cannot succumb to temptation, but because He knew that, with the help of His grace and under the inspiration that trust itself gives, man possesses the qualities that can enable him to make the right choices. God did not despise the work of His hands.

Cannot young people in an institution be trained in responsibility without there being a mayor and a judge and elections and town meetings and commissioners and the bank?

Undoubtedly they can, but not without a suitable pedagogical system. This is not easy to find. How can one give a hundred or more teenagers concrete responsibilities day after day? How can one plan to have these increase gradually to fit the different ages and the varied capabilities of each youngster? How can this be done in such a way that the boys and girls themselves will readily accept them?

My fear is that, unless one is able to elaborate a way of community living that adheres as closely as possible to the realities of life, one may easily fall again into a system that satisfies the adults by solving the problem of discipline and still leaves untouched the real problem of education.

Gino was one of the first citizens to enter the Boys' Town of Rome. He was the youngster who had sat so quietly in the restaurant that first evening, who had answered each question with "I don't know; I am no good."

We had presumed that Gino's depressed state had been brought on by the double shock of his father's death in an accident and his mother's internment in a mental home. Soon we became convinced that it was not as simple as that. One day our social worker was allowed to visit the mother.

"How long has your sinus trouble been bothering you?"

"Ever since Gino was born"—a deep sigh—"everything started when Gino was born."

Was there a hint of resentment?

A few weeks later the social worker met Gino in the garden.

"I saw your mother recently. She was very happy to have such good news of you." Silence from Gino.

"You are very fond of your mother." It was half statement, half question.

"Yes."

"She is very fond of you."

"No, she isn't. She never has been." The words burst forth like a torrent overflowing. Nothing could hold back the story of how, for as long as he could remember, his mother had been critical of him. "When I was tiny, I broke a cup and she said: *Sei il solito stupido.*[1] You can't even handle a cup." Whatever he did: "Why can't you be like other boys? You're no good at anything."

Now that we had discovered the root of his trouble, we knew where to start: to make him understand that it was his mother's sickness, not a lack of love on her part or any fault on his, that had provoked her resentful attitude.

Our second task was more difficult: to make up for the years of lost growth, to build up the self-confidence that had been so consistently undermined. Hearten him with praise? Praise can be a dangerous weapon. If it is not deserved, a boy may reflect: *I must be really hopeless: they have to lie to encourage me.* Little by little, we had to find out what were the tiny things that Gino could do, praise him when he deserved praise and so help him to persevere.

Gino's first reaction to self-government had been a negative one. The only spark of interest he had shown was when he applied for a job. He became a street-cleaner. It was a job that even he could handle.

The first week went by, and pay-day came.

"I earned this today."

Gino had run into my study to show me his first pay-check. It was the first time I had seen him enthusiastic about anything. After his outburst, he was embarrassed. He edged toward the door.

"Well, so long. I must go to the store to buy a copy-book and some candy."

It was history repeating itself. I thought of Johnny Smith. He had been brought to us one evening in 1946 by an American Red

[1] "You are stupid as usual."

Cross worker. Standing there in his diminutive American uniform, he had been unhappy and defiant. The GIs had picked him up near Salerno, treated his head-wound, given him his name. He had stayed with them as a mascot, eighteen months from Salerno to Germany. They had been sorry when their ship sailed for home and they had to leave him on the dockside in Leghorn. He had been desperately unhappy, contemptuous of anything that was not American. Go to an Italian Boys' Town? He'd rather die. He had about fifty dollars in his pocket when he arrived. How would he ever come out of the dream-world, where he had been everyone's pet and yet had felt like a man amongst men? How could he become a child again, do all that a child must do, learn a step at a time the hard realities of life: that candies and money do not fall from trees, that good things must be earned by conscious effort?

I had felt pessimistic about Johnny and his continued refusal to adjust, until the evening I drove back late from Rome. He had come into the dining room to keep me company while I ate.

He had put his hand into his pocket and pulled out the aluminium disks that were the primitive coins of Boys' Town. "I earned twenty merits today."

There had been the same quality of pride that I now detected in Gino's voice as he showed me his pay: the pride of a youngster who has started to become a man.

A visitor and I met Giulio as we were walking down Peace Avenue.

"This friend of ours would like to see the Boys' Town currency."

"I don't have any on me. My brother Duilio has all my money."

Later on I saw Duilio and joked about his being the banker in the family.

"We are saving up for something."

"Yes?"

He blushed. "We want to buy the black and silver tea-service in the ceramic shop. We are going to give it to our mother for Christmas."

Their mother was an invalid and a widow. Her husband had died when they were very young.

Angelo was another boy who seemed to be saving his money. One day at table the boy manager of the candy store remarked to him: "You must have a nice fat savings account. You never spend anything in the store."

"No, I don't have too much money in the bank," Angelo replied, without further elaboration. The subject was dropped. Some time later, however, when Angelo met me outside, he himself brought up the matter, as though he owed me an explanation.

"You know the old aunt who is taking care of my little sister? She is very poor. I send her my savings each month. I hope you don't mind."

"Mind? Of course not. It is your money and, anyway, that is a wonderful way to spend it. But don't you ever buy yourself any candy or a coke or anything?"

"Oh, I don't need anything. I have everything I want."

Tonino brought me a five-hundred lire note. "Will you get me a money-order, please?" He gave me a scrap of paper with the name and address.

"Who is Mario?"

"I heard about him on the radio. He is only thirteen and he has been a cripple for years. He can't run about but he is always cheerful. All the boys in his village go to visit him. He tells them stories and helps them with their homework. I wish I were like him."

"You are sending him a gift?"

"Yes. He probably doesn't need it but I want to send it. At least he'll know that a lot of people know about him and admire him."

"How dreadful to let young people play-act as mayor and give themselves airs as judges and commissioners and what not. And then pretend that this is an educational system."

I have always kept this cutting from an Italian educational review, hoping that some day the author might leave his university rostrum and visit one of the Boys' Towns. He must come to Rome from time to time and the Boys' Town of Rome is very close to the city. Or perhaps he has already met some of our ex-citizens who have gone out into the world, not to play-act but to live as they learned to live in their democratic self-governing communities, as responsible men with a deep sense of brotherhood and an optimistic view of a world where they know by experience that mutual trust can exist.

CHAPTER THIRTY-SIX

Guidance

IF THE boys and girls do so much in the Boys' Towns and Girls' Town, what is left for the adults to do? Instruct them; that is obvious. Give them guidance, based on love, respect and trust. See that they get the inspiration they need.

Nine years have passed since the founding of the Boys' Town of Rome. None of the original citizens are left. Giuseppe is in the second year of the Faculty of Commerce and Industry at the University of Pisa; Nicola is in an American University; Romano is a cashier in a bank near Naples; Franco is an inspector for a gasoline station company; Tonino is in France; Fausto is in England. They were not sorry to leave Boys' Town. It was the logical conclusion of the training they had received. There was the pang of separation, and nostalgia afterwards, but, just because Boys' Town was so close to each one of them, they knew that the bond would not be broken, that, no matter how far they might travel, it would always be their home.

Yesterday's citizens are an inspiration to our teenage citizens of today. They are a proof of the validity of their own effort, of the tangibility of their own dreams and aspirations.

Inspiration! Does the word remind one of Paul on the way to Damascus, or John on Patmos? The inspiration I mean is not the shaft of light from on high. It is God speaking to us through nature, through the palpitating flow of everyday life, through the example of those round us.

To open up every possible avenue of inspiration for a child: this is the privilege of the adult world.

It was July, 1946. To celebrate the first birthday of the Boys' Village and to give "Zio Pietro" and "Zia Maria" a chance to visit their daughter in Northern Italy, we had decided to interrupt the daily routine and take the boys to camp. We loaded them on to army trucks, borrowed some dilapidated tents and headed for the Lake of Vico.

The immediate result of the temporary suspension of the self-governing system was the re-emergence of the gang.

The city-bred boys, the black-marketeers of yesterday, instinctively gravitated together and gave their group of three tents the name of the "gang of the butt-collectors". Their newly assumed air of superiority towards the others—"they're only kids"—was highly irritating; their escapades became an increasing problem.

One day it was a trial of strength with an American sergeant. He had brought an Italian lady-friend in his jeep to spend a quiet day at the lake. With a threatening air he ordered our youngsters to leave his part of the shore. They did, except for the "butt-collectors".

"What right has he to send us away? This is a public beach."

They pretended to withdraw until the sergeant had changed into bathing trunks, inflated the inner-tube of a tyre and settled himself comfortably on the water. Then, swimming rapidly under the surface, they applied vigorous pinches to his well-padded area wedged tightly in the rubber circle. He was very angry and came stalking up to camp.

"Is that what you are teaching this band of ruffians?"

Each day brought some new problem. There was a subtle defiance of authority in their systematic lack of punctuality, in the exaggerated laughter with which they greeted the camp-fire entertainment of the other boys. Yet I felt that this novel situation was offering a challenge that might eventually prove to be constructive. It did not escape me that Pietro, one of the roughest diamonds, was regularly giving up several hours of play each day to help the cook. Of course he made up for it by bossing the other boys arrogantly when he served the soup, but still . . . ! It was Totarello, another member of the gang, who swam far out into the lake and saved two teenage girls from drowning.

After ten days of activities close to the camp, I invited the "gang of the butt-collectors" to accompany me on a fifteen-mile hike. Afterwards they accused me of having tricked them into it.

"What do you mean? I only told you I was sure you couldn't do it. You proved I was wrong."

After two miles they had already asked if they might take off their shoes and walk in their bare feet. After four, what little enthusiasm they had had for the venture had completely disappeared. They sat down sullenly: "We are not going any farther." They were looking at me as though I was Herod ordering another slaughter of the innocents.

"Fine! I could see you were getting tired. There is a nice spot over there where we can sit in the shade. Of course, we will just have to eat dry bread. If we don't go on until we find water, we can't cook the spaghetti or make the sauce. But that's O.K."

They plodded on, mile after mile. Their spirits had revived. They had caught a serpent and carried it tied to a branch suspended between two right shoulders. Our throats were parched and now it was I who was beginning to worry. Then, unexpectedly, like the sweetest music, came the sound of water gushing from a crevice in the rock.

As we rested in the shade after lunch, I told them the story of a man who had walked the same countryside, bare-footed, centuries before, and how he had suffered thirst until he found a crystal-clear spring.

"See how God loves Brother Francis to have put Sister Water here for his refreshment."

The sun and the water, the trees and the birds, our fellow-creatures and manifestations of God's love for us.

There was no mockery or resentment in the bold eyes of the boys sprawling contentedly under the chestnut trees. They were proud now of their effort. There would be the same long walk home, but what of it? Perhaps, from this day forward, the sun and the moon and the stars, the sea, the wind and the rain, the calm and the storm, the autumn and the spring, might begin to speak to them, might acquire an ever-increasing power to inspire.

Lola, our first dog in the Boys' Village, lay exhausted. She did not have the energy even to look in the direction of the two newly-born puppies.

Saverio and Gianfranco—alarm in their eyes—stumbled bare-footed up to my tower room. "Lola is dying!"

I was their everyday doctor. I took their temperatures and gave them their pills. I would surely know what to do for a suffocating dog! Their anxious gaze rested confidently on my hand as I stroked the slender white head. There were only a few remedies in the tiny medicine cabinet: cough syrup, laxatives, sulphur ointment, coramina. Coramina! For the heart! I added ten drops to a spoonful of sugared water and forced it through the closed jaws of the dog. Three minutes—a shudder—a sigh—a heave of the body—and six more puppies, one after the other, came to light.

The sun touched the pomegranate trees with gold, gave texture to the dirty-grey stucco walls, rested upon the faces of the boys. Their eyes—black, with sultry depths; soft brown, with little specks of green; blue-grey, with nordic lights and a touch of southern warmth—beautiful eyes made more lovely by the glow within: a warm, compassionate radiance, giving a glimpse of the miraculous potentialities of the human soul.

Lola growled as each tiny hand reached out, to be hastily withdrawn. She licked my fingers as they caressed the squirming puppies, her faithful eyes imploring: "Please be gentle with them; they are very tiny."

"You see, she knows Monsignor saved her life." It was *Morto* —"The Corpse"—a pale-faced youngster, speaking. My prestige as a dog-doctor was firmly established.

Five years later: Luigi and Ezio had found a puppy trapped in a shed close to a disused quarry. They had carried it gently back to the village. It was immediately obvious that there was no hope. The puppy, starving for days, was nearing its end. We placed it on an old strip of felt, near the still-warm embers of the fire. Luigi brought back a bowl of hot milk from the kitchen. The puppy had lost consciousness.

Bed-time came and went. The two youngsters, squatting by the hearth, sat on in silence. From time to time they touched the tiny head with gentle, soothing motions. Luigi and Ezio would be tired in school tomorrow.The teacher would probably be annoyed at their homework left undone. Let them stay on. Compassion is more important than homework; it is something that cannot be learned so easily in school.

Midnight!

"Go to bed now, boys. There is nothing more you can do. I will stay here."

Sadly they stroked the little body, and stood up to go.

"Goodnight and God bless!"

January 1, 1957. Midnight Mass had started the New Year. Afterwards the boys, the teachers, the farmworkers and their wives and daughters had gathered in the dining hall for hot chocolate, panettone, oranges and nuts.

"Sante! Sante!" A farmboy had burst into the party to call the cow-man. *"Bianca sta per partorire."*[1]

By the time we reached the cow barn, the calf had been born. Bianca was licking him inch by inch, motherly pride in each methodic flash of the tongue.

The boys clustered around in admiration, laughing joyfully at the long thin legs and the quivering body.

"Happy birthday to you!" Who started it? The robust harmony swept up to the barrel-shaped vault, shocking the wondering cows out of their placidity.

Another creature had come into the world; the miracle of life had given its welcome to a New Year; the inspiration of birth was doing God's work in the impressionable souls of youth.

There are many little homes within the confines of each Boys' Town. The director and his family, the driver, the cook, the men in charge of the winery, the dairy farm and the tractors, their wives and children. Their presence is essential for the welfare of each youngster. They are the educators *par excellence*. They are the models for tomorrow's reality. Ten-year-old girls carry their baby brothers in their arms; little children play little children's games in the farm-village square. There is a potent message for all of us in those tiny children's eyes: innocence and purity and trust!

The other day I thought of Pasqualina. She must be a wife and mother now. It was in 1942 that I first met her, a six-year-old child in the Calasanctian Sisters' Orphanage in Rome. She had beautiful limpid eyes.

"Pasqualina," I said to her, "there is a wounded sailor-boy in our hospital with a name like yours. He is called Pasquale."

[1] "Bianca's going to give birth."

She had shown immediate interest. "I will say a prayer for him."

"Do," I said. "Ask God to make him a good man."

When I paid my next visit to the home, one of the sisters remarked laughingly: "Ever since you told Pasqualina about Pasquale, she has been running into the chapel a dozen times a day."

The little episode had a sequel that I had not foreseen. Pasqualina went to town one morning with one of the sisters. Passing the hospital, she asked to go in to see me. The head nurse told them that I had not yet returned from the Vatican.

"It doesn't matter. I really went to meet Pasquale."

The young sailor was surprised to see the little girl with the bobbed hair and enormous brown eyes approaching his bed.

"Hello, Pasquale!"

"Hello! How do you know my name?"

"Oh, I do. I say a prayer for you every day."

"Yes? What for?"

"I ask God to make you a good man."

When I returned and heard the story from the nurse, I thought that now the fat was really in the fire. Pasquale was the most difficult case we had in the hospital. Even at Christmas he had refused to make his religious duties. Immobile in his plaster cast, he watched me as I drew near. He did not give me time to utter a word.

"Father, I want to go to Confession."

Gregorio stood stiffly in front of me. He knew why I had sent for him.

"Sit down, Gregorio."

There was a pause.

"Did you see the doctor's little boy, Mark, this morning? He is big for his two years. Wolf was so excited when he saw him. He jumped all around him and sniffed him. He must have thought he was a lamb in his white woolly coat."

We both laughed. Little Mark had been an amusing sight, waving his two tiny fists at the big dog, amazed but not alarmed at his antics.

"Tiny children have such trust in everybody, big dogs included. And they seem to sense how wonderful a child's innocence is.

They let them pull their ears until their eyes water; they know there is no malice in them."

Another brief pause.

"Do you ever think, Gregorio, that it will not be long before you have a little boy like Mark?"

Gregorio smiled sheepishly. "That's a long way off."

"Why? You are sixteen. Carlo, who was here the other day, has a little boy and girl, and he is only twenty-three. It seems no time at all since he was your age. I remember him sitting in the same chair where you are now. That is one of the reasons why you are working so hard to become a really competent mechanic. You will be well able to provide for your family when you marry."

"Yes. I have thought of having a home of my own some day. I don't know when."

"You will, and you will be just as proud of your little boy as the doctor is of his and as Carlo is. That is the great joy of being a father, to be able to say: *I gave life to this little human being; it is my responsibility to protect him against all harm and to see that he grows up to be a fine man.*"

Another pause.

"Gregorio; what would you feel at such a moment if someone told you that your little fellow, so innocent and so trusting, would one day—when he is eleven or twelve years old—meet an older boy who would teach him dirty things?"

There was a shocked silence. Gregorio had forgotten the fear he had had when he entered and had not seen where our casual conversation was leading. He bowed his head.

I walked to the window and opened it. Boyish laughter from the swimming-pool wafted into the room.

"You never looked at it that way, did you? Maybe you knew that Lelio had nothing to learn, even though he is only twelve? That may be so. I don't know. There was a time, however, not very long ago, when he, too, was an innocent little fellow. Innocent or not, now, it must not be you to push him down any farther. You must protect everyone younger than yourself, as you would want someone to protect your little chap tomorrow."

I pretended to ignore that Gregorio, a husky sixteen-year-old, was crying. I gave him a light punch on the shoulder. "Run along now. The lunch bell will soon be ringing."

Some of the older boys in Boys' Town go to the city each morning for higher studies. They have to catch the 6.45 bus. Before they leave, many of them go to the chapel to receive Communion. By so doing, they limit their breakfast time to four or five minutes. They are strapping young men, members of the football and basketball teams, careful about their choice of a tie and the cut of their hair.

The younger boys do not comment on this daily occurrence. Some of them go to daily Mass; many of them do not. I know, however, that they are conscious of the young men who make their way spontaneously each morning to the chapel. A question-mark is forming itself in their heads. Why do they go when no-one forces them to? Inspiration is not a gale. It is a breeze so gentle that only gradually does one awaken to the pleasure of its blowing.

Inspiration! As I said—before mention of the word led my thoughts so far afield—the inspiration to which I am referring is not the shaft of light from on high. It is the finger pointed upwards by someone who stands at our side.

Christ gave us the example. To inspire, the Supreme Teacher became a servant. He humiliated Himself, becoming obedient unto death, even to the death of the Cross.

The professor at his cathedra, the priest in the pulpit, are teaching figures of authority. Sometimes the height and the detachment become too great. Socrates among his pupils. Paul VI in the crowd on the Way up to Calvary are figures of greater inspiration.

Educators often stress their authority lest others forget it, not realizing that their very fear is a discernible sign of weakness to those they seek to inspire. My own father was a formidable person to many people: a man of vast culture, fond of his own opinions. I remember him as a humble man, not preaching at me but changing his comfortable slippers for his outdoor shoes even when he was tired, even when it rained, to go to evening Benediction.

Driving back to my Boys' Republic one evening in 1947, I took a friend with me. He watched in amusement as the boys ran up to give me a hug and the older ones a punch on the arm.

"Is that how you treat Monsignor? Don't you know he is a big shot in Rome?"

The boys froze. They were still the sensitive youngsters of the war. Only Raimondo found words to answer. He spoke slowly, almost sadly: "Here he is our brother."

To inspire, one cannot set oneself up on high. One must identify oneself in brotherhood, even with the tiniest child, even with the drunkard, even with the fallen. Only then does heart speak to heart in the common language that belongs to the children of God.

I learned my lesson when I was a very young priest, newly ordained. I had dropped in at Veritas House on Abbey Street in Dublin to see my good friend Dr. Reilly. In the morning mail he had received a letter from Father Webb, a Jesuit Father in England, who needed a priest to help him with his mission in Worcestershire during the hop-picking season. I had a long vacation ahead of me and I readily agreed.

In Worcestershire I found a room prepared for me at the home of Lady Winnington. Each day a car took me to and from the farms where the hop-pickers were working. There was no doubt that the car and the livery won grudging respect from the farmers, who were not too kindly disposed towards Catholic priests. None the less, after a few days had gone by, I presented my apologies to my kind hostess and moved into a toolshed on one of the farms, next to the miserable stables where the pickers lived. They slept on straw. I slept on the bare boards. They cooked their supper over a camp-fire. I cooked mine over a primus-stove. At noon the farmers allowed me to eat in the kitchen after the farmhands had been served.

It would have been a disheartening experience if one had allowed oneself to be discouraged. The few Catholics among the pickers were inclined to hide themselves in the crowd. The rest were hostile, and then indifferent. Under the circumstances it was natural that the children should become my main concern. They were tough youngsters, girls as well as boys. Their language reflected the knowledge of life that they had picked up in the streets of Birmingham and London. In the evening, when their day's work with their parents in the hopfields was done, they gathered outside my hut for games and singing and a talk.

One afternoon there was great excitement: a Church Missionary Society had brought a film on Palestine to a neighbouring farm. For once I would have a quiet evening to myself. Instead, at five-fifteen, as I was still lingering over the pot of tea I had prepared, there was the usual scuffling outside my hut. Sure enough, when I opened the door, six tousle-headed youngsters were waiting there.

"Don't you know there is a film over at Myrtle Farm?"

It was Arnold who took it upon himself to reply. He was a well-built boy, with heavy black eyebrows and a snub nose.

"We know all right. But we are not going."

The others chimed in to insist that they were not interested in going to a film. I probed a little deeper. At last, it was Arnold again, red in the face and scraping his boot self-consciously against the leg of the table, who told me the truth.

"You are here every evening. It isn't right that just because *they* come with a picture we should leave you."

It was my first contact with a tough boy's fierce loyalty and his no less fierce affection.

I sent them off to the film and they shot away, overjoyed. I, too, felt pleased with myself. Maybe I was not such a failure as I had come to believe.

It soon appeared that it was not only the children that had adopted me. After a showing of the film, one of the missionaries had spoken to the adults, warning them against the Papist priest in their midst. Normally this would have met with general approval. Not now. Maggie, the matriarch of the camp, had stood up in front of them all and—good Protestant that she was or at least claimed to be—had belaboured the speaker with her tongue.

When the children ran to bring me the news, I felt sorry for the poor man. The mere sight of Maggie—a huge woman, with a loud voice and an unprintable vocabulary—had never failed to scare me. Later that evening she was at her usual place by the iron cauldron over the camp-fire. With her greasy hair flowing down her back she looked more than ever like a witch. I tried to hurry by as usual, but this time she stopped me. "That so-and-so! I told him." Profanity flowed freely. "I said to 'im: "*Look here*, I said. *We know how that poor little man lives. Like we do. He don't come in no ruddy car. He don't go home to no soft bed at night.* Oh, I told 'im." And Maggie beamed at me with cheerful self-satisfaction.

When the hop-picking season ended and the big trek back to the cities began, many of the pickers and their families came to say good-bye. To most of them I had probably not said ten words in two months, yet all of a sudden we were old friends. "Will we see you next year?" "Good luck, Reverend." "Look after yourself."

Arnold and five other tough teenagers trooped up, with packs on their backs. "So long! See you sometime. We may not be coming here next year." They were embarrassed at first to hold out their hands. Len, who prided himself as a boxer, made a jab towards my ribs. "Well, so long! See you sometime. So long!"

Strange how scared a boy can be of showing emotion!

Now I could confess to myself that I had been scared many times during my first weeks in the hopfields, so ill-equipped to go among people and mingle freely with them. Perhaps, after all, it may not be essential for one to have the gift of story-telling and putting people immediately at their ease by making them laugh. Perhaps people do not mind a little self-consciousness and timidity, so long as it is not stand-offishness; perhaps God can use one's very shyness to establish a bond.

There had been a bond between these people and me; the bond of our living the same life, at the same level; the bond of their coming to realize that I must have cared—as I did—if I had wanted to share their daily lot.

Isn't it difficult to deal with boys who are almost men? Don't they become restless? Have problems? Isn't it particularly difficult in a community, where—no matter how one may try—it can never be the same as having one's own father and mother and brothers and sisters?

Of course they become restless. Of course they have problems, and many of them. Every adolescent, every teenager, boy or girl, entering into manhood and womanhood, has big problems, that touch the very essence of their being, the meaning and purpose of their life. Of course all this is potentially more difficult in a community that is not one's home.

This is the time when the guidance that boys and girls have received in the preceding years, the certainty they have of being cared for and trusted and esteemed, the habits and the outlook they have formed, the strength of character they have acquired, are going to make the new transition a vigorous step forward and not a weak regression into the past.

This is the time when the living example of the men and women with whom they have come into daily contact—and how essential it is for boys and girls to have had this daily closeness to adults of both sexes—will be a powerful element in giving them the courage to make the right choice.

It is evident that, without the potent force of example, even the wisest counselling would lose its effectiveness. Yet, this should not lead one to believe that guidance is by any manner of means a passive operation. It is not enough for young people to have a model to observe or to feel that they are accepted by adults for whom they nourish affection. They need positive, vigorous help in solving their problems. Even the psychic structure of the independent teenager would rebel at the thought of being abandoned to his or her own devices.

How to give this guidance effectively? That is the question. The dictatorial parent, who solved the problem of his adolescent children by rigorously laying down the line of conduct to be followed, is largely a figure of the past. His place has been taken by the perplexed parent, only too willing to delegate his task to the school, the summer camp and the church. In many educational establishments, however, authoritarian paternalism still survives. It is not to be wondered at if there, too, adolescents rebel at the attempts made to solve their personal difficulties *en masse*. It is true that their problems are generally common to every young person of their own age and sex, but they feel—and rightly so—that they are also very special to themselves.

All parents, at some time or another, are shocked to realize how little they really know about their growing children. Other educators often appear to be supremely confident of their knowledge of youngsters whom they have only known for a relatively short time.

Common sense is not enough. To counsel effectively, one must have humility, know that one is not infallible, that one does not have the solution to a difficulty at one's fingertips, that another adult may be more effective than oneself in providing guidance for a particular child. There must be knowledge acquired by study and careful observation. There is a right moment and a wrong moment,

a right way and a wrong way of proposing a solution for each
human problem of each individual child.

Day by day the adult must train for his task. Learn to know
each boy or girl, with their individual stories of sorrow and
frustration, with their good qualities and their defects, to lead
them, not like a mule-driver, but as a friend anxious to promote
their just desires. Not afraid to correct, not afraid to be firm when
a youngster's own good requires it. Affectionate understanding
must not deteriorate into weakness. Deep down, young people do
not want an adult to tell them they are right when they are wrong;
they want to have the comforting knowledge that there are
grown-ups in whom they can have confidence because they are
sincere. Men are good at discovering motivations; so much so,
that they often get them wrong. Children do it by intuition, and
with surprising accuracy. Self-righteousness, self-glorification,
self-centredness are easily perceived. They irritate and delude.
They are the negation of what a boy and a girl instinctively seek:
the altruism, the humility, the sincerity of the love that alone can
inspire.

CHAPTER THIRTY-SEVEN

The Ways of Providence

FROM THE podium I looked out over the vast multitude that thronged the Singer Bowl in the New York World's Fair. There was laughter and shouted salutations and a buzz of expectancy. Very shortly a cortège of cars, escorted by motor-cyclists, would enter the arena, and President and Mrs. Johnson would be greeted with a thunderous ovation.

"Dear brothers and sisters"—a hush fell as I began to speak —"is it not a remarkable thing that it should be the voice of an Irish priest working for homeless children in Italy to open this, the 50th Anniversary Convention of the Amalgamated Clothing Workers of America?

"It is because of your desire to help create a world where your children and your children's children may live together without prejudice that you have granted me your friendship and support in working for the fatherless youngsters of another land, thousands of miles away. You felt as I do, that it is a privilege that God has given us, to be able to open the confines of our family and take other children into our arms and into our hearts, to breathe into them the life that is our love."

As I left the stadium, I would meet a little Jewish woman, well on in years. She would pat my face with her wrinkled hand as though I were her son. Her own son and daughter were long-time supporters of my Boys' Towns. She herself had canvassed her baker, her grocer and her butcher each year, to add their dollars to the donations she sent me.

Outside the gate, I would run into an official of the International Longshoremen, whom I had first met some years before at the Convention of their Southern Conference. It was they who had invited me to address them, but I was embarrassed that sweltering

June day in Jacksonville, Florida, to find that the overwhelming majority of my audience were negroes, giant men, perspiring in the heat and tired after several hours of discussions. What could I say that might possibly interest them? I had ended talking about children: hungry children, children without homes, children without love. They had crowded to the aisles as I left, to shake my hand and wish me luck. How great is the capacity of man's heart when the voice that speaks to it is that of a child!

Sometimes, today, when quiet descends, and my mind goes back over the years, I realize how far my travels have brought me.

In November, 1959, Pius XII had died. As I knelt by the iron bedstead in the Papal Villa at Castel Gandolfo, where only a few years ago the poor and the persecuted had sought refuge, I knew that a light had gone out in the world. Twenty years had passed since the Conclave, since I stood in the Royal Hall, outside the Sistine Chapel, waiting for the door to open and allow the tall figure in white to emerge. I had never lost my sense of awe in his presence, so great had been the spiritual stature of the man. Yet, how often on those occasions had the seemingly incongruous words of Christ come to my mind: "Unless you become as little children, you shall not enter the Kingdom of Heaven"!

It had been his quality of childlike innocence that all those who had had close contact with Pius XII had found so deeply moving. His joy when a tiny bird perched on his hand during meal-time, the ease of his approach to little children, the simplicity of his complete absorption in the everyday human problems that an unending procession of the humblest people brought to him: these were the memories that remained to overshadow even the acuteness of his intellect, his rapid intuition, his almost unerring diplomacy.

His successor was dissimilar in many ways: in physical build and appearance, in temperament and attainments, but not in his essential childlike candour, not in the firm realization that the mission of the Church must be to unite men and not to divide them.

"Young men," Pius XII had said to the soldiers who visited him, "you will be visiting many lands and seeing many peoples.

Remember that all men, for all their differences, are members of the same great, human family under God."

"The great rule in life," said Pope John to the Harlem Globetrotters when I took them into audience, "is to keep one's feet on the ground and one's eyes on heaven. You trot round the globe and obviously keep your feet firmly planted on the ground. While doing so, keep your eyes focused on the heavens and on the will of Him who is the Heavenly Father of us all."

I was amused that day to see the quizzical expression in the Holy Father's eyes as I translated his long speech into English. He was not used to hearing a translation greeted with so much laughter. "Is this Monsignor telling them my jokes or putting in his own?"

Little did any of us realize, in those first months after his election, what a gigantic step forward the new Pontificate would take in opening the windows and door of the Church in charity unto all mankind.

Another day, another audience. This time it was a group of supporters of Boys' Towns of Italy being received by the Holy Father. He motioned them to the circle of gilt chairs at the far end of his study: "They were placed here for the Cardinals; today you are my Senate—a Senate of Charity."

Pope John was warm in his admiration of the extraordinary structure of Boys' Towns of Italy, that had united men and women of every faith into a closely-knit and active family.

"May God enkindle the wills of all so that they may break through the barriers that divide them, cherish the bonds of mutual charity, understand others, and pardon those who have done them wrong. By virtue of His action may all peoples of the earth become as brothers, and may the most longed-for peace spring forth and reign always among them."[1]

It was a day late in November, 1963, that I found myself in the airport at Los Angeles on my way back from a Congress in Mexico. My plane from the south had been delayed and I had missed my connection for New York. I took advantage of the delay to telephone to a friend in Glendale.

It was the wife who answered: "Wait until I call my husband. He is in the garden. He will be surprised."

[1] Encyclical *Pacem in Terris*.

"Oh, good! He is at home? I was afraid he might be at work."

"Today is Thanksgiving."

An hour later I was sitting down to a home-cooked Thanksgiving dinner.

"Thank heavens we bought a turkey. We were undecided, there just being the two of us, and the children don't eat much meat." The young wife was in a flurry of excitement. Only when all the trimmings had been served, did she take her place at table. Even then her attention was taken up by the children: Vincent Jr., Joseph aged two, and Maureen, a demure little maiden of four, who sat next to me.

"Vincie was a bad boy this morning. He took a coke out of the icebox without permission. I think I had better send him to Boys' Town to learn how to behave."

"Will you come back to Boys' Town with me, Vincent?"

"No!" said Vincent with great emphasis.

"You're right. You wouldn't leave your Mummy and Daddy and there would be no Thanksgiving turkey if you were in Italy."

How clearly defined the personalities of these children, young as they were! Each one coming to bloom in the security of the love that surrounded them.

How different from so many thousands of other children I had known! My thoughts went back in particular to a little boy I had met one cold November evening during the war. It had been difficult to discern the tiny figure that emerged from the dark arches of the Colosseum. Under his ragged soldier's jacket he had no shirt. From between the top of his baggy trousers and his bare skin he had pulled out a package of American cigarettes. I had not bought the Camels but I had found him a place to sleep. Some months later, when Boys' Town was founded, he had become one of its citizens. Now, seventeen years later, I was sitting in his home in Los Angeles, admiring his ease as a father and thanking God, with him and his family, for many blessings.

We sat on the porch after dinner, watching Vincie and Joseph playing on the tiny lawn. Some day, I thought, Vincent will sit here and tell his children the story of the war and how he lost his parents and wandered the streets. He will describe how he went to Boys' Town, such a poor place but so rich in human warmth and understanding.

We talked about Tommaso in Australia, and Mario and his brother in the Argentine, and Giacomo in England, and Tonino in France.

"Tommaso is probably an Australian citizen by now and Giacomo an Englishman. They will laugh when they hear that I am an American. I used to make such fun of the Americans for having flour as white as chalk and liking jelly with their meat." He paused. "Give everyone my love . . . Beppe and Memmo and Nando and Giovanni, when you see them. I don't know any of the boys who are at the Villaggio now, but give them my love just the same."

On the plane back to New York, I studied my air-route map of the world. What a tiny space Italy occupied on the face of the globe! Rome and Naples and Milan were mere pinpoints of red. As for the Boys' Towns, all of them together would not merit even an infinitesimal dot.

Yet, one could fly on to the farthest places on earth, to Sydney and Perth and Hong Kong and down the American continent from Toronto and Los Angeles to Buenos Aires, and still meet the men who had once been citizens of those microscopic communities. In New Zealand, Australia, South Africa, Nigeria, India, Egypt and Alaska one could speak to the priests who had spent the earliest years of their apostolate in the Boys' Towns of Italy.[1]

They had returned to their own lands to work for other children, black and white, yellow and brown; for new victims of neglect, children tortured again by strife and prejudice, by fresh tragedies and upheavals; for boys and girls subject to the same heart-aches, responsive to the same affection, capable of the same generous response as the Italian youngsters they had come to know so well.

In a few days another plane will take me across the Atlantic and over France and down the rocky coastline that leads to Rome. I will see on the heights above Leghorn the little villa where four generations of little ones have found a home. At Civitavecchia, the old tower and the Sea Village round it, and, across the Aurelia, the Industrial Village and the Farm. The Leonardo Da

---

[1] Father Elliston in Dunedin, Fathers Castles and Costigan in Melbourne, Father Boardman in Cape Town, Father Louis in the snowy wastes of the north, Father Vanigasorijar in Calcutta, Father d'Souza in Allahabad, Father Geohargi in Cairo.

Vinci airport and, close by, the oasis of green in the brown countryside, the pattern of white cottages and streets and squares that is the Boys' Town of Rome. Children will be there to greet me, young ones from the Garden City, sturdy young men from the Industrial City. And among them the children of other nations, Venezuela and Canada, England and Spain, Germany and Russia and Belgium, whom the ebb and flow of life has brought to the doors of a tiny community where the gates are never closed and the light in the window is never spent.

Strange that so many people so far apart should look to this little spot on the outskirts of Rome, to these Boys' Towns and Girls' Town, as a part of themselves. Protestants and Orthodox, Catholics and Jews: this is the fruit of their charity, the partial realization of a common dream.

It is not difficult in this place of paradox, in this warm fraternity of children, to imagine a world where men of goodwill will share in each others' sorrows, rejoice in each others' joys, help carry each others' burdens along the road that is the brief pilgrimage of life.

I kneel in the little chapel where Christ in the splendour of His manhood raises Lazarus to life.

Perhaps it was necessary, dear God, for us to have seen evil triumphant for a time and humanity beaten to its knees. In the loneliness of desolation our souls cried out for the solidarity of our brothers and through sorrow we awoke again to the possibility of love.

Perhaps it is good for us to feel tired sometimes in the evening, and discouraged when indifference is encountered. In our continued dependence on the charity of others, in the poverty disguised under the smiling aspect of our towns, we are obliged each day to recognize anew the providential intertwining of our lives.

I saw Pope Paul VI the other day. He welcomed me with the quiet gentleness of manner that has always been characteristic of him.

It is several years now since Monsignor Montini visited the Shoeshine Hotel and stayed to dinner with the boys, since we sat together on a terrace overlooking Lake Vico, watching a crowd of exuberant youngsters from Boys' Town running back down the hill to their first summer camp. He nodded towards them: "There lies the key to the future."

Some time had gone by after that when he sent a Prelate from the Secretariat of State to see me. He wondered whether I was not hiding myself away in my Boys' Town at Civitavecchia and whether, now that the emergency of the post-war period had ended, there might not be more important things for me to do.

I am still grateful for the delicacy with which this suggestion was made. Today, however, even more than yesterday, I feel that my choice was right. Not merely because of the buildings that have since been erected—the Nurseries, the Schools and the Children's Villages—but because of letters such as the one I received this morning.

"My wife was so happy to have met you. She was overwhelmed by all that she saw at the new Boys' Town, by all that you are doing for those youngsters who one day will say: *To have known Monsignor was the most beautiful happening in my life.* You have been everything to me; you know what my many negative qualities were and my few good ones; you gave me back faith and the courage to know how to live. I hope that all of us, near and far, feel as close to you as I do."

One does not ask oneself how objective is his judgment. The knowledge that one of yesterday's children looks back with gratitude is a source of great joy. Perhaps, in this one instance, one has been a not too ineffective instrument in the hands of God. Every time that a child has entered one's door, sad beyond measure and with a hundred little miseries hidden away, one has been awed by the immensity and the delicacy of one's task. To do one's best and leave the rest to God: this has been one's only true source of strength, the words of St. Paul one's only consolation: *The foolish things of the world hath God chosen, that He may confound the wise; and the weak things of the world hath God chosen, that He may confound the strong.*

It has not been sad work. How could it be? There has been sorrow sometimes, but joy always, and in such abundance that the trials have seemed negligible in comparison. The happiness has been so great that one has been afraid and has welcomed other trials that might in part restore the equilibrium of earthly living.

There has been the happiness of giving and of being able to give and it has not been enjoyed alone. Twenty years ago I began and most of the people who started with me are still at my side. They have given of themselves more meritoriously than I, lacking so many of the consolations that I have had and yet bearing the daily grind so cheerfully and so silently that their sacrifices have tended to go unnoticed.

The family of the Boys' Towns of Italy: it has not been an empty phrase. There has been a family where administrator and secretary and driver and cook and teachers and farmers and bricklayers and technicians have worked together, united by a common bond: the service of God's children.

The children have felt the joyfulness and unselfishness of this service, and it has reassured and inspired them. They have seen other men and women, too, many of them faraway, working for them, dedicating a great part of their lives and of their substance to helping them, men and women who have learned, each in his or her own way, the great lesson of life, that the secret of happiness is to love and the essence of love is to serve.